THE
MEANING
OF
MARIAH
CAREY

THE
MEANING
OF
MARIAH
CAREY

MARIAH CAREY

with MICHAELA ANGELA DAVIS

Andy Cohen Books

Henry Holt and Company   New York

Andy Cohen Books
Henry Holt and Company
Publishers since 1866
120 Broadway
New York, New York 10271
www.henryholt.com

Andy Cohen Books® and ⚑® are registered trademarks of Macmillan Publishing
Group, LLC.

Distributed in Canada by Raincoast Book Distribution Limited

Library of Congress Cataloging-in-Publication Data

Names: Carey, Mariah, author. | Davis, Michaela Angela, 1964–
Title: The meaning of Mariah Carey / Mariah Carey with Michaela Angela
 Davis.
Description: First edition. | New York : Andy Cohen Books, 2020.
Identifiers: LCCN 2020020198 (print) | LCCN 2020020199 (ebook) |
 ISBN 9781250164681 (hardcover) | ISBN 9781250164698 (ebook)
Subjects: LCSH: Carey, Mariah. | Singers—United States—Biography. |
 LCGFT: Autobiographies.
Classification: LCC ML420.C2555 A3 2020 (print) | LCC ML420.C2555
 (ebook) | DDC 782.42164092 [B]—dc23
LC record available at https://lccn.loc.gov/2020020198
LC ebook record available at https://lccn.loc.gov/2020020199]

Our books may be purchased in bulk for promotional, educational, or business
use. Please contact your local bookseller or the Macmillan Corporate and
Premium Sales Department at (800) 221-7945, extension 5442, or by e-mail at
MacmillanSpecialMarkets@macmillan.com.

First Edition 2020

Designed by Meryl Sussman Levavi

Printed in the United States of America

1   3   5   7   9   10   8   6   4   2

BVG

To my legacy, my children, Roc and Roe,
You are the physical embodiment of unconditional love.

To my lineage, my ancestors, all of them . . .
You may have come from two different worlds
that were often in struggle with each other,
yet the best of you lives on inside of me, finally, harmoniously.

And to Pat, my mother, who, through it all,
I do believe actually did the best she could.
I will love you the best I can, always.

Now faith is the substance of things hoped for,
the evidence of things yet unseen.

Hebrews 11:1

CONTENTS

PREFACE

Irefuse to acknowledge time, famously so. I've made a lot of jokes and memes about it, but it's a very real belief for me. I cried on my eighteenth birthday. I thought I was a failure because I didn't have a record deal yet. That was my only goal. It was as if I was holding my breath until I could hold a physical thing, an album that had "Mariah Carey" printed on it. Once I got my deal I exhaled, and *my* life began. From that day on, I calculated my life through albums, creative experiences, professional accomplishments, and holidays. I live Christmas to Christmas, celebration to celebration, festive moment to festive moment, not counting my birthdays or ages. (Much to the chagrin of certain people.)

Life has made me find my own way to be in this world. Why ruin the journey by watching the clock and the ticking away of years? So much happened to me before anyone even knew my name, time seems like an inadequate way to measure or record it. Not living based on time also became a way to hold on to myself, to keep close and keep alive that inner child of mine. It's why I gravitate toward enduring characters like Santa Claus, the Tooth Fairy, and Tinker Bell. They remind me we can be timeless.

It is a waste of time to be fixated on time. Often time can be bleak, *dahling*, so why choose to live in it? Life is about the moments we create and remember. My memory is a sacred place, one of the few things that belong entirely to me. This memoir is a collection of the moments that matter, the moments that most accurately tell the story of who I am, according to *me*. It will move back and forth, up and down, moment to moment, adding up to the meaning of me now.

But then again, who's counting?

THE
MEANING
OF
MARIAH
CAREY

PART I

WAYWARD CHILD

AN INTENTION

My intention was to keep her safe, but perhaps I have only succeeded in keeping her prisoner.

For many years, she's been locked away inside of me—always alone, hidden in plain sight before masses of people. There's significant evidence of her in my early work: often she can be found looking out of windows, dwarfed by a giant frame, barefoot, staring at an empty rope swing swaying from a lone tree against a purple dusk sky. Or else she's two stories up in a brownstone, watching the neighborhood children dancing on the sidewalk below. She's shown up in a school auditorium in OshKosh overalls, holding a ball on the sidelines, waiting and wanting to be chosen. Sometimes she is caught in a rare moment of joy, on a roller coaster or flying by on skates with her hands in the air. Always she lingers, though, as a dull longing just behind my eyes. She's been scared and alone for so long, and yet through all the darkness, she's never lost her light. She has made herself known through my songs—her yearning heard over the airwaves or seen on screens. Millions of people know of her, but have never known her.

She is little Mariah, and much of this will be her story, as she saw it.

Some of my earliest memories are of violent moments. Because of that, I have always carried a heavy blanket with which I cover up large pieces of my childhood. It has been a burden. But I can no longer stand the weight of that blanket and the silence of the little girl smothering beneath it. I am a grown woman now, with a little girl and boy of my own. I have seen, I have been scared, I have been scarred, and I have survived. I have used my songs and voice to inspire others and to emancipate my adult self. I offer this book, in large part, to finally emancipate that scared little girl inside of me. It is time to give her a voice, to let her tell her story exactly as she experienced it.

Though you cannot dispute someone's lived experience, without a doubt, details in this book will differ from the accounts of my family, friends, and plenty of folks who think they know me. I've lived that conflict for far too long, and I'm weary of that too. I've held my hand over the mouth of that little girl in an attempt to protect others. Even "those others" who never tried to protect me. Despite my efforts to "be above it all," I still got dragged and sued and ripped off. In the end, I only hurt her more, and it almost killed me.

This book is a testimony to the resilience of silenced little girls and boys everywhere: To insist that we believe them. To honor their experiences and tell their stories.

To set them free.

EXISTENCE

Early on, you face
The realization you don't
Have a space
Where you fit in
And recognize you
Were born to exist
Standing alone

—"Outside"

There was a time in my early childhood when I didn't believe I was worthy of being alive. I was too young to contemplate ending my life but just old enough to know I hadn't begun living nor found where I belonged. Nowhere in my world did I see anyone who looked like me or reflected how I felt inside.

There was my mother, Patricia, with paler skin and straighter hair, and my father, Alfred Roy, with deeper skin and kinkier hair, and neither had faces with features just like mine. I saw them both as riddled with regret, hostages of a sequence of cruel circumstances. My sister, Alison, and brother, Morgan, were both older and darker, and not just in terms of the hues of their skin, though they were slightly browner. The two of them had a similar energy that seemed to block light. They had an approach to the world that made little room for whimsy and fantasy, which was my natural tendency. We shared common blood, yet I felt like a stranger among them all, an intruder in my own family.

I was always so scared as a little girl, and music was my escape. My house was heavy, weighed down with yelling and chaos. When I sang, in a whispery tone, it calmed me down. I discovered a quiet, soft, light place inside my voice—a vibration in me that brought me sweet relief. My whisper-singing was my secret lullaby to myself.

But in singing I also found a connection to my mother, a Juilliard-trained opera singer. As I listened to her doing vocal exercises at home, the repetition of the scales felt like a mantra, soothing my frightened little mind. Her voice went up and down and up and up and up—and something inside me rose along with it. (I would also sing along with the beautiful, angelic, soulful Minnie Riperton's "Lovin' You" and follow her voice up into the clouds.) I would sing little tunes around the house, to my mother's delight. And she always encouraged me. One day, while practicing an aria from the opera *Rigoletto*, she kept stumbling on this one part. I sang it back to her, in perfect Italian. I might have been three years old. She looked at me, stunned, and at that moment I knew she saw me. I was more than a little girl to her. I was Mariah. A musician.

My father taught me to whistle before I could talk. I had a raspy speaking voice even then, and I liked that I sounded different from most other kids my age. My singing voice, on the other hand, was smooth and strong. One day, when I was around eight years old, I was walking down the street with my friend Maureen, who had porcelainlike skin with warm brown hair and a sweet face like Dorothy's from *The Wizard of Oz*. She was one of the few little white girls in the neighborhood who was allowed to play with me. As we walked, I began to sing something. She stopped suddenly, frozen in place on the sidewalk. She listened for a moment in silence, standing very still. Finally, she turned to me and said, in a clear and steady voice, "When you sing it sounds like there are instruments with you. There's music all around your voice." She said it like a proclamation, almost like a prayer.

They say God speaks through people, and I will always be grateful for my little girlfriend speaking into my heart that day. She saw something special in me and gave it words, and I believed her. I believed my voice was made of instruments—piano, strings, and flutes. I believed my voice could be music. All I needed was someone to see and hear me.

I saw how my voice could make other people feel something good inside, something magical and transformative. That meant not only was I not unworthy, valid as a person, but I was valuable. Here was something of value that I could bring to others—*the feeling*. It was *the feeling* I would pursue for a lifetime. It gave me a reason to exist.

CLOSE MY EYES

It took twelve cops to pull my brother and father apart. The big bodies of men, all entangled like a swirling hurricane, crashed loudly into the living room. Within an instant, familiar things were no longer in my sight—no windows, no floor, no furniture, and no light. All I could see was a chaotic mass of body parts in motion: dark pants and strong arms bursting out of dark sleeves, enormous hands grabbing, fists punching, limbs tangled together and tearing away, heavy, polished black shoes scuffling and stomping. There were quick flashes of shiny things: buttons, badges, and guns. At least a dozen pistol handles, stiff and sticking out of dull leather holsters, a few cradled in palms and thumbs, sat on wide black belts around broad hips. Chaos filled the air with the sounds of cursing, grunting, and howling. The entire house seemed to be shaking. And somewhere in the eye of this storm were the two most important male figures in my life, destroying each other.

I always thought of my brother's anger as weather—powerful, destructive, and unpredictable. I don't know if it was a singular act or an ongoing illness that made him so volatile, but it was all I had ever known.

I was a little girl with very few memories of a big brother who protected me. More often, I felt I had to protect myself from him, and sometimes I would find myself protecting my mother from him too.

This particular fight with our father had escalated more quickly than most, however. A shouting match became a tornado of fists in what seemed like a matter of seconds, banging through the room, knocking things over, and leaving havoc in its wake. In that moment, the rage between my father and brother was so forceful that no one person could have stopped it. No one would have dared.

By the time I was a toddler, I had developed the instincts to sense when violence was coming. As though I was smelling rain, I could tell when adult screaming had reached a certain pitch and velocity that meant I should take cover. When my brother was around, it was not uncommon for holes to be punched in walls or for other objects to go flying. I never really knew how or why the fights would begin, but I did know when tension was turning into an argument and when an argument was destined to become a physical fight. And I knew this particular one was going to be epic.

My Nana Reese was there, which was a bit odd because it was rare that she or anyone from my father's family, who lived in Harlem, was at our house. We were in Melville, a predominately white, affluent-adjacent town in Suffolk County on Long Island, New York, though I would eventually move thirteen times growing up. Thirteen times to pack up and go, to try to find another place—a better place, a safer place. Thirteen new starts, thirteen new streets with new houses full of people to judge you and wonder where or who your father is. Thirteen occasions to be labeled unworthy and discarded, to be placed on the outside.

Pastor Nana Reese, the Good Reverend Roscoe Reese, and their African Methodist Pentecostal Church were where my father came from. Roy was the only son of Addie, Nana Reese's sister. My father never lived with his father, and there was always a potent distance between them, a mystery that inevitably held a misery. These people, living in the village of Harlem, were his people. They had come up from Alabama and parts of North Carolina and other regions of the South, bringing with them traditions, traumas, and gifts—some of which were ancient, African, and mystical in origin.

Nana Reese and I found each other right before all hell really broke loose. The thunder of profanity, fists, and feet drowned out all other sounds, so I didn't hear when the cops burst in.

I didn't know if they had come to save us or kill us. It was Long Island in the 1970s, and two Black males were being violent—the appearance of the police almost never meant that help had arrived. On the contrary, their presence often complicated and elevated the existing terror and escalated violence. That hasn't changed, but this was my first encounter with the fact. I had no benefit of experience; I had no benefit of any kind. My cousin LaVinia, Nana Reese's daughter, always said, "You kids had all the burdens of being Black but none of the benefits." It took me a long time to understand the reality of her observation.

This, of course, was not the first vicious fight between my father and brother—for as long as I could remember, their relationship had been a war zone. But it was the first time the troops had been called in. It was also the first time I witnessed the possibility that a member of my family could brutally die in front of my eyes. Or that I could die too. I wasn't yet four years old.

Before my mother and father found their marriage unbearable, they lived together in Brooklyn Heights. Though the neighborhood had seen a stream of bohemians arrive as early as 1910, and the 1950s brought in a wave of urban activists—liberal folks with money who loathed the suburbs—in the 1970s it was still a pretty eclectic mix of mostly working- and middle-class families. It was pre-yuppie and ungentrified. If there was a tolerant place for a young mixed-race family in that era, Brooklyn Heights was probably the closest you could come to it.

Throughout my childhood, I would live in many obscure places, mostly on Long Island, and feel very much like a castaway on this island-off-the-island of Manhattan. Both my parents worked very hard so we could live in neighborhoods where we could glimpse that elusive "better life" and feel "safe." Conventional wisdom, however, suggests that "better" and "safe" are synonymous with white.

We were not a conventional family. Was it better to live in a place where my white mother would often walk alone through the front door first, ahead of my Black father with her mixed kids—for their safety? What does that do to the psyche of a man who is supposed to be the head of the household? How can such a man keep his family safe, and what does such an indignity signal to his Black son?

🦋

After the squad of policemen managed to separate my father and brother, though there was still a considerable amount of yelling, everyone was alive. The truly dangerous part of the storm was over; the thunder had stopped. The next thing I knew I was cradled in Nana Reese's arms, crying and trembling. She had scooped me up like a sack of laundry and set me close beside her on what the kids used to call "the rocking couch," a cheap, flimsy structure the color of dirt, rust, and olive, dotted with flecks of mustard. Sometimes I think it was that couch that planted the seed of my eventual preference for Chanel. We kids called it the "rocking couch" because it was missing a leg, and if you shifted your weight back and forth it would, well, rock. This was a noble attempt to find humor amid broken things, a talent I shared with my brother and sister. In the midst of the violence and trauma, a great comfort came to me on that sad sofa.

Nana Reese held me tight until my little frame stopped shaking and my breathing became normal. From disorientation I returned to the room, I returned to my body. She turned my face up toward the light and made sure my eyes were focused and locked on to hers. She placed her delicate hand firmly on my thigh. Her touch immediately steadied any aftershocks still pulsing through me. Her gaze was unusual—not that of a great-auntie, a mother, or a doctor. It was instead as if she looked directly into the essence of me. In that instant we were not a frightened little girl and a consoling elder but two souls, ageless and equal.

She told me, "Don't be scared of all the trouble you see. All your dreams and visions are going to happen for you. Always remember that."

As she spoke, a warm and loving current spread out from her hand to my leg, gently coursing through my body in waves and rising up and out the top of my head. Through the devastation a path had been washed clear; I knew there was light. And somehow I knew that light was mine and everlasting. Before that moment I hadn't had any dreams I could remember. I had very few memories either. I certainly had yet to hear a song in my head or have a vision.

From around when I was four years old, after my parents' divorce, I didn't see my Nana Reese much. My mother and my father's families remained locked in conflict, and since I lived with my mother, I was largely cut off from Nana's life of healing and holy rolling in Harlem. I did later learn that people called Nana Reese a "prophetess." I also learned that she was not the only healer in my lineage. Beyond all that, I believe a deep faith was awakened in me that day.

I understood on a soul level that no matter what happened to me, or around me, something lived *inside* me that I could always call on. I had something that would guide me through any storm.

And when the wind blows, and shadows grow close
Don't be afraid, there's nothing you can't face
And should they tell you you'll never pull through
Don't hesitate, stand tall and say
I can make it through the rain

—"Through the Rain"

THERE CAN
BE MIRACLES

When I was six years old, my mother moved my brother and me into a tiny, nondescript house in Northport, Long Island. It sat sadly atop a stack of long, winding concrete steps.

The dull little structure had a few tiny rooms running along either side of a steep, creaky staircase, which led up to even smaller rooms. My mother was often working or out at night, so Morgan was left to babysit me. He had no skills to look after a little girl. He would leave me alone and go run wild with his teenage friends. One night, while left alone, I was watching a special on *20/20* about children being kidnapped—totally inappropriate for a six-year-old. And it so happened that at that moment, some kids in the neighborhood decided to throw rocks at the window. Their voices broke through the dark night, chanting, "Mariah, we're gonna get you!" I was terrified by the news, by the kids, by the night, by the house, by my absolute aloneness.

I wanted my brother to love me. I was impressed by his strong energy, but it also scared me. This little house couldn't possibly bear the weight of all of our pain and fear—especially my brother's. It was such a raw time. I was a scared little girl, my mother was profoundly heartbroken, and my brother—well, let's just say he was more than simply an angry teen, especially in high school. He'd outgrown anger by middle school and had graduated to full-on rage. As a young teen, my brother was bursting with creative and athletic promise. But earlier in his life he had been bullied and beat up for having a disability and being a mixed-race kid. The visible difference he wore on his skin always distanced him from the white boys in Long Island and made him a target. Children can be mean, but when ordinary meanness is combined with racism, it takes on a peculiar brutality, one very often sanctioned by (and learned from) adults. My brother most likely caught some hell from the Black kids too. I'm sure his distance from their kind of detectable Blackness, the kind that gets you roughed up by the cops for nothing, stirred up a resentment in them that came out in the form of physical blows and name-calling.

My brother was broken early on, and the only tool he had to defend himself was destruction. He would fight everything, his demons and everybody else, especially our father. The relationship he had with our father was not one that helped him rebuild—instead, it ground him down even further into his inner outrage. A broken man cannot fix his broken boy. My brother was shattered into pieces, scattered to the wind, and our father's outdated tools of militaristic discipline were inadequate to help him collect himself and prepare him for manhood. The misunderstanding and emotional distance with our father was my brother's perpetual and crushing agony, and it resulted in his absolute rage.

For most of my childhood I was caught between my brother's fury and my mother's sad searching. Rage and despondence are both highly damaging, but, I think, one turns inward and the other turns outward. When they collide, it can be catastrophic. By the time I was in kindergarten, catastrophe was already routine to me. When we lived in Northport, mini explosions erupted between my mother and brother daily. I conditioned myself to be still and wait for the outbursts to pass over. Most of the time I tuned out the words and reasons behind their fights—the "why" was big-people territory. To me, their arguments were just a blur of intense voices at high volume, punctuated by ruthless cursing.

One particular night, however, I distinctly knew the source of the argument: my brother wanted to use my mother's car, and she wouldn't let him. Certainly they'd had hundreds of fights over the car, but for some reason this night felt different. I was paying attention. Typically, their fights would start off the way I imagined normal fights between most teenagers and parents did, but this one wasn't like that. It began at blow-up level and rapidly escalated into violent obscenities being hurled across the room. Hurtful words flew back and forth like bullets ricocheting off the walls, gaining strength with each new round. There was no escaping the crossfire; the screaming shot room to room, up and down the stairs, and the entire house became a battlefield. There was no safe place. I felt the air tighten as my mother and brother came face-to-face, mere inches of electrified anger between them. I was terrified. My whole body stiffened. Eyes opened wide, I fixed on the space between them and cried out, "Stop it! Stop it!" over and over again, through my tears. I was hoping maybe my cry could slip into that space and disarm them for a moment.

Suddenly there was a loud, sharp noise, like an actual gunshot. My brother had pushed my mother with such force that her body slammed into the wall, making a loud cracking sound. I saw her frame go rigid; for a moment she appeared frozen against the wall, pinned up like a painting, her feet lifted several inches off the ground. Next thing I knew she was totally limp, as if her bones had melted, folding onto the floor. It was a split second. It was an eternity. My eyes were still fixed in place, only now I was looking at my mother collapsed in a crumpled pile on the floor. My brother stomped out and slammed the door, shaking the house one last time, and sped off in her car.

I stood there for a moment in the eerie silence. I could hear myself breathing, but I couldn't tell if my mother still was. A chilling clarity came to me, just as a soft part of my childhood left. Without taking my eyes from my motionless mother, I pulled myself together. Picking up the receiver of our one telephone, I felt it heavy and cold, pressed against my small ear. My little fingers pushed down the square buttons in a familiar sequence. It was the number of one of my mother's friends, whose house she would sometimes visit to hang out. Since I was only six years old, hers was one of the few numbers I had memorized.

Clearing my voice so I could be heard over the telephone's static hum, choking on tears, I did my best to calmly tell her, "My brother really hurt my mother, and I'm home alone. Please come help." I don't remember what she said. I hung up still feeling focused, my eyes still fixed on my mother's body. I went into a sort of trance.

I don't know how long I stood there, just that I snapped out of it at the sound of a loud banging on the door. I scurried to open it for my mother's friend, and several policemen rushed in. I couldn't understand what anyone was saying, but I watched as they hurried over to where my mother was lying. Next thing I knew, she was moving. The moment I realized she was alive, the spell of shock broke, and a gush of fear and panic rushed over me—the dawning realization of what had actually happened, what had almost happened, and what unknown future was waiting. I tucked my small body into a ball, held on to myself tightly, and quietly began to cry. I could hear the faint sound of my mother's voice as she stirred back to consciousness. Then I heard a crystal-clear voice, ringing out just above my head. It was a man's voice, a voice that I will never forget.

One of the cops, looking down at me but speaking to another cop beside him, said, "If this kid makes it, it'll be a miracle." And that night, I became less of a kid and more of a miracle.

WHEN CHRISTMAS COMES

I don't want a lot for Christmas
There is just one thing I need
I don't care about the presents
Underneath the Christmas tree

—"All I Want for Christmas Is You"

My mother added a leaf to her tiny wooden table, making it *almost* family-sized for the day. With a few simple decorations, the table became the festive centerpiece, along with a Charlie Brown-ish tree, of an otherwise makeshift furnished living room in the run-down house where the two of us lived. Despite our circumstances, my mother wanted us to have a "wonderful life."

The days leading up to Christmas were an event. My mother always kept an Advent calendar. We would open a new flap each day. I'd read the portion of a story or a poem printed there, and she would give me the chocolates hidden inside. The mulled wine she made camouflaged the dankness of the house with a warm spicy aroma. I was well aware we didn't have much money, so while I never really anticipated getting any extravagant presents or popular toys, I loved that we'd make an effort to get into the spirit and do what we could to create an ambiance of joy and jubilance. We'd clean up, we'd decorate, and of course we would sing. Christmas carols sung in my mother's operatic voice brought a feeling of spaciousness to our cramped daily existence.

Mother wasn't much of a cook, but for Christmas dinner she tried—we both tried. We tried to put all the trauma and drama that infected the rest of our lives on hold and just have a peaceful Christmas meal. Too much to ask? I think not. I was a child craving a childhood, in a house filled with disappointment and pain.

Throughout the years, my sister and brother would rarely communicate all year, let alone come to visit where my mother and I were living. Christmas was one rare occasion when we would all be together under one rickety roof. The four of us would sit around the table, eyes avoiding eyes, often unable to talk, clogged up by all the things none of us had language for. I was very young and had not yet accumulated enough of a past to be broken by it. My siblings and my mother wouldn't communicate for most of the year, so by Christmas dinner my brother and sister would come stuffed with hurt and anger, starving for attention. Eventually, inevitably, they would all explode in a torrent of verbal abuse. I would sit there in the center of the chaos, crying and wishing: wishing they would stop screaming, wishing my mother could stop them from screaming and cursing. Wishing I could be somewhere safe and merry—somewhere that felt like *Christmas*.

My sister and brother clearly couldn't stand each other, but their deep resentment toward me was a constant, silent menace simmering right below the surface. I was the third and youngest child, and our parents were divorced by the time I was three. I was what *they* considered a golden child: lighter hair, lighter skin, and a lighter spirit. I lived with our mother, and they were exiled from each other and us. They existed in a different kind of pain, absorbing whatever hostility under-loved, troubled, mixed kids do in any neighborhood, Black or white. I believed they believed I was passing. There I was with my blondish hair, living with our white mother, in what they considered a safe white neighborhood. Their resentment toward me was perhaps the one thing they had in common; they seemed bound in that bitterness. I actually understood why they were angry and hateful toward me, but at the time, I couldn't fathom why every year, they just had to ruin Christmas.

But my wishing was more powerful than their pain. I wished with exuberance. I set about creating my own little magical, merry world of Christmas. I focused on all the things my mother struggled to create; all

I needed was a shower of glitter and a full church choir to back me up. My imaginary Christmas was filled with Santa Claus, reindeer, snowmen, and all the bells and trimmings a little girl's dreams could hold. And I loved contemplating a sweet baby Jesus, taking in the powerful joy the true spirit of the season brings.

Not every Christmas was ruined by my family.

My mother was culturally open when I was young and had a diverse group of friends. I remember I had a friend—let's call her Ashley—whose mother was gay (Ashley had no clue). My mother was very matter of fact: "Ashley's mom is gay, and she lives with her partner." No big deal. And it really wasn't. Two of my favorite people were my guncles (gay uncles), Burt and Myron. They were wonderful, and so was their home. It wasn't a grand spread, but theirs was a charming midsized brick house set back on a sweet piece of wooded land. Wild raspberries grew in the backyard, and they had a golden Labrador named Sparkle. When they traveled, my mother and I would house-sit for them. I reveled in the cleanliness and comfort.

Burt was a schoolteacher and photographer, and Myron was, as he put it, a "stay-at-home wife." Myron was a *vision*. He wore a perfectly coiffed beard and his hair was always blown out in cascading layers, which he would finish off with a shimmering frosting spray. He was perpetually tanned and sashayed around the house in spectacular multicolored silk caftans. Burt would bring me out in their yard to take photos of me (I just adored showing off in front of a camera), and he totally encouraged my exaggerated poses. He fully supported and understood my propensity for extraness.

I distinctly remember one Christmas photo session we staged. I was dressed up in a green dress with flowers, and, as a special Christmas miracle, I had decent-looking bangs. I pretended to be placing an ornament on the tree as I coyly looked back over my shoulder and Burt snapped the picture: fashion-feature festive.

I enjoyed Burt and Myron's lovely, cozy little home year-round, but especially at Christmastime. They put so much care and personality into preparing for the season. The house would be perfectly clean, and there would be pretty decorations, precisely placed, and a fire roaring in the fireplace. The house smelled like a new oven with something roasting inside; they always had little savory morsels to nibble and served fancy drinks like brandy Alexanders. I remember being stuck at their house one holiday during an ice storm, which I hoped would never end. Burt and Myron gave me my first taste of what a homey Christmas really felt like. They provided an example of a homey lifestyle in general.

My guncles supported the showgirl in me. Whenever I wanted to put on my own little production (which was frequently), they would pay full attention to me. They never tried to tame my over-the-top imagination. It was from my little girl's spirit and those early fantasies of family, and friendship, that I wrote "All I Want for Christmas Is You." Think of how it begins: ding, ding, ding, ding, ding, ding, ding, ding . . . the delicate chimes are reminiscent of those little wooden toy pianos, like the one Schroeder had on *Peanuts*.

I actually did bang out most of the song on a cheap little Casio keyboard. But it's the feeling I wanted the song to capture. There's a sweetness, a clarity, and a purity to it. It didn't stem from Christian inspiration, although I've certainly sung and written from that soulful and spiritual perspective. Instead, this song came from a childlike space; when I wrote it, at twenty-two years old, I wasn't that far away from being a child. I recorded an entire Christmas album, which was a risk. You just didn't see Christmas videos on MTV back then. In fact, it was almost unheard of for anyone—let alone such a young singer, so early in her career—to write and record an original Christmas song that was a legit smash hit.

Though I was accessing the private dream world of my childhood in the song, I wasn't in the happiest place when I wrote it. My life had changed so quickly, yet I still felt lost, wandering the wild borderlands between childhood and adulthood. My relationship with Tommy Mottola, who would eventually become my first husband (and so much more) was already getting weird, and we weren't even married yet. But to his credit as the head of my record label, he encouraged me to make my first Christmas album, *Merry Christmas*.

I was feeling nostalgic too. I've always been a tragically sentimental person, and Christmastime embodies that sentimentality for me. I wanted to write a song that would make me happy and make me feel like a loved, carefree young girl at Christmas. I also wanted to deliver it like the greats I grew up idolizing—Nat King Cole and the Jackson Five—who had tremendous Christmas classics of their own. I wanted to sing it in a way that would capture joy for everyone and crystallize it forever. Yes, I was going for vintage Christmas happiness. I also believe that somewhere inside I knew it was too late to give my brother and sister peace, and my mother her wonderful life, but I could possibly give the world a Christmas classic instead.

THE FATHER
AND THE SUN

Thank you for embracing a flaxen-haired baby
Although I'm aware you had your doubts
I guess anybody'd have had doubts
—"Sunflowers for Alfred Roy"

My father always reminded me of a sunflower—tall, proud, and stoic, but also bright, strong, handsome, and self-possessed. He labored hard to reach up and out of the harsh ground in which he was rooted. He was determined to transcend the limitations faced by his parents, their siblings, and their whole generation. He was the only child of his father, Robert, and mother, Addie. He was embarrassed by Addie's third-grade education. Addie was tough on her son, and so he grew to respect and rely on order and logic. By his own strength, he hauled himself out of the violent, oppressive environment that had driven one of his uncles to kill another. My father craved discipline, culture, and freedom, so he joined the military—a logical choice for a man who'd had no say over the time or skin into which he was born.

The military may have taken my father out of the Bronx, but it did not remove him from the perils of being a Black man in America. While he was enlisted, a white woman at the base where he was stationed said she was raped and that a Black man did it. On no evidence other than his not being white, my father was accused of the crime and placed in a jail on the base. To add extra suffering, and to serve as a warning to other Black soldiers, the white officers in charge assigned a Black officer to supervise my father—a deliberate reminder that a US military uniform did not camouflage their race. Much like assigning a Black overseer on a plantation, it was an effective technique of terror.

My father was mortified, but mostly he was scared. Like many Black men, he lived in fear of arbitrary brutality, abduction, or death. Yet perhaps above all he feared exhibiting fear—because he knew for that transgression, death was the certain punishment. My father was eventually released, without any apology, support, or counseling. The military's only explanation was that they had apprehended the actual culprit. With a government-issued gun in hand, he walked straight out of that prison to the top of a hill. Consumed with trauma and rage, he thought of pulling the trigger—and he was not contemplating suicide.

My father took surgical care with everything he did. His lifestyle had a truly austere quality: part military barracks, part Shaolin monastery. His kitchen was small and impeccably kept. The contents of his pantry were precisely indexed by size and category. There was no room for extravagance or waste of any kind in his home. There were no multiples of anything: one TV, one radio. In his closet hung just the amount of shirts needed for a week, nothing more. He didn't consider a bed properly made unless the covers were tucked in so tightly that you could bounce a quarter off its surface.

My father's approach to most things was efficient and militaristic. He considered the act of snacking frivolous. If I was hungry while waiting for dinner, he would give me one Ritz cracker. *One.* The allure of that bright-red box, with its iconic swirl of golden, sunflower-shaped crackers rising out of their wax sleeves, was intoxicating. He would pull out one tall column of crackers, undo the meticulously folded sleeve top, slip a single cracker from the stack, and hand it to me delicately, as if it were a precious gem. Then he would carefully refold the paper, slide the stack back into the box, and return it to its place on the shelf, where it would stay.

I'd hold the buttery, salty, crunchy goodness up to my nose, close my eyes, and breathe in one long, luxurious sniff. With precision, I would take one teeny-weeny bite along the scalloped edge. I'd chew ever so slowly, letting the savory sensation linger on my tongue. Turning the golden treasure ever so slightly, I would nibble off another little piece of the edge, relishing every grain of salt and crumb, making my one cracker last as long as I could. (Ironically, the slogan on the box was "there's only *one* Ritz"—and for me, there really was!)

By today's standards my father would have been considered a hipster. After the military, he moved to Brooklyn Heights, drove a classic Porsche Speedster, and prepared authentic Italian dishes in his kitchen. Oh, how I lived for my father's cooking! He made a mean sausage and peppers, and delicious parsley meatballs, but his linguine with white clam sauce was *sublime*. The scent of garlic in hot olive oil, boiling pasta, and the salty sea are what the best Sundays smell like to me. I loved Sundays. Those were the days I spent with my father—and our meals together were what I looked forward to the most.

One Sunday, my father's mother, Addie, was there—a rare occasion. I don't think I was more than five years old. It began as a typical Sunday, my father spending the entire day meticulously preparing his signature dish. He shucked and cleaned every clam, sliced the garlic, and chopped the aromatic flat Italian parsley. It was such a process—a ritual, rather. As per usual I hadn't eaten all day, save maybe *a* Ritz cracker (and I probably hadn't had a full meal the day before; Saturday night at my mother's house could be a bit haphazard). Between reading and coloring and tummy rumbles, I eyed the pantry. The air was perfumed with the freshness of my father's ingredients. I'd waited all week, waited all day; I just needed to hold out until dinnertime. Soon I would be reveling in my favorite dish.

I smelled the pasta softening in the boiling water and knew it wouldn't be long. "It's dinnertime!" my father finally sang. I jumped up and rushed to sit at the small Formica table in the kitchen. Addie, with a fabulous red wig and a red printed caftan to match, was on a tangent, telling some story only the grown-ups would be interested in. I could barely hold my head up, as I'd probably started to swoon and drool waiting for the deliciousness that was about to appear before me. I watched my father put the pasta on my plate, then scoop up the heavenly sauce and artfully pour it around the linguine. I followed his every move as he lowered the steaming white plate down in front of me. It was time! And then, just as I was picking up my fork, Addie—who had not paused in her story to take a breath—whipped out a green canister of grated Parmesan cheese and proceeded to shake its unsavory, powdery contents all over my elegant fresh linguine.

Noooooooo!!!!!! I screamed in horror. But it was too late; my plate was covered with it. My father *never* put that cheese on white clam sauce! Where had it even come from? Did she have it in her pocketbook?! Unable to control my shock and revulsion, I ran to the bathroom, slammed the door, and exploded into tears. "Roy, you better make her eat that pasta. Make her eat that food!" I heard Addie telling my father in defiance. That was the only time I remember my father's perfect pasta being foiled, and I think it was the last time Addie joined us for Sunday supper.

My father taught me that words have meaning and thus, they have power. Once, on a lovely summer Sunday afternoon, I heard the faint jingle of the ice cream truck coming down the street outside my father's house. Upon recognizing the mystical melody that promised so much pleasure, I let out an excited cry: "*Aaaaa! The ice cream man!*" The song was loud and clear now, so I knew the truck had stopped somewhere nearby. The pattering of running feet and the happy squeals I heard confirmed it—the ice cream man was right outside our door. My mind was racing. *I gotta go!* I thought to myself. *He's going to leave!*

"Can I borrow fifty cents, please, please?!" I nearly shrieked at my father, dangerously close to hyperventilating.

"Do you want to *borrow* fifty cents? Or would you like to *have* fifty cents?" he replied in a cool, calm tone.

A mild panic was creeping in. "Uhhhh," I stammered. I didn't know what to say. All I knew was that I had to get some money for the ice cream man. "I don't know!"

I wasn't thinking clearly. Again, my father spoke in a patient, level manner that only enhanced my frenzy.

"There's a difference between borrowing and having. Are you asking me to *give* you fifty cents?"

I was in a state and unprepared to make distinctions at that moment, so I blurted out, "I just want to borrow fifty cents. I'll give it back! Please!"

He reached in his pocket, pulled out two shiny silver quarters, and dropped them in my anxious little palm. Like the occasional Ritz cracker, they felt like precious jewels. I burst through the doors of the building, barely touching the steps, and ran to the truck like a gazelle being chased by a lion.

I had gotten my ice cream, but my father made it clear I would have to repay the money I had *borrowed*. At seven years old I wasn't earning any money yet, so I asked my mother for the quarters. She couldn't fathom why my father would barter with his little girl, and she gave them to me. They had always had opposing parenting styles. I kept my promise and gave the money back to him the next Sunday. The ice cream man incident was a lesson not only in respecting the meaning of words but in integrity and money management. My father was a man who had saved the very first dollar he ever made.

Being a single father was a fairly new notion back then, so he wasn't prepared to plan girlie playdates or fun, child-centered activities. For the most part, I was simply the child accompaniment to his regular adult life—keeping busy and out of the way as he cooked, cleaned, and tinkered with his car while listening to football on the radio. And he *adored* his Porsche. It was his only true luxury. He bought two of them in his lifetime, one before children and one after, both used. His Speedster was apparently always in need of some sort of repair, so he was *always* messing around in it.

The car was in a perpetual state of being "prepared" for full restoration. It was a vague, matte noncolor, because it was covered in gray primer, not paint. I once asked him why the color of the car was so dull. He explained that it was primer, but that the original color had been candy apple red. "Oh, so one day you're going to make it candy apple red?" I asked.

"They don't make that color anymore," he said flatly. I was confused. Why not just make it another color, then? But if it couldn't be the original color, he'd rather it not be any color at all.

He was incredibly patient with the Porsche, spending hours with it, believing deeply in its exotic beauty and high performance. It was very cool and chic—a soft-top convertible with two seats. He loved the freedom of putting the top down and the intimacy of only having room for one passenger. We would go on long drives without much chatting. If the radio was on, it was tuned to the news ("1010 Wins—you give us ten minutes, we'll give you the world"). Every now and then we would sing one of those funny, folksy songs that go on and on, like "There's a Hole in the Bottom of the Sea."

There's a wart on the frog, on the bump, on the log,
in the hole in the bottom of the sea

He also liked to sing "John Henry," a folk song about a Black man who worked as a "steel-driving man."

John Henry was a little baby, sitting on his Daddy's knee

When he would sing "knee," he'd hit an impossibly low note that would always make me laugh. I liked singing those songs because they would help the time and the miles go by. Back then I thought just driving was such a bore. But now, oh, what wouldn't I do to sit next to him, one more time, in those leather seats, on the open road, with just the hum of the engine and the swishing of the wind as our accompaniment. My mother, the opera singer, taught me scales, but my father taught me songs that made me laugh.

Thank you for the mountains
The Lake of the Clouds
I'm picturing you and me there right now
As the crystal cascades showered down

—"Sunflowers for Alfred Roy"

Occasionally we would go to Lime Rock Park, a racetrack in Connecticut. It was a slightly more glamorous experience than a typical NASCAR venue. Paul Newman had a team there, and world-class drivers like Mario Andretti were regulars. I found the racetrack pretty boring, but going to the races was a favorite activity for Alfred Roy, and he made all of his kids join him. This was one rare thing we kids all could agree on: cars going around and around in a circle wasn't high entertainment.

When we were on our drives or at the racetrack, I was often just *around* while he did regular adult things. While he listened to or watched football (which he loved, and which I found extremely boring) I would be close by, quietly reading or drawing—observing the ways of an adult.

My father did have a few books just for me in his house. The one I remember most distinctly was about a little Black boy who was blind. The cover was white, with large red, orange, and yellow circles. It was full of colors and told the story of a boy who saw the world through touching and feeling shapes, rather than through color.

When I think of that storybook, I think of Stevie Wonder. Reading it, I wondered if this was the reason why Stevie Wonder could create such vivid worlds and emotions through his songs: he was seeing without eyes; he was seeing with his soul. Stevie Wonder is by far the songwriter I respect and love the most. He is beyond genius; I believe he writes songs from a holy place. I think that having this book about the blind Black boy was one way my father attempted to introduce the concepts of racism and perception to me, because we really didn't talk about it. We didn't talk about the shades and the shapes of *us*.

Perception was also very important to my father. Once, while drawing alongside him on a quiet Sunday afternoon, I made what I thought was a very clever cartoon. It was a picture of our family with the caption, "They're weird. But they're okay." But when I showed it to my father, he got really upset.

"Why would you say we're weird?" he demanded. I was shaken by his stern tone, and I had no idea why the idea made him angry.

"I don't know. I probably heard it somewhere," I said. In my cartoon I had also added, "But they're okay," which I thought was optimistic. It was a little tongue-in-cheek.

With an absolute seriousness that chilled me, he said, "Don't ever say that."

I never intended to offend him, in fact, I'd wanted to delight him. I felt really bad that day. But the heavy load he carried, his deep desire to be accepted as a full human being, was something I wouldn't learn about until much later—something I am still trying to make peace with.

At the time, I didn't have the language to tell him that weird was how I felt. I didn't know how to say that was how I felt other people saw us—as *weird*. I thought everything was weird. My hair was weird; my clothes were weird; my siblings and their friends were weird; my mother and all the shabby places we lived with her—they were all *weird*.

I thought the Unitarian Universalist Fellowship was a *weird* church. We had started attending when the family was still together. The five of us would go to this old medieval-style stone castle with thick walls and a tall tower, filled with a congregation of what looked like every odd person on the Island. To my little-girl self it appeared like the Church of Misfit Toys at a Renaissance fair. The pastor, who was formerly Jewish, had changed his name from Ralph to Lucky. *"Reverend Lucky?" Okay.* The teens would go up in the tower and do whatever weird things teens did. Even as a little girl, I knew this was not *my* scene. But my father, though the only Black person, felt like he was accepted there among the other outsiders, so he stayed at the fellowship forever.

I don't think my father understood how different we were from everyone in the neighborhoods I lived in with my mother. It was weird to be living in a makeshift apartment on top of a deli when *everyone else* lived in a house. We lived in a small commercial section of Northport where there was a strip of stores on the ground level of a cluster of Victorian houses. They were small-town businesses: a bicycle shop, maybe a general store, and then the deli. A staircase alongside the deli's entrance led up to a small, dim railroad-style apartment where I lived with my mother and Morgan.

I had a room at the end of the hall, no bigger than a typical walk-in closet. The apartment was small, the floors were covered in pea-green carpeting, and the walls and doors were thin; the sound of laughing and voices often kept me awake at night. I had very few things in that tiny room that brought me comfort. The most precious, perhaps, were gifts from my father—a little ceramic bunny and a sweet molasses-colored teddy bear named Cuddles, which I kept until it was destroyed many years later after a flood in a Manhattan apartment that was on top of a bar and nightclub (apparently, there are levels to living on top of establishments, and I have gone through all of them).

I remember when you used to tuck me in at night
with the teddy bear you gave to me that I held so tight

—"Bye Bye"

Even with Cuddles by my side, I frequently had nightmares, and it was in that dismal apartment where my troubles with sleep first began.

I don't recall anyone else *living* around there, and there were certainly no other Black people for miles. Morgan's was the only Afro in sight. Once, after he got in trouble, my mother meekly admonished him to "stay in his room." Shortly after, the owner of the deli downstairs called my mother to inform her that he was watching her son jump from rooftop to rooftop above the other stores. Morgan had climbed out of the window onto the roof and was making a daring escape. He eventually went through a phase when he shaved his head bald and would wear karate pants, with a snake casually draped around his neck. He would walk through the town looking like a punk ninja, full of anger, hoping to find a fight. Even without his hair he was impossible to miss.

My father might not have liked me calling the Careys weird, but weird things certainly happened to us. Every now and then, Alison would crash into the apartment like a meteor, and friends of hers and Morgan's would hang out all night.

One night Alison booked *me* as the entertainment. Earlier that day she'd taught me the song "White Rabbit" by Jefferson Airplane. It was an odd selection for sure, but I figured maybe she liked it because the refrain of "Go ask Alice" sounded close to her name. When I was brought out to the living room to perform, all of the lights were out, and I was surrounded by burning candles and a circle of teenagers (as well as my mother). Watching Alison's face for approval, I let out the first verse:

One pill makes you larger, and one pill makes you small
And the ones that Mother gives you, don't do anything at all
Go ask Alice, when she's ten feet tall

A song about taking drugs and tripping is not typical (or appropriate) lyrical content for a little girl. But I sang it because my big sister taught it to me. I loved nothing more than learning and singing songs, but this one was full of scary images ("the White Knight is talking backward /and the Red Queen's off with her head") and what seemed to me like creepy nonsense ("the hookah-smoking caterpillar"—what?).

Of course, I wondered what this song was about and why I was singing it in the dark. It was past midnight, and while all the other kids my age were nestled in their beds, I was belting out, "Feed your head!" for a candlelit gathering of wannabe-hippie teens conducting a pseudo-séance. Tell me that's not weird.

"See you next Sunday!" That was our thing. My father and I gave that little promise to each other with a wave each week as I left him to return to life with my mother. But as I grew a little older, my seriousness as a singer-songwriter began to swiftly envelop my whole world. I was in the profession by the time I was twelve. My father did not see it or support it, largely because he did not understand it.

Music, as a career, was not logical to him. When I talked about writing poetry and singing, he would shift the conversation to grades and homework. He didn't see the focus and discipline I was cultivating as an artist. He didn't see how I was learning the craft, sitting in on jam sessions with accomplished jazz musicians with my mother and developing the skills of scatting and improvisation. He never saw how I spent hours writing, enriching my ear, and studying popular music trends on the radio. Above all, we had a fundamental difference in belief: I followed my heart, while he was guided by his fear of not being accepted. From that awful and auspicious day when Nana Reese laid her hands on me and spoke into my heart, I truly *believed* anything I wanted was possible. It was real to me. Absolute. My father did not believe anything was possible. On the contrary, he expected the world to vehemently deny his desires, not the least of which was dignity.

Alfred Roy was a man who lived his entire life under threat of humiliation and dehumanization as a result of his identity. He placed all his hope in the notion that societal respect would be awarded him through his discipline, diligence, and excellence on traditional institutional tracks like academics, service to your country, and respectable work. His other two children had all the makings of great students. When they were younger, he demanded that they produce all As on their report cards, and mostly they did (yet he would still sometimes question why each A wasn't accompanied by a plus). The only class I excelled in was creative writing, in which I was always in the advanced groups. But I was *tragic* in mathematics and really couldn't connect with most other subjects or material.

The two potential academics took terrible turns in their teens, fulfilling a Black father's greatest fears. The boy had been "institutionalized," placed in the precarious "care" of the state, the first stop on a dangerous fast track to becoming a statistic. And the girl, pregnant before her sixteenth birthday, had already arrived at one. And I, the baby, who wasn't a wild one, rejected the traditional, "safe" route to a secure career and began to pursue what he saw as an improbable, mysterious, and dangerous path. My father was extremely strict with my siblings, and they would often complain or joke about his tight and eccentric ways to my mother. However, in an effort to shield me from their harsh perspective, I often overheard her tell them, "Don't say that in front of Mariah."

There were moments when my father did disappoint me. After Alison was no longer living with him, he went from being a divorced single father to a true bachelor. There were times he wouldn't show up for our dates.

As a child, there were them times
I didn't get it, but you kept me in line
I didn't know why
You didn't show up sometimes
On Sunday mornings
And I missed you

—"Bye Bye"

So, over time, our Sunday ritual became sporadic. My music was driving so much of my time and energy by that point. I worked on it every moment I could. I was determined to rise above my conditions, rise above all the people who didn't believe I was going to make it, rise above the sad place my sister had fallen into, rise above my brother's angry dysfunction. I was going to rise above it all—even if that included my father, the one stable family member I had. After paying for one summer at a performing arts camp, the most my father ever did for my career was to warn me about how uncertain and treacherous the entertainment business could be.

Years later, I called my father and played "Vision of Love" from the recording studio, putting the phone receiver right up to the Yamaha speaker.

"Wow," he said, "you sound like all three Pointer Sisters!" He wasn't a big music man, so this comparison was high praise coming from him. It meant he had noticed all of the layers of the background vocals, in addition to the strong lead. He was really *listening* to my song. And I could tell he was happy with it and with me. After all those years, it was truly validating.

Yet, even after all I had accomplished I wasn't immune to the perfectionism he had projected onto his other children. After I had garnered two Grammys within my very first year in the industry, he remarked, "Maybe if you were a producer you could win more, like Quincy Jones." That same year, the legendary Quincy Jones took home seven Grammys for his epic project *Back on the Block*, which spanned the entire history of Black American Music and featured giants from Ella Fitzgerald and Miles Davis to Luther Vandross.

I had done astonishingly well as a new artist (who had written her own hit songs), and here my father was, comparing me to arguably one of the greatest musical giants the industry has ever known, with decades of experience and endless accolades and honors to his name! I was immediately thrust back to my childhood, as if my two Grammys were two A's on my report card and he was asking me what had happened to the pluses. I think my success in music scared him because he had no idea about, and seemingly no influence on, how I'd arrived. He didn't ask and I didn't tell.

Gradually, "next Sunday" turned into a month of Sundays. I had to let go of our Sundays so I could manifest my own day in the sun.

COLORING OUTSIDE
THE LINES

It's hard to explain
Inherently it's just always been strange
Neither here nor there
Always somewhat out of place everywhere
Ambiguous without a sense of belonging to touch

—*"Outside"*

My first encounters with racism were like a first kiss in reverse: each time, a piece of purity was ripped from my being. Left behind was a spreading stain, which seeped so deeply inside of me that to this day, I've never been able to completely scrub it out. Not with time, not with fame or wealth, not even with love. The earliest of these encounters happened when I was about four years old and in preschool. The activity for the day was to draw a portrait of our families. Laid out on the table was a stack of heavy-stock construction paper the color of eggshells and small groups of crayons for us to pick from. While I much preferred sing-along and story time to coloring, I was excited about the project and determined to do my very best. I thought if I did a good job maybe the teacher would decorate my drawing with a gold-foil star sticker.

I chose my supplies carefully, found a quiet corner, and got busy with the assignment. At that point, our family of five had not yet fractured. For a short time, I had a father, a mother, a sister, and a brother, and we were all living together in what felt to me like relative peace. I wanted to create a family portrait I could be proud of. I wanted to draw all the different unique things about everybody—their clothes, their heights and proportions, their facial features—all the little details that would make my portrait come to life. Father was tall, and Mother had long dark hair. My brother was strong and my sister had her pretty ringlets. I wanted to capture all of it. The sound of crayons rubbing on thick paper created a dull hum as the faint, comforting scent of Crayola wax wafted through the room.

Deeply engaged with perfecting my masterpiece, I was curled over with my head down, nose nearly touching the paper, when I felt a tall shadow fall across my quiet corner. I knew instinctively that it was one of the young student teachers looming over me. At four years old I had already begun to develop a keen watch-your-back instinct, so I immediately stopped moving my hand. Tension rose up and stiffened my little body. For a reason I did not yet know, I sensed danger and felt suddenly protective. I held absolutely still until she spoke.

"How ya doin' there, Mariah? Let's see."

Relaxing a bit, I lifted the paper toward her and proudly presented my family picture in progress. Immediately, the student teacher burst into laughter. She was soon joined by another young woman teacher, who also began to laugh. Then a third adult came over to join in the fun. The cheerful buzz of children working with crayons stopped. The whole room had turned to stare at what was happening in my little corner. A brew of self-consciousness and embarrassment boiled up from my feet to my face. The whole class was watching. I managed to speak through the stifling heat in my throat.

"Why are you laughing?" I asked.

Through her giggles, one of them replied, "Oh, Mariah, you used the wrong crayon! You didn't mean to do that!" She was pointing at where I'd drawn my father.

As they kept laughing, I looked down at the picture of my family I had lovingly and diligently been creating. I'd used the peach crayon for the skin of myself, my mother, my sister, and my brother. I'd used a brown crayon for my father. I knew I was more like the color of animal crackers and my brother and sister were more like Nutter Butters, while my father's skin tone resembled graham crackers. But they didn't have any cookie-colored crayons, so I'd had to improvise! They were acting like I'd used a *green* crayon or something. I was humiliated and confused. What had I done so wrong?

Still cackling hysterically, the teachers insisted, "You used the wrong crayon!" Every time one of them made the declaration the whole gang laughed, laughed, and laughed some more. A debilitating kind of disgrace was pressing down on me, yet I managed to pull myself up slowly, eyes burning and brimming with hot tears.

As calmly as I could, I told the teachers, "No. I *didn't* use the wrong crayon."

Refusing to even give me the dignity of addressing me directly, one of them said to the other snidely, "She doesn't even know she's using the wrong crayon!" The laughter and taunting seemed like it would never end. I stood glaring up at them, working very hard not to vomit from embarrassment. But despite my nausea, I did not break my glare.

Eventually the laughter started to subside, and one at a time they backed away from the picture and from me. I watched them across the room, huddled together and whispering. They had only ever seen one member of my family of five: my mother, who dropped me off at school each day. *She* was the color of the peach crayon. They had no idea and no imagination to suspect that the light toast of my skin, my bigger-than-button nose, and the waves and ringlets in my hair were from my father—my handsome father who was the color of warm maple syrup. His complexion was a crayon color they didn't have; brown was as close to right as I could get. It was the teachers who had got it all wrong. But despite their cruel and unwarranted attack, they never apologized for the public humiliation, for their ignorance and immaturity, or for demoralizing a four-year-old girl during coloring time.

By the time I made it to first grade, my family of five had crumbled like cookies. My parents divorced, but although they were living a short car ride away from each other, racially their neighborhoods on Long Island were worlds apart.

In first grade, I had a best friend named Becky. She was cute and sweet and looked just like the Strawberry Shortcake cartoon to me. She had big blue eyes, smooth strawberry-blond hair that was naturally sun-kissed and hung perfectly straight down like heavy drapes, and reddish freckles sprinkled across her whipped cream–colored cheeks. In my mind, she looked like what little girls were *supposed* to look like. She looked like the little girls who were adored and protected; like the little girl my mother might've had with a man *her* mother would've approved of.

One Sunday, our mothers made arrangements for Becky and me to have a playdate at my house. I was delighted because Becky and I really had fun together. When Sunday finally arrived, my mother picked up Becky in whatever ragtag car she was driving at the time, and we headed to my father's house. We pulled up to the brick town house, and Becky and I hopped out of the car. I grabbed her hand and skipped excitedly up the steps. Curiously, my mother hung back and watched—ordinarily she would have driven off. Just as our feet hit the top of the stoop, my six-feet-two-inches-tall, dashing father emerged through the door with a hearty grin. He looked like a movie star.

"Hiya, Mariah!" he called out, giving me my usual greeting. As he neared us, Becky suddenly released my hand. Her body froze stiff and, like a bursting raincloud, she exploded into tears. Confused, I looked to my father for help, but I could see that he was frozen too, and breathless, a mortified look twisting his strong features. In a state of shock, my mind scrambled as I tried to process the abrupt and painful turn of events. Becky in hysterics, my father in silent agony: how had we gotten here in a single instant?

I didn't know what to do. I was stuck there, unmoving, for what felt like hours but was likely merely moments. Finally, my mother came up behind us on the stairs, to Becky's rescue. Without even a glance in my direction, she gently placed her arm around the distraught little girl and wordlessly guided her down the stairs and into the backseat of her car. My mother sped off with the strawberry blonde, without ever making any attempt to clarify what had happened. There was no consolation, no mediation, no acknowledgment of the devastation to me or my father. In the wake of Becky's storm, my father and I stood quietly together on the stoop and waited for the ache to pass. Nobody ever mentioned it after that, but we never played together again, and the moment remained with me forever. And, believe it or not, her name really *was* Becky.

No one ever outwardly questioned my ethnic background when I was alone with my mother. They didn't dare ask about, or else could not detect, the differences in our hues and textures. Becky, and most likely her mother too, had probably just assumed my father was also white, or maybe something exotic—but certainly not *Black*. That day on the stoop I learned, beyond the shadow of a doubt, that I was not like the people I went to school with or who lived in my neighborhood. My father was totally different from them, and they were afraid of him. But he was my people; I came from him. That day, I saw firsthand how their fear hurt him. And his hurt deeply hurt me too. But what was perhaps most painful, that afternoon, was that he saw that *I* saw their fear of him. He knew it would impact me forever. He knew I could never return to the innocence all children deserve.

HODEL

Singing was a form of escapism for me, and writing was a form of processing. There was joy in it, but it mainly was survival (and it still is). My voice was recognized as pure talent not only by my mother but also by my teachers. A friend of my mother's was my music teacher, and she was exceptional. As a child I was in a few school plays, and I would sing for friends at random events. Singing onstage (or anywhere), imagining I was someone else, was when I felt most like myself. Walking around alone and coming up with melodies while singing to myself was when I felt the most whole. To this day, I escape to my private vocal booth to shut out all the demands of life and feel myself in my space, singing alone.

I was in the fifth grade when I first got the opportunity to attend an exclusive performing arts summer camp. This was a breakthrough! I could finally be around other young aspiring artists and hone my craft, undistracted by the confusion and chaos at home. I landed the role of Hodel, one of the five daughters in the camp's production of *Fiddler on the Roof.* I lived to go to rehearsals. It was my favorite time and place. I was confident, quickly learning the songs and studying their meanings. The act of practicing came naturally to me; I liked to do things over and over again.

I loved the experience of witnessing my performance getting better with each try, finding new and better ways to deliver a song.

The drive to practice music was also something my mother recognized and encouraged in me early on. She rehearsed the *Fiddler* songs with me at home, playing along on her Yamaha piano. Even as a little girl I was interested in exploring the details that made up a great song. And I was fascinated by the storytelling in the musical. I even managed to make a "camp friend" in the community of largely Jewish and mostly wealthy kids. We bonded through our love and seriousness of singing. We even kinda looked alike. She was Israeli with thick curly, almost kinky hair. So we both had tangled textures. We tried to dress alike when we could, we had the same pink onesie. Because people saw us together, saw some physical similarities, I think they thought I was a blondish Jewish girl from means.

I loved Hodel because she fell in love with a revolutionary boy and went to the ends of the earth to follow her passion. My big number was in the second act, a song called "Far from the Home I Love." It was a well-suited song for my breathy tone, and I remember I sang it in a purely emotional way. The song opened with these lovely, memorable lines:

> *How can I hope to make you understand*
> *Why I do what I do?*
> *Why I must travel to a distant land*
> *Far from the home I love.*

My father was coming up to the camp for the show's opening night, and I was thrilled. He was a practical man who *wasn't thrilled* with my artistic passion, but he had reluctantly paid half of my hefty tuition for camp that year. So while he was certainly coming to support me, he was also checking in on his investment. I didn't have the privilege of trying all different kinds of hobbies, like the kids I went to school with—it was this camp, or bust. So I knew I had to get all I could from it. There was no flitting from tennis lessons to guitar to dance class. Not that I would ever step foot in a dance class, even if we could afford it. I was traumatized early on about dancing.

One time when Addie was at my father's house, she looked at me, with my unruly flaxen hair and peach-crayon-colored skin, and said, "Roy, that ain't your baby." Then, as if to prove her point, she addressed me: "Girl, lemme see you dance." While I was surrounded by music, there wasn't much dancing in my childhood. My mother didn't dance; I never saw my siblings dance. My father didn't dance until later in the eighties, when he took hustle lessons.

In my mind, dancing became a measurement for Black acceptance, for belonging somewhere and to someone—for belonging to my father. I didn't dance for Addie that day. I didn't dance much at all after that. I just couldn't recover from the fear of not dancing "right" for my father. I stood there terrified to move, fearing if I didn't dance well enough or if I moved the wrong way, it would somehow prove that my father wasn't my father.

That day at camp, as Hodel, I sang and smiled and pranced about the stage and sang some more. I sang in a very distinct lullaby style. I was good, and everybody knew it. I could hear the loud clapping as I took my bow; it was like another kind of grand music, giving me energy, giving me hope. As I raised my head I saw the widest smile on my father's face. His smile was like sunshine itself. He walked up to the edge of the stage, his arms filled with a big bouquet of sunny daisies tied with a lavender ribbon. Beaming with pride, he handed me the flowers as if they were a prestigious award. At first we were both too giddy to notice that people were staring at us— and not in a way that felt good, not because I had given the outstanding performance of the night. They were staring because my father was the only Black man in sight, and I belonged to him. That night, the teachers, the parents, and all the other campers learned that my father was a Black man, and I paid the price for it. I got my thunderous applause and I got my flowers, but I never got another major role in a play at that camp again.

Please be at peace father
I'm at peace with you
Bitterness isn't worth clinging to
After all the anguish we've all been through

—"Sunflowers for Alfred Roy"

LIGHT OF MY LIFE

Letting go ain't easy
Oh, it's just exceedingly hurtful
'Cause somebody you used to know
Is flinging your world around
And they watch, as you're falling down, down, down,
Falling down, baby

—"The Art of Letting Go"

Y ou've always been the light of my life."
My mother told me this over and over when I was a child. I
wanted to be her light. I wanted to make her proud. I respected
her as a singer and a working mother. I loved her deeply, and, like most
kids, I wanted her to be a safe place for me. Above all, I desperately wanted
to believe her.

But ours is a story of betrayal and beauty. Of love and abandonment.
Of sacrifice and survival. I've emancipated myself from bondage several
times, but there is a cloud of sadness that I suspect will always hang over
me, not simply because of my mother but because of our complicated
journey together. It has caused me so much pain and confusion. Time has
shown me there is no benefit in trying to protect people who never tried
to protect me. Time and motherhood have finally given me the courage
to *honestly* face who my mother has been to me.

For me, this is the steepest cliff edge. If I can make it to the other side
of this truth, I know there is relief of epic proportions awaiting me. Those
people who have hurt me, over and over, whom I have escaped or walled off,
are deeply significant in my story, but they are not central to my existence.

Removing myself from toxic people I love has been excruciatingly painful, but once I found the courage (with prayer and professional help, of course), I simply let go and let God. (I'll add, though, that there's a huge difference between simple and *easy*. It ain't easy, baby.) Yet, there is no "artful" way of letting go of my mother, and our relationship is anything but simple. Like many aspects of my life, my journey with my mother has been full of contradictions and competing realities. It's never been only black-and-white—it's been a whole rainbow of emotions.

Our relationship is a prickly rope of pride, pain, shame, gratitude, jealousy, admiration, and disappointment. A complicated love tethers my heart to my mother's. When I became a mother to Roc and Roe, my heart grew two times over; as my capacity for pure love expanded, the ability to tow heavy pain from my past diminished. Healthy, powerful love did that for me: it illuminated the dark spots and unearthed buried hurt. The new, clear light that emanates from my children's love now rushes through every artery, every cell, every dark nook and cranny of my being.

Even after all this time, a part of me fantasizes that one of these days my mother will transform into one of the caring mothers I saw on TV as a child, like Carol Brady or Clair Huxtable; that she will suddenly ask me, "Honey, how, was *your* day?" before she gives me a report on her dog or her bird, or asks me to pay for something or do something—that she will have genuine, sustained interest in me and what I'm doing or feeling. That one day she will know me. That one day my mother will *understand* me.

To a certain extent, I know how my mother became who she is. Her mother certainly didn't understand *her*. And her father never had a chance to know her; he died while her mother was pregnant with her. She was one of three children raised by a widowed Irish Catholic woman. My mother was known as the "dark one" because her hair wasn't blond and her eyes were a mix of brown and green, not pure blue like her brother's and sister's. Blue eyes were a symbol of the purity of whiteness, and being of 100 percent "pure" Irish descent was central to her mother's entire identity.

My mother grew up in the 1940s and 1950s in Springfield, Illinois. It was the capital city at the center of a state at the center of the country. But Springfield was also a center of insidious institutional racism. In 1908, a white woman was allegedly raped by a Black man (the same accusation leveled against my father and countless other innocent Black men), which ignited a three-day riot by white citizens in which two Black men were lynched and four white men were shot to death by Black businessmen protecting their property. In the 1920s, when my mother's mother was coming of age, the Ku Klux Klan had a strong presence in the city and the city government, holding several key positions and setting the moral compass for the community. Springfield was a city openly cloaked in hate.

One of the few stories my mother told of her childhood was of being in kindergarten and sharing her mat with a Black boy at naptime. For this, the nuns at her Catholic school publicly shamed her. Obviously there was a rancid repertoire of slurs for Black people in my mother's youth, but she also told me of the odd slurs and degrading names they had for Italians, Jewish people, and all "others" when no one else was around. She made me privy to the hierarchy of racism in their white community. Ironically, even among her beloved Irish there was a social caste system that divided the "lace curtain Irish" from the "shanty Irish." The lace curtain Irish were "pure," well off, respectable, and "properly placed" in society (think of the Kennedys), while the shanty Irish were characterized as dirty, poor, and ignorant. There was a critical and pitiful *need*, in this system, to have a host of others to look down on. To my mother's mother, all "others" were below the Irish. But Black? Black people were always at the absolute bottom of the order. Nothing was below Black.

My mother not only ignored the moral code of her hometown, she rebelled against it, later becoming active in the civil rights movement. By the standards of her environment and family, she was a liberal eccentric. She was interested in life outside of their tiny, tight, white world. She was intellectually curious and drawn to culture, especially to classical music. She recalls that one day, while listening to a classical music station on the radio, she heard an aria. It was the most beautiful sound she'd ever heard, and she was determined to chase it, inside herself and out in the world. She decided to start her quest in New York City, which seemed a million miles away from her family and the small-minded place they inhabited.

Young Patricia had big dreams—many of which she realized. She was extremely gifted and driven. Winning a scholarship to the prestigious Juilliard School for music, she would go on to sing with the New York City Opera, making her debut at Lincoln Center. My mother built an exciting, artsy, bohemian life in New York City. She was in the downtown scene and dated a diverse cast of men by whom *her* mother would have been mortified. Her pure Irish Catholic mother wouldn't approve of her dating anyone who wasn't lily-white. (Of course, in turn, the white supremacists of Illinois weren't crazy about the Irish *or* Catholics—the WASPs [White Anglo-Saxon Protestants], as they were referred to at that time, always needed a fresh supply of people to have beneath them.) An Italian guy would have been a problem, a Jewish man, a tragedy. My grandmother would've come completely undone if she knew my mother had had a steamy affair with a rich, older Lebanese man named François, right before she fell in love with, and married, a man her mother could not even conceive of. My father. A beautiful, complicated Black man. This, to my grandmother (and her community) was the *worst* thing her daughter could do to her and to the family lineage. Talking to a Black man was considered a shame; befriending one, an outrage; carrying on with one, a major scandal, but *marrying* one?

That was an abomination.

It was the ultimate humiliation. My mother's marriage to my father was beyond betrayal to her mother; it was a high crime against her white heritage, punishable by excommunication.

To her mother, who grew up in a time and place where the KKK openly held mass rallies and were active in government, marrying a Black man carried a burden of shame she could not fathom. Her mother was raised not to drink from the same fountain as Black people, not to sit in the same seat as Black people or swim in the same pool. She was taught, *and believed*, that Black people were dirty and that Blackness could rub off. After all, the United States is the birthplace of the "one-drop rule," the racial classification system that asserts that any person with an ancestor possessing even one drop of Black blood is considered Black.

In my grandmother's view, my mother loving my father made her a bottom-feeder, procreating with the lowest human group and making mulatto mongrels—me and my siblings. Needless to say, my grandmother completely disowned her daughter. She told no one else in the family her daughter was married to a Black man (and pregnant with a son). Save for a few sporadic, secret phone calls, my mother became almost entirely disconnected from her mother. She wouldn't go back to her hometown for many years to come.

Even the most gifted, compassionate, progressive person cannot easily overcome being completely rejected by their mother. To have the love of a mother is too primal a need. Whatever soft place my mother might have had to land was hardened like concrete by her own mother's ignorant, fearful family and upbringing. Even her marriage to my father and the births of three beautiful children couldn't fully heal the deep wound of maternal rejection—nothing can. I also doubt loving a Black man and having mixed children is the cure-all for generations of belief steeped in white superiority, and my mother and her family were steeped down to the white of their bones.

I've often wondered why my mother defied her mother, family, and her-itage by marrying my father. What was her *full* motivation? Was it all in the name of unconditional love? It was never "we belong together" between them. She never reminisced to me about their romance, nor was there any physical evidence of it: no photos, no poems, no letters, no trace of a great love. (Well, there were three children.) Maybe my mother wanted to keep her history and memories of my father private, though I can't help but won-der if her marriage wasn't, in part, a rebellion against her mother. Did she do it for the attention, the drama of it all? More than once over the decades, I've heard my mother order her coffee "Black, like my men." She's often done it in front of me and one of her young Black grandsons—*awkward*.

To be honest, I don't know if my mother ever wanted to get married and have children so young. I could understand her wanting to create a safety net, a new family of her own, and to continue blazing trails, leaving her backward home and family behind. But what I couldn't understand was her abandoning her promising singing career to do so. From very early on I decided that I didn't want the same fate; I couldn't have a man or an unplanned pregnancy take me off my path. Witnessing my mother's and my sister's detours was a sad and stinging warning. Watching their dreams go up in flames burned a cautionary tale into my mind.

In 1977, my mother recorded an album she titled *To Start Again*. But by that time, she'd already had a troubled interracial marriage, three kids, a divorce, and one child still living with her, me. Did she think a record company would suddenly discover her? This is one of many miscalculations that as a child I observed my mother make and placed in a file labeled "What Not to Do."

Time rolled by after my parents' divorce, and eventually my grandmother allowed my mother to visit her with her granddaughter—but *only* her youngest granddaughter. I was a twelve-year-old little girl and didn't quite understand why she only invited me. Looking back, I suspect it was because I was blond-*ish* and very fair for a mixed kid. I didn't raise much suspicion to the culturally untrained eye. I was too young to know how my mother and her mother interacted with each other, and I never knew what happened between them at that point: Was there an apology from Pat's mother for disowning her daughter and withholding family from her? Did she reckon with her racism? Was there forgiveness? I don't know. What I do remember is that she was stiff and formal. She had stark white hair that she wore neatly away from her face with one big wave in the front. On her stern face she wore black cat-eyed glasses. Her house was not warm, and there was no smell to the place. I recall her coming into the quiet, sterile bedroom where I slept while I was there, after my mother had put me to bed. She sat on the side of the bed in the dark and, in a whisper, taught me the Lord's Prayer.

> *Give us this day our daily bread*
> *And forgive us our trespasses,*
> *as we forgive those who trespass against us.*
>
> Matthew 6:11–12

That's all I remember of that visit to see my grandmother. In an unusual twist of fate, she died on my mother's birthday, February 15. After that, oddly enough, my mother pretty much sainted her. As an adult, my mother was never a practicing Catholic, but for many years she went to light a candle for her mother on that date. Strange how death can make people forgive those who trespassed against them and their children.

🦋

For most of my early childhood it was just my mother and me. We moved constantly. After an exhaustive search, she found us a place by the water. She wanted to be in a more peaceful setting where she could take long walks with the dog and go down the road to the beach. The two of us moved into what she referred to as a "quaint cottage" but I later learned the entire neighborhood called it "the shack." I found the neighbors' description to be more accurate.

It was a small, rickety structure covered in a wavy faux-brick siding that had buckled under the elements. Inside, a layer of dank sadness seeped through the floorboards and walls, which were covered with cheap "imitation of wood" paneling that was paired with filthy flea-ridden carpeting. No matter the time of day, it was always dark inside. Prior to us moving in, the place had been abandoned and had become a hangout where teenagers would smoke, drink, and mess around. It was set off of a rough, unpaved driveway of rubble and stones and faced a big white Victorian house, which made it look like something the big house had belched out. It was marked, and so were we. My mother and I were the eccentric lady and her little girl who lived in "the shack." How . . . quaint.

🦋

The first chapter of Marilyn Monroe's autobiography, *My Story*, is entitled "How I Rescued a White Piano." In it she writes about her mission to find her mother's 1937 baby grand piano.

Gladys Monroe Baker, mother to Marilyn Monroe (born Norma Jeane Mortenson), was in and out of psychiatric institutions all of her life. It's been documented that she suffered from paranoid schizophrenia, an incurable disease that performs a violent dance with the mind, releasing it to lucidity for brief moments, then, without warning, spinning it back into hellish delusion. As a result of her mother's inability to maintain sanity, Marilyn spent most of her childhood in orphanages, followed by a series of foster homes. During one of Gladys's rare healthy periods, she and little Norma Jeane lived together for a few months in a small white house near the Hollywood Bowl. The most prized possession in their modest abode was a baby grand piano. When her mother's illness reared its ugly head again, dragging her back into darkness and into another institution, the few furnishings and the piano were sold off.

After Norma Jeane's transformation into Marilyn Monroe The Movie Star, she spoke very little of her childhood, her mentally ill mother, or her unknown father. And though Marilyn had made herself into a radiant icon, I imagine there was a piece of her still searching for an uninterrupted childhood, longing for her mother to be whole. I see how the piano must've become a symbol of a time when she and her mother were together in relative peace and harmony. Pianos are elegant, mystical, and comforting—from them simple tunes and majestic compositions can spring forth and fill a dismal living room, a dank bar, a concert hall, or even a shack with joy and glory.

Marilyn went on a mission to find her mother's piano. As the story goes, while still a struggling model and actress, she found and purchased the piano at an auction and kept it in storage until she was able to move it into a home of her own. It accompanied her to all her residences. One of its final homes was the lavish Manhattan apartment Marilyn shared with her third and last husband, renowned playwright Arthur Miller, where she custom-coated the instrument in a thick, shiny white lacquer to match the apartment's glamorous, angelic décor—"a world of white," as her half sister, Berniece Miracle, called it. "My happiest hours as a little girl were around that piano," Marilyn said. I imagine when your childhood was fraught with insecurity and fear like Marilyn's and like mine, the romance of those lost happy hours is extremely valuable. I understood why she searched for, bought, stored, and cared for the piano—so much so that I rescued it at auction at Christie's in 1999. It is a treasure and my most expensive piece of art. And now, Marilyn Monroe's white baby grand piano is the centerpiece, the pièce de résistance, of my own glamorous Manhattan penthouse. Marilyn was my first vision of a superstar that I could relate to, on an almost spiritual level.

We did without a lot of things when I was young, but what my mother couldn't live without was a piano. We always had a piano, and I had many happy and formative hours around it with my mother. My mother would go through songs and scales with me, and of course I would hear her practicing her dramatic operatic scales. It was at the piano where I would sit and make up little tunes of my own.

My mother never had much money, but one of her greatest contributions to my development was exposing me to all kinds of people, especially musicians. She made a few dollars here and there by giving voice lessons at our house. Her practicing was a constant, but what I treasured most were the jam sessions. Accomplished musicians would come and hang out and play music at my mother's bohemian spot "by the bay," and I would jam with them. Live music was the best thing about living with my mother. I was surrounded by the love of music, but even more importantly, by the love of *musicianship*—the love of the craft, the love of the process. When I was a little girl, my mother introduced me to the world of sitting in with musicians: improvising, vibing, and singing.

I particularly remember her singing from a Carly Simon songbook, she would play from it all the time. If I asked her to play a song for me to sing, she'd happily oblige. She never pushed me to sing or practice, but she encouraged me. She knew early on I had her advanced ear for music. When I was five she arranged for me to have piano lessons for a short time. But rather than read the music, I would play "Mary Had a Little Lamb" by ear. "Don't use your ear, don't use your ear!" my teacher would implore. But I didn't know how *not* to use my ear. Because music was a gift of freedom in my world of scarcity, the one place I felt unrestrained, I resisted the repetition and discipline required to learn how to read music and play the piano. Hearing and mimicking came so easily to me. This is one of several times I wish my mother *had* pushed me and made me sit and stick with it.

My mother and her guitarist friend would also sing standards from the 1940s (of course that's the era I loved, not only for the glamour but because the melodies were so strong). She particularly loved Billie Holiday and would often sing her songs. I remember hearing my mother sing "I Can't Give You Anything But Love." I learned it and we would sing it together, and I would instinctively scat, which I *loved*. It felt like my little-girl version of catching the Holy Spirit.

I learned several jazz standards from my mom and her musician pals, and some of them took note of my ear and natural abilities. At about twelve years old I would sit with her and Clint, a piano player. He was a big brown teddy bear, and he could play his ass off. He would sit and work with me and treat me like a serious musician. When I would sit with him and sing, we were just two musicians working together. He taught me jazz classics, and one of the first songs I remember learning was "Lullaby of Birdland," made famous by the great Ella Fitzgerald. I will always have a profound respect for Ms. Fitzgerald and all the jazz legends who laid such a fertile musical foundation for musicians of all genres. It was not an easy song at any age, but for me at twelve, it was beyond advanced. With its intricate melody, full of vocal shifts and changes, it was composed for one of the most nimble jazz vocalists of all time. Learning and listening to live jazz helped train my ear and shape my creative wiring. I was learning how to *feel* when to modulate and when to scat. Being introduced to jazz standards and a jazz discipline gave me my appreciation for sophisticated modulations in a song and how to employ them to communicate emotion. (Stevie Wonder is the absolute master of this.)

For me, songs are always about emotion. My mother may not have taken me to church, but jamming with jazz musicians was close to a spiritual experience. There's a creative energy that flows through the room. You learn to sit and listen to what the other musicians are doing, and you get inspired by a guitar riff or what the pianist is playing. When you are in a zone, it is a miraculous madness. For me, it was always an exquisite escape, which I desperately needed and always sought.

By the time I was eleven or twelve my mother was taking me to a supper club on Long Island to sit in with her and other musicians. There was a dining room on the ground floor where they would serve dinner, and upstairs was live jazz. I was in the sixth grade, up in there at all hours of the night, any day of the week, sitting in with grown-ass musicians. I'm not sure if my mother just wanted to be able to hang out at night and sing and not be stuck in the shack—I mean "cottage"—with a kid, or if she was consciously developing me as an artist, or if maybe she wanted to present to her friends her little protégée? I do remember her encouraging me while I sang. I felt more welcomed (and natural) with jazz musicians at night in the club than with my classmates during the day—those kids who asked incessantly, "What *are* you?" those kids who judged me by the way I looked and had no idea what my life was really like. I always knew that the world of suburban Long Island wasn't for me. I was a fish out of water, and though I survived it, I knew that no one there really cared about me, and I *certainly* knew I wasn't staying.

And my mother wasn't just any old mom supporting me—she was a Juilliard-trained musician. Music was something we genuinely connected on, and without pushing or becoming one of those overbearing stage mothers or "momagers," she instilled in me the power of believing in myself. Whenever I mused about what I'd do "if I make it," she would cut me short and say, "Don't say '*if* I make it,' say '*when* I make it.' Believe you can do it, and you will do it."

The fact that I believed I could become a successful artist is one of my greatest strengths. Around the same time, my mother entered me in a talent competition in the city and I sang one of my favorite songs: "Out Here On My Own" by Irene Cara.

I felt "Out Here On My Own" described my entire life, and I loved singing that way—singing to reveal a piece of my soul. And I won doing it. At that age, I lived for the movie *Fame*, and Irene Cara was *everything* to me. I related to her multicultural look (Puerto Rican and Cuban), her multitextured hair, and, most importantly, her ambition and accomplishments. She won an Oscar for Best Original Song for "Flashdance . . . What a Feeling" (which she cowrote), from *Flashdance*, making her the first Black woman to win in a category other than acting. (She won a Grammy, a Golden Globe, and an American Music Award for the song too.) But "Out Here On My Own" was such a pure song that touched my heart, and I couldn't believe I won a trophy for singing a song I loved. It was the first time I'd received validation as an artist. What a *feeling*.

It wasn't just music my mother exposed me to. She had friends who treated me like family, which helped offset all the shabby places we lived and the disheveled way I often looked.

My mother had a friend named "Sunshine," who was short and quite a large woman, with a warm and generous heart. She wore her hair in two long ponytails, like Carole and Paula from *The Magic Garden* (a popular local kids' TV show I loved, which was hosted by two young, hippie-esque women with a pink squirrel sidekick, who sang folksy songs and told stories, in the seventies and early eighties). Sunshine had big, older sons and no daughters, so she took an interest in me, especially in my disorderly and neglected appearance. She would often bring me cute, girlie clothes that she made herself. On my sixth birthday, she outfitted me in a white embroidered shirt paired with a blue skirt, white tights, and Mary Jane shoes. She even got my hair to lie down in pigtails (maybe being a Jewish woman and having textured hair gave her some insight). My birthday crown sat nicely right on top. She even bought me a birthday cake decorated like a lamb! A *lamb*! It is one of the few times I remember feeling beautiful as a child. Sunshine lovingly made sure I looked put together and cute. She was never anything but caring and sweet to me. Years later, when I was going into junior high, she came by with some clothes for me that I felt were too childish. I rejected them rudely, in the cruel fashion of an angsty preteen. To this day, I regret how mean I was to such a considerate caretaker—one of the few in my whole life.

I tried my hardest to accept all my mother's unfortunate choices in men. I even tried to impress them. (Some of the names have been changed to protect the dickheads.) Tales of a certain man in my mother's life right before my father loomed large in our household. We knew his name, François, we knew he was Lebanese, and we knew he was rich. Despite her great talents, my mother, like many women of her era, subscribed to the belief that a man was her most reliable source of security. The time between the relationships she had with François and with my father was not long; it was even sometimes suggested there had been some overlap, which led to the suspicion that *perhaps* Morgan was not my father's child. Drama.

After the divorce from my father, my mother and François reconnected, and she planned an epic reunion with "the rich man who got away." My mother got Morgan and me excited about the fantasy that a wealthy, exotic man would come and sweep us up out of our run-down digs, and we would be set for life—all we had to do was impress him. I could do that, I thought. Maybe my mother and I could sing a song at the piano? The night of their big date arrived, and while my mother and François were out, I pulled together the best little outfit I could to greet him. I was nervous, because my mother wanted to be rescued *bad*, and I wanted to be in a nice, safe place too. The stakes were high.

I was home alone when my mother and François returned (I was home alone a lot as a child). Determined to do my part to make this relationship work for my mother, I ran to the door. François came in ahead of her. He was a tall, imposing older man in a dark suit with sharp, mysterious features. "Hello!" I began cheerily, perhaps throwing in a curtsy for dramatic effect. "*Shut up!*" he barked. "*Where is my* son*!?*"

The force of his words crushed every bit of enthusiasm out of me. He was *scary*. I was only a kid, and this big stranger had stormed into my house, dismissed me, and screamed at me. I ran crying to my mother's bedroom. She tried to calm me down, but I was inconsolable. I'm not sure if François ever saw Morgan (who had our father's Black features running all up and through him). But needless to say, no rich, heroic man saved us that day; no man "saved" us any day.

I did not like or trust most of my mother's men. She had one older Black boyfriend, Leroy, who tried to "protect" us from Morgan during one of his more violent episodes by saying, "I got my piece," and flashing a pistol. Imagine that: your mother's boyfriend carrying a gun and threatening to use it on her teenage son, your brother. Sadly, it did make me feel safer; Morgan had become a scary presence to me by then.

However, my mother's men were not all bad. Nothing and no one is ever *all* bad. There was a sweet man in my mother's life named Henry. He was my favorite. He was about ten years younger than my mother and a horticulturalist. He drove an old red pickup truck, outfitted for the field; his many gardening tools, tree cuttings, mulch, and other supplies would stick out from the back. He knew his trade. He was very well educated and grew extraordinary plants that towered over me (mainly some species that were illegal at the time). He also grew an impressive Afro that seemed to float around his head. My mother and I lived in a few different places with Henry, but for a while the three of us were in a small house on a grand estate, where he was the gardener. The place gave me plantation vibes, and we lived in the modern equivalent of the servants' quarters. But still, Henry's house was nicer than most of the houses we'd lived in and gave me a brief moment of stability.

I was in the third grade when we lived there, and Henry built me a swing on a big, old tree that was near what looked to me like a mini-mountain made of garbage. One day he brought home two rescue kittens, one for me and one for him. I liked his better; he was orange, with a very special spirit. Ultimately he became mine. He grew to be big and squishy, and his name was Morris, like the icon. I'd sit and swing with him on my lap. We truly loved each other. I confided in him when I had a really hard day at school, which was often. I never fit in with the kids, who were all white and most of whom lived in the estates in that neighborhood. I was the child of the girlfriend of the hired help, and they let me know it. I brought my troubles to Morris. Even if I had had any friends I wouldn't have wanted them to see I lived near a trash dump. Once, when I was really upset after having a pretty big argument with my mother, I ran out of the house, grabbed my cat, and headed for *my* place. While swinging over the hill o' garbage with Morris in my lap, the smell of rotting food wafting over my face, I promised myself no matter what, I would never forget what it felt like to be a child—a moment I re-created years later in the "Vision of Love" video. (Sans the garbage. I wanted to be sentimental, not *bleak*.)

I really liked Henry; he was an Aries just like me. We would dance, and he would pick me up and twirl me around. He provided me with glimpses of what the life of a carefree little girl could be. Henry was kind, and he paid for my second year of performing arts summer camp. I remember his mother, who used to work for Estée Lauder and was an exceptional cook. One day she laid out a divine soul food spread, ending with a German chocolate cake, which I had never had before. It was a delicious, warm, gooey, homemade pile of happiness. But with all that love also came darkness. Henry was a Black Vietnam veteran and was severely damaged by the consequences of both of those identities. I suspect he suffered from post-traumatic stress disorder (PTSD), and, even as a kid, I was aware of his occasional psychedelic drug usage. I believe the fallout from his experiences of war and racism was the root cause of why he and my mother broke up.

One day near the end of my third-grade school year I got home and my mother was up in arms. She announced, "We can't stay here anymore. We have to leave now."

She already had our things packed and in her car. Henry was sitting in a chair in the middle of the kitchen. The lights were off, and I could see the strong silhouette of his Afro. He was holding a long double-barreled shotgun in one of his hands. Staring down at the white linoleum floor, he said very calmly, "You're not leaving me. I'm not gonna let you guys leave." He never raised his head or voice and seemed to be in a kind of trancelike state.

"I'm not going to let you guys go," he said. "I'm going to chop you up and put you in the refrigerator and make you guys stay here." Well, after he said *that*, I rushed to get into the car. My mother started the engine.

"Morris!" I screamed. "I have to get Morris; he's still in there!" Panicked, I jumped out of the car. I was determined to get my cat. That cat represented too much for me; he *was* unconditional love to me.

"Be careful," my mother said, as she let me reenter a house occupied by an armed man who had just threatened to chop us up. (Henry never did anything to hurt me and perhaps she believed he wouldn't now, but *still*.) I had to pass the kitchen, with Henry and the shotgun, to search the other rooms for Morris. When I finally found him, I scooped him up in my arms, ran out of the house, and jumped in the car. As we sped off, my heart was going a mile a minute. "Hallelujah, I got Morris!" I triumphantly exclaimed.

I never knew what happened between her and Henry, and I never saw him after that day. I heard that many years later, while he was riding down the road in his same vintage red pickup, "'Vision of Love,' by Mariah Carey," came bursting through his old radio. I was told that he rolled down the window and yelled out into the fresh air, "She made it! She made it!" I really hope Henry made it too.

My mother did occasionally try to give us *moments*. She would save up a little money so we could do things like go to dinner in New York City. And it was on these excursions that I developed a taste for "the finer things." I have a distinct memory of one night when we were riding back from the city. I was looking out the back window at the New York City skyline, and I said to myself, This *is where I'm going to live when I grow up. I want to have* this *view.*

I always knew we lived in shitty places among other people's nice houses in the suburbs. I never dreamed I'd get married and live in a big white Victorian house, or even a cozy little home like my guncles. But I did envision something *grand*. I remember watching *Mommie Dearest* and seeing Joan Crawford's pristine manor. *That's what I want*, I thought.

I even believed I could surpass its splendor. Even then, I saw myself living in a mansion or more, because I *knew* I would realize my dreams. And when I saw the New York skyline, looking like a giant silver crystal encrusted with multicolored jewels, I envisioned I would live somewhere where I could see *that*. And I do. I see it clearly; I see the entire city from the rooftop of my downtown Manhattan penthouse. As a result of a lot of hard labor, I went from swinging over garbage to singing in a mansion in the sky.

So yes, my mother exposing me to beauty and culture gave me encouragement and lifelong lessons that contributed both to my art and to what is good in me. But my mother also created persistent turmoil, which caused trauma and deep sadness. It has taken me a lifetime to find the courage to confront the stark duality of my mother, the beauty and the beast that coexist in one person—and to discover there's beauty in all of us, but *who* loved you and *how* they loved you will determine how long it takes to realize it.

Looking back now, I can see that in my early years, there was significant neglect. For one, there were the people my mother let be around me, particularly my violent brother, my troubled sister, and their sketchy cohorts. And I often looked a mess, though I believe that was likely a result of my mother being oblivious (in the name of being bohemian) rather than malicious. However, I noticed a shift in our relationship when I was about fourteen years old. One night, as we were riding together in the "Dodge dent," as she called it, "Somebody's Watching Me," by Rockwell, came on the radio. It was a huge international hit on Motown Records at the time, and I loved it, largely because Michael Jackson sang the hook. We were driving and bopping along with the song when my mother broke out into Michael's signature part of the chorus. "I always feel like / Somebody's watching me."

She sang it in an elaborate, operatic style, and I turned my face to the window to hide my giggle. I mean, it's a very eighties R & B record, with the hook sung in Michael Jackson's impeccably smooth signature style, so to hear it delivered like Beverly Sills (a popular Brooklyn-born operatic soprano from the 1950s to the 1970s) was pretty hilarious to my teenage singer's ears.

Oh, but Mother was not amused. She whipped the volume knob down and glared at me, her brownish-green eyes narrowing and hardening to stone.

"What's so funny?" she spat. Her seriousness quickly swallowed up the silliness of the moment. I stuttered, "Um, well . . . that's just not how it goes." She stared at me until every bit of lightness faded. Almost growling, she said, "You should only *hope* that one day you become *half* the singer I am." My heart dropped.

Still, to this day, what she said haunts and hurts me. I don't know if she meant to cut me down to size or it was just her bruised ego talking; all I know is that those words that shot out of her mouth pierced my chest and were buried in my heart.

These words were there in my heart in 1999 when I was acknowledged and respected for my voice and my compositions by two of the greatest opera talents of all time. I was invited to join Luciano Pavarotti in "Pavarotti & Friends," a prestigious annual fundraising concert for children in war-torn countries, hosted by the great tenor, the maestro, in his hometown of Modena, Italy. (The concert was directed for TV by Spike Lee, ya dig?) It's an ancient town known for producing fancy sports cars like Ferraris and Lamborghinis as well as balsamic vinegar— and I'm sure whatever indulgences the maestro desired were imported. I brought my mother and my wonderful little nephew Mike with me. I was proud and happy to be able to treat her to a glamorous trip and to introduce her to one of her idols. In a strapless pale-pink silk taffeta sheath gown, my mother watched me share a grand outdoor stage in front of fifty thousand people with one of the greatest and most famous opera singers of all time. Not only did we sing together, he sang *my* song: Pavarotti sang an Italian version of "Hero" with me, for the whole world to see. For my mother to see.

Then, in May 2005, I met the phenomenal soprano Leontyne Price (the first Black woman to become a prima donna at the Metropolitan Opera and the most awarded classical singer) when she was being honored at Oprah's illustrious Legends Ball, which celebrated twenty-five African American women in art, entertainment, and civil rights. The historic weekend began on Friday with a private luncheon at her Montecito home, where the "legends" were greeted by the "young'uns," including Alicia Keys, Angela Bassett, Halle Berry, Mary J. Blige, Naomi Campbell, Missy Elliott, Tyra Banks, Iman, Janet Jackson, Phylicia Rashad, Debbie Allen, myself, and many more.

And throughout the extraordinary weekend, we young'uns paid homage to the legends for their great contributions. My mother would often boast, "Oh yes, Leontyne and I had the same vocal coach," and here I was hanging out with her (at Oprah Winfrey's *house* no less)! Madame Price remembered my mother, and she also validated my talent.

On the day after Christmas that year, on the most elegant, thick, eggshell-colored stationery I received a letter from her:

"In the difficult, demanding business of performing arts, you are the crown jewel of success. To achieve your level of success as a multidimensional artist is an outstanding measure of your artistic talent." It went on to say,

It was a pleasure to visit with you during the Legends Weekend and to tell you in person how much I admire you and your artistry. Your creativity and performances are superb. You present your compositions with a depth of feeling that is rarely, if ever, seen or heard. It is a joy to watch you turn all of the obstacles you faced into stepping-stones to success. Your devotion to your art and career are praiseworthy. This brings you a standing ovation and a resounding Brava! Brava! Brava!

Dead

I guess to my mother, I may not have been half the singer she was, but I was the whole singer and artist I was.

This was my first glimpse into how misguided words from a mother can really affect a child. What a simple difference a laugh along from her would have made. Whatever had connected us before, a fragile mother-daughter bond, was shattered in that moment. There was a distinct shift: she made me feel like the competition, like a threat. In place of our previous bond grew a different tie, a rope tethering us through shared biology and social obligation. In no way did my mother crush my dreams of being successful that day; my faith had grown too strong by then.

Having people you love be jealous of you professionally comes with the territory of success, but when the person is your mother and the jealousy is revealed at such a tender age, it's particularly painful. I was going through some heavy shit then, and for her to expose her insecurity to me in that way, at that time, was damaging. I'd already had so many years of insecurity around my physical safety. Though a subtle, brief moment, this was the first big blow in a long line of times when people close to me would try to put me down, put me in my place, underestimate me, or take advantage of me. But she, above all, was the most devastating, because she was the most essential. She was my mother.

DANDELION TEA

A flower taught me how to pray
But as I grew, that flower changed
She started flailing in the wind
Like golden petals scattering

—"Petals"

She called herself Dandelion—the hearty, bright-yellow wildflower with small tooth-shaped petals that gives the early signal that spring is near. After its flowering is finished, the petals dry and the head becomes a ball of lacy dust feathers carrying seeds. The legend goes that if you close your eyes, make a wish, and blow the feathery pieces into the air, your wish will scatter into the world and come true. The English sometimes call them Irish daisies. And the tea made from the root and leaves is widely believed to have healing benefits. But these wildflowers can also be a menace, poisoning precious flowers and growing grass—weeds to be uprooted and discarded.

When I was a little girl, my older sister seemed to live on the wind. She was always somewhere far away. Childhood memories of her exist in my mind as flashes of lightning and thunder. She was exciting but unpredictable—her torrential gusts always carried inevitable destruction with them.

The distances between my mother, my father, their first daughter, and myself are far reaching. Unlike her, growing up, I never spent any significant time as part of a whole interracial family. Most of my experiences were with one parent at a time—me with my mother, or me with my father. I have no recollection of them as a happily married couple. It is bizarre to me that they were even married, not just because of race, but how different they were as people. But before I was born, the Carey family consisted of a Black father, a white mother, and a mixed boy and girl. The four of them would walk down the street, and people would *know*. This rebel Carey quartet experienced the spectacular ignorance and wrath of a society woefully unprepared to receive or accept them; *Loving v. Virginia*, the Supreme Court decision that struck down the law banning interracial marriage in the United States, wouldn't happen until three years after my mother and father's marriage. As a result of the hostility from their community and country, Morgan and Alison were instructed by our parents to refer to them as "Mother" and "Father," in the hope, I imagine, that the formality might elevate their status to respectable. My parents seemed to think that if neighbors or other onlookers heard their girl and boy say, "Good morning, Mother" or "Hello, Father," they wouldn't perceive them as disgusting.

Morgan and Alison were beautiful children and were very close when they were young. Alison had skin like creamy butterscotch pudding, with a head of thick, deep, dark curls and eyes to match. She was extremely intelligent and curious and she loved to learn. I was told she brought home good grades, got into good schools, and loved music too. But she lived firsthand the discomfort and animosity directed at her and her offbeat Black and white family. She saw their neighbors throw raw meat studded with broken glass to their dogs, and their family car blown up. She saw things inside the family too, things a child should never see and I will never know. I do know that what she experienced damaged and derailed her girlhood.

She was fully aware when the family unit unraveled and our parents turned on each other; she absorbed the full pain of a family coming undone. She also saw another daughter come into the clan, breaking the symmetry and changing her status as the only girl and youngest. I was the new little one. When my mother and father could no longer live together without emotionally torturing each other, they tore themselves apart to survive separately. The three of us children would be plagued by pain, resentment, and jealousy for a lifetime.

Alison and Morgan both believed I had it easier than they did. Our father was very strict with them. He was not harsh with me because three or four years old was the oldest I had been when we were all together. During one of their countless fights, I vaguely remember my mother yelling at him something like, "This one is mine! You *will not* beat this one." I was *her* little one. She often said she "didn't have the strength" to challenge my father's aggression when my siblings were growing up.

I only have one memory of all of us having dinner together. It was a sort of "restorative dinner"—my parents trying one more time to see if we could pull it together and be a family. We were all sitting around the table, and I started singing.

My father said, "Children should be seen and not heard."

The entertainer in me took that as a cue, so I got up from the dining table, walked the few feet to the living room area (which was in plain view and well within earshot), stood on top of the coffee table, and continued to sing at the top of my lungs. Alison and Morgan dropped their heads, ducking before the wrath of our father that they were certain would inevitably ricochet around the room. But my mother gave him a look, and he didn't say anything. My sister and brother were flabbergasted. I was not hit, yelled at, punished, or even *stopped*. They would have never, ever dared defy our father. No wonder they hated me.

Needless to say, the dinner didn't save us. Divorce was inevitable. My mother and father made the final decision to break up before all was broken. I remember I was taken to our neighbors' house, and they gave me popcorn while my family was next door discussing the dismantling of the Careys. After several violent encounters involving the police, by court order my father and brother could not live together. At one point Morgan had been taken to Sagamore Children's Psychiatric Center, a care facility for seriously emotionally troubled children and families in crisis. Morgan was a crisis. I also heard a psychiatrist had concluded that a significant contributing factor in Morgan's behavioral problems was Alison, who had a talent for instigating and manipulating Morgan to his breaking points. Alison is *very* clever. So Morgan had to live with my mother, and she had made it clear to my father that he would not have me. That left Alison scattered.

I've heard Alison express that she felt like my mother tossed her away, that she clearly loved Morgan and me more than her. I've also heard my mother say Alison chose to live with our father because she felt bad and didn't want him to be alone. There is likely some truth in both of their perspectives. I was too young to really understand.

I don't really know what life was like for my sister living with our father, just the two of them, broken and angry. It must've been dangerously claustrophobic—a constant clashing of feelings of abandonment and resentment toward my mother under their roof. They had no real space to resolve, no chance to heal. Order and obedience was how my father tried to make sense out of the chaos of society and the rubble his family structure had become.

The child now in his sole care was a bitter, broken teenage girl, and he had no tools to deal with her dysfunction and hurt. Eventually my father and Alison did form a bond, united in their disdain for my mother. I believe they also bonded over the inevitable visibility of their Blackness.

Predictably, Alison turned to boys and sex in an attempt to fill the family-sized hole of rejection in her heart. At fifteen she met a handsome Black nineteen-year-old military "man," and Alison got pregnant. Our mother wanted her to have an abortion. Our father told her she could have the baby if she got married. The young man was stationed in the Philippines, and with our father's permission Alison followed him, and they got married there. Before she left, I recall sitting on the bed with her in her room at our father's house. What I remember of her room was that on her wall was a shelf of books and a shelf of fancy dolls—the ones with big, poofy lace *quinceañera*-type dresses. I would look up at those dolls, far out of my reach—there for show, not for playing.

I was staring at them when she pointed to her belly and said, "There's a baby in there." A baby *where*? In her *stomach*? I was too young and didn't understand at all what she meant. I didn't understand much about Alison then.

I'll never forget her bizarre combined baby and bridal shower at my mother's house. They put a little girl on the cake—a doll, not one that looked like a grown woman but a little baby doll with dark brown hair like my sister's. The whole thing was so confusing to me. I was a little girl, wondering, *Is this a baby-is-coming party or a girl-is-going party?* I couldn't tell if it was a festive or tragic occasion. My mother was pacing and pissed off. My teenage sister had a swollen belly, and she kept pointing at it and saying to me, "There's a baby in here; look, there's a baby in here." And there was this weird cake with a little doll on it. How was a little girl supposed to understand all of this?

And so, for a long time afterward, I always thought, "Okay, so I guess at fifteen is when people have kids and get married."

It twisted my reality. But it also focused me. I made the promise to myself that was *not* going to be me. My sense of self-worth, or rather, my sense of self-preservation was born at that bon voyage/bridal/baby shower. I vowed I was not going to be promiscuous ever. This promise to live a different life led me to become a very prudish person. I knew then—suddenly finding myself an auntie before I was eight years old—that Alison's path was not going to be my life. Once the last slice of baby-bridal cake was gone, my sister was gone too, for several years.

I will never understand what happened to her in the Philippines. But I do know when she left my father's house, the remainder of her fragile childhood was left behind.

After a few years in the Philippines, Alison returned to Long Island. I was about twelve years old, and she was twenty. Whatever had happened to her over there, or on Long Island, or in a back room somewhere, had taken its toll on her. That super-smart, beautiful girl with the dark curls who was my big sister had hardened into a strange kind of absence. Something, or many things, must have happened to her to lead her to barter her body for money and drugs, as she went on to do for years. Back then, there was so much I didn't know, but there also was so much I should have never found out, certainly not so young. The years between us might as well have been centuries.

When Alison came back, she would drift from place to place and man to man, occasionally crashing with us at my mother's house between the many random relationships with men she collected and discarded. There was one older man—I guessed he was about sixty. He had half a head of hair, all of which was gray. He was polite to my mother and would sometimes fill our refrigerator with food, so I guess she *trusted* him? One evening at the shack, Alison and my mother got into one of their innumerable epic arguments, and for some unknown reason Alison took me with her to this older gentleman's house. There's little of his house, or that night, that I remember because when we arrived, Alison sat me down on a light-brown couch and handed me a little chalky ice-blue pill with a crease carved down the middle and a glass of water.

"Here, take this," she said.

I took it. Within minutes (I think) I was in a heavy, scary darkness, pushed down into a place beneath sleep, and I couldn't pull myself out. I don't know how long I was knocked out. I felt like I'd been absorbed into the couch (the only reason I remember the color). It was harrowing.

At twelve, I probably weighed eighty pounds soaking wet, and Alison gave me a whole Valium. I don't know why my sister drugged me. I don't know why my mother let me go with her and this man. Perhaps they both wanted me out of their hair for the evening, but my life was in jeopardy in her hands. This may have been the first time that year she could have seriously hurt me, but it certainly wasn't the last.

Even though by her twenties Alison had already gotten married, given birth, gotten divorced, traveled thousands of miles away, and done dreadful things, she could still be zany and spontaneous. The worst had not yet happened between us, so I was genuinely happy for the wild stray visits she made to my mother's house. On her good days she was a bright burst of energy in our often-bleak little dwelling. She seemed mature and had a hollow kind of glamour. She took a new interest in me as a preteen now rather than a little girl. She paid attention to the obviously neglected outside of me, swooping in and correcting my disastrous attempts to make myself pretty, which to a twelve-year-old means everything. After I accidentally made my hair all kinds of shades of ugly orange, she took me to get a toner for my hair and made it one color. She took me to a place that made my eyebrows beautiful. She took me shopping for my first bra. She and I would make earnest attempts at being *normal*. We were trying to be sisters—or so I thought.

Even though I was young, I knew my sister was doing things that were not good. I mean, she had a beeper, and only drug dealers, rappers, and doctors had beepers back then. She wore a nice manicure—bright-pink nail polish, sometimes decorated with rhinestones. Once, as she was dropping me off in front of my mother's house, she dipped a sharp pink nail tip into some white crystal powder and held it up to my face, saying, "Just try it, just try a little bit; who cares?"

I knew it was cocaine, and it scared me to death. Thank God, I didn't take the sniff. I played it off and calmly replied, "No thanks! Bye; see you later." I shudder to think what could've happened if I'd walked into her trap and then that house. I don't know what would've happened if I'd snorted cocaine right before seeing my mother, or ever in my life.

It was all such a setup. Alison began bringing me around her friends, and I started looking forward to our secret outings—though for all the initial glamour and excitement, it was a very scary time in my life. Even though it was a long time ago, I still have nightmares about it. Alison did not choose how her life began, and I know she went through trauma too. It seemed as though she'd turned completely away from the light.

One day, she explained that it was time for me to meet her fabulous boyfriend, John, and the other girls she hung around, who she'd been telling stories to me about. John was tall, with green eyes, a large, fluffy Afro, and a strong charisma. Christine, a seventeen-year-old runaway white girl, an older woman named Denise—"older" meaning she was maybe twenty-eight—and my sister, then in her early twenties, all lived in a house together with John. I looked up to Christine; she had a worldly air about her, yet she also seemed like a little girl. Her pale skin was sprinkled with tan freckles, and she had medium-blond hair that fell softly to her shoulders, which were long and thin like the rest of her body. She could've been in a teen movie, but instead she was there, in that house. She was damaged.

John's house was nicer, brighter, and cleaner than where I lived. They had a brand-new couch. There was a television, and I could watch whatever shows I wanted. They had all the snacks I could want. They had Juicy Juice. We couldn't afford any of that at home. A couple of times my sister came to where I lived and filled the refrigerator with the stuff I liked. This was part of the confusion I felt about our relationship. It sometimes felt and looked like she cared, but her motives were always unclear. Was she being a nice big sister, or was she creating an appetite in me for what I knew I could have all the time at John's house? It was manipulation masquerading as love.

My sister told me not to tell anyone I was going to the house where she lived with John, especially not my brother. She told me that my brother didn't like him because John had beat him at backgammon. Being so young and naïve at the time, I believed their animosity was about a board game, not a prostitution and drug operation. So there was no one who knew, no one to protect me. Dysfunctional families are ideal prey for abusers, the exposed little ones vulnerable to being picked off. Now, of course, it's clear to me that the fun house was a whorehouse. I think my sister was kind of like the hustler, the talent scout. But at the time, I had no idea; after all, I was only a twelve-year-old girl. Winning me over was so easy—literally like giving a kid candy, but instead of candy it was a hair rinse, a bra, and a Juicy Juice box.

John, my sister, and I would drive to the city together. I remember one time we were going somewhere, and the radio was playing a song he loved. He loudly screamed out the lyrics, while my sister and I giggled at his strangled singing. They let me smoke cigarettes in the backseat of the car. I felt cool and free.

We would go to IHOP to get pancakes. They took me to Adventureland and I played Pac-Man. In those moments, I almost felt like someone's precious little sister. I was having all these fun adventures and thinking to myself, *I finally know what it feels like to have a big sister who's in my life for good. And I like this easy breezy guy, John.* This was what I'd been missing. I was starting to feel something resembling stability, a sense that I had something that looked like a normal family and was moving toward somewhere I belonged.

But confusing and curious things quickly started happening.

The closer I got to my sister, the more clearly I could see her broken parts. She had secretly gotten me my own phone line, which only she called me on. She would have these desperate bouts of drug-induced hysteria and call me late at night, in the middle of an episode. I'd talk her down off the ledge, then try to go back to sleep, get up early in the morning, and complete the seventh grade. No one at school knew that frequently, just a few hours earlier, I had subdued my suicidal big sister. Killing herself became a common threat that she shared with me in the wee hours before I went to the school bus stop.

Then the calls stopped for a while. Finally, one day, Alison phoned and said she and John were coming to pick me up. I was excited to think of the three of us together again, riding, laughing, smoking, singing, and playing. But John showed up alone.

We began driving, but there was no radio blasting, no talking. It wasn't fun at all, and I felt that something wasn't right.

Finally I asked, "Where is my sister? When are we going to pick her up?"

John kept his eyes forward and assured me, "Oh, she'll be here later." I was sitting in the front seat, and I could clearly see the handgun resting against his thigh.

John, his gun, and I made two stops: a card game and a drive-in movie. There's a look, a feel, and a smell to rooms where grown men play in the dark. It was dank and cluttered. The air was dense with cheap booze, stale menthol cigarette smoke, and unspoken perversions. There were no pretty things. It was hard for me to see and hard to breathe.

I don't know exactly how many men there were; I don't know how many guns, how much money, or how many vile thoughts were at the table—but I do know it was all men, and me. I sat in a corner on the sticky floor where I could see the door and held onto myself. I stayed still and kept my eyes down as the grown-man jokes, grown-man cussin', grown-man hungers, grown-man fears, and grown-man fantasies flew above my head. Every now and then I'd catch a glimpse of one of them leering at me or hear a lewd reference to me in their conversation.

I don't remember how I got from the card-room floor back into the front seat of his car. What I do remember is feeling dirty from the sticky floor and the men's filthy words. I knew my sister was not coming to clean me up this time. A panic bubbled up in my throat. *Where am I going? Why am I alone with my sister's boyfriend? Why did he take me around those disgusting men? Why can't we just go to IHOP? Where is my sister? Where is she?* I began to pray.

Our next stop was the drive-in, where almost immediately John put his arm around me. My body went stiff. My eyes were fixed on his gun. John pushed in closer and forced a hard kiss on me. I was nauseous and scared; I felt immobilized. From the corner of my eye I noticed an elderly white man pull up and park next to us, peering directly into John's car.

The look on the man's face was a mix of revulsion and recognition. He clearly saw an adult man—John, with his round Afro—and a little girl, small with blond coils of hair. He saw the powder-blue car and John's light-brown skin. He saw the details, and even if he didn't detect my distress, he could see this was no place a little girl would ever want to be. John pulled out of the drive-in slowly and drove me home in silence.

I committed that man's face to memory. He is still there, fresh and frozen in that terrible time. I believe he was a prayer in person.

After a couple of days back in my room, the phone began ringing again, but this time I wouldn't pick it up. I resumed pretending I had a regular seventh-grade life. I wanted to be a child again. Sometimes all the kids in my neighborhood would play chase (tag) at night. Most of them lived in nice houses with two parents, and sisters who didn't burden them with thoughts of suicide and set them up with pimps. I longed to blend in to a typical summer night in an everyday Long Island neighborhood, to play and clown around with other regular kids. I just wanted to outrun my drama through a game of chase.

We often played in an area not far from the beach that had a kind of roundabout. We would hang out at that spot and sometimes build a fire, make funny voices, and sing. One night we were deep in a group game of chase, kids scattered about running and weaving, when I saw a car coming down the road. I immediately recognized it as John's car. It was creeping along, ever so slowly, as if the driver was looking for something or someone. Panicking, I instinctively ducked behind a house, pretending to hide from whoever was "it." There was no way I could tell my friends that I was "it" to a pimp with a gun.

John eventually drove away. Though I had narrowly escaped him again, the fear of men followed me for a very long time. When I got home I unplugged the phone from the wall and disconnected from trusting my big sister forever.

I had nobody to tell what had happened. I couldn't tell my mother. I didn't have any real, close friends. I had never really fit in. Even if I did, how could I have explained it to a kid from a regular household who ate dinner at six o'clock, went to bed at nine thirty, and got in trouble when they didn't brush their teeth? They'd never be able to understand. Big sisters are supposed to protect you—not pimp you out. So I didn't tell or trust anybody.

But as a girl, you still want your big sister, and dandelions are still flowers when they first bloom.

One visit from my sister, among all the visits and memories, marked me the deepest.

We tried to have tea. Tea was a thing in my mother's house, but it was anything but proper. There was no cheery, whistling kettle; we boiled the water in a small beat-up saucepan on an old stove in the tiny, flavorless, dingy, grime-colored kitchen. Matching cups and saucers were certainly nowhere to be found; we had mismatched cups and mugs, the kind found in the box marked "Free" at yard sales on Long Island. English breakfast was the staple tea flavor; we each had a cup with a steeping tea bag. I had a thick ceramic brown drip-glazed mug that was chipped at the lip. I was holding the steaming, fragrant black tea with both hands when the phone rang.

"Oh hello, Al," we heard our mother answer. It was our father.

We were both a little shocked. My father rarely called my mother's house, and if he did, it was almost always to scold us about something. Alison and I exchanged a quick glance—who had done what now? Suddenly my mother looked in my direction, and I could tell they were discussing me. I vigorously shook my head "no" and mimed refusal. Alison and I were just about to have tea, maybe even a rare light moment, and I knew I'd have to get serious when it came to talking with our father. And who knew what Alison might have done that I'd have to hear about.

But Mother didn't cover for us. "Yes, she's here; hold on," she said, holding the phone out and shaking it at me. Whatever "normal sister moment" Alison and I were trying to create was totally blown. I straightened my face, got up begrudgingly, and took the phone. Then I shook it and stretched the cord over to Alison, gesturing for her to take it.

"Nooooo, you take it," she said back. A silly back-and-forth commenced between us for a few moments—a game of who would take the burden of talking to Father. It was almost fun.

Finally I put the receiver to my ear. "Hi, Father. I'm fine," I said, repressing the urge to let out a little giggle. As I went through the mechanical niceties of the conversation, my sister began gesturing wildly, shaking her head and slicing her hand across her throat, signaling for me not to let on that she was there. As I tried my best to carry on the conversation with our father, I made silly faces back at her, doing all I could not to break into laughter. My sister could be pretty theatrical, and in that moment I found her extra hilarious. I thought we were playing a game. Eventually I figured it was her turn to try and talk seriously to our father while I tried to make her laugh, so I said, "Guess what—Alison is here! Want to talk to her?" Laughingly, I motioned at her to take the phone.

But she wasn't looking at me. She was looking down at her mug of still-steaming tea in her hand, and when she lifted her face, her eyes were rabid, without a trace of their former playfulness. Before I realized what was happening, she yelled "*No!*" and, in a flash, threw the boiling-hot tea on me.

The next thing I remember I was stripped down to my waist, and a doctor was removing the remaining bits of my white-and-turquoise diagonal-striped top, which was embedded into the flesh of my shoulder, with large tweezers. The doctor had had to slice off my shirt with an instrument, as some of the fibers had begun to fuse with my skin. (I fucking loved that top—one of the very few cute pieces I had, and now it was out of rotation, stuck to my back.)

My back was splattered with third-degree burns. I couldn't recognize it as mine, as it turned different shades of maroon from the violent scalding I received at the hands of my sister. The horrific physical sensation had been so intense that I blacked out. Afterward, my back was numb and couldn't be touched without causing me excruciating pain. It took years before I could accept a simple pat on the back, as most of my skin had to completely renew and repair itself.

The deepest injury, though, was from the emotional trauma. Feelings are not like skin; there are no fresh new cells coming to replace ruined ones. Those scars go unseen, unacknowledged, and unhealed. The truly irreversible damage to me came from the burn of my big sister, not the tea. Her arson was deliberate—she burned my back and my trust. Any faint hope I'd held up to that point of having a big sister became scorched earth.

I know my sister was deeply wounded. She is the most brilliant and broken person I have ever known. I may never understand what hurt her so badly that it made her hurt so many others in return, but to me, she was her own most permanently damaged victim. From my perspective she chose to take up permanent residence in "Victimland." The promise of her life was squandered in a tragic series of cheap bargains rather than being redeemed through the difficult, lifelong work of recovery and rebuilding oneself.

Alison has burned me in many ways and more times than I can count. Over and over I have tried to be her fire department, financing treatments and paying for stays in premium rehabs. But even with substantial resources, there is no way to rescue someone who doesn't realize they're burning. The scars I carry from my sister are not just a reminder, they are lessons. They have taught me that perhaps our worlds are far too different to ever overlap, hers made of fire and mine of the light.

I always hoped and wished Alison would get better, so *we* could get better. I understand she was severely emotionally injured and had to take her enduring pain out on someone. She chose me. Through the years, both my sister and brother have put me on the chopping block, sold lies to any gossip rag or trashy website that would buy or listen. They have attacked me for decades. But when I was twelve years old, my sister drugged me with Valium, offered me a pinky nail full of cocaine, inflicted me with third-degree burns, and tried to sell me out to a pimp. Something in me was arrested by all that trauma. That is why I often say, "I'm eternally twelve." I am still struggling through that time.

And I miss you, dandelion
And even love you
And I wish there was a way
For me to trust you
But it hurts me every time
I try to touch you

—"Petals"

DETANGLED AND
SWEPT AWAY

In the photograph, bright rays of sun shine down on me like a spotlight, and the hot dog I'm holding has a big, happy bite taken out of it. My hair is a range of gold highlights, raw sienna, wheat blond, and sweet lemon, lit by the sun. Soft, thick waves of it are blowing in layers away from my face as a few ringlets sweep up off my shoulders. There is a tenderness in my gaze, cut slightly with seriousness at the edges of my eyes.

This photo is one of my favorites from my childhood. In it, I look like a typical first grader on summer break. I look like I belong to somebody who knows how to look after me. I appear well cared for. But I wasn't.

My childhood was rife with neglect. There were many things about me that my mother didn't understand how to nurture or maintain—but the most obvious, most symbolic, and most visible was my hair.

My hair was rooted to no one. No one *did* my hair. No one knew how. We didn't have conditioner (or "cream rinse," as it was called back in the day) at my mother's house. There were no pomades, wide-toothed combs, or hard-bristled brushes. There was no Sunday ritual of getting my hair washed and braided; certainly, there was no greasing of the scalp. There was no order made in my hair. I never felt the tidiness or security of having my hair *done*.

As a result, my hair was often a matted, tangled mess. And no one around me could fully understand the particular humiliation of being a nonwhite little girl with unkempt hair. I didn't have the language for it, but I carried the burden of how it felt. My neglected hair was a siren, signaling that I was different from all the little white girls—and from little Black girls too. My wild, mixed, and mangled curls made me feel inferior, unworthy of receiving proper attention.

There was no going to the salon, *dahling*. I don't recall my mother ever going to a *salon*. She fully subscribed to that bohemian, no-fuss beauty philosophy of the 1950s and '60s. For her, a full beat face was eyeliner—a little cat wing, if she was being extra fancy—a swish of mascara, a touch of blush, a lip, and voilà! Flawless face. Her hair was fabulous, either up or down. Even if she had believed in seeking professional grooming services, for her or me, we could never afford it. And besides, there were no salons in that part of Long Island that could comprehend the contradictions of my tendrils, the sheer complexities of the needs of my hair. At that time there weren't mixed-texture professionals anywhere, really, nor were there any specialized products. I was living tangled in between an Afro Sheen and a Breck Girl world.

The two constant representations of female beauty I saw on a daily basis were my mother and TV commercials. I admired and deeply desired the dark, smooth perfection of my mother's long, luxurious hair. The contrast between how my mother's hair looked when she woke up in the morning and how mine did was *profound*. She would shake her head, and thick, straight hair would tumble down like a yard of heavy silk crepe, draping into an elegant pool across her shoulders. I, on the other hand, had smashed-down, fuzzy, sweaty clumps, exploding in a cacophony of knots, waves, and curls all over my head.

And then there was the hair I saw on TV, the magnificent, sunshine-filled, slow-motion-blowing-in-the-wind-while-running-barefoot-through-fields-of-flowers hair. I was enchanted by those commercials, especially the ones for Clairol Herbal Essence shampoo. It was as if Eve herself was in the Garden of Eden, bottling the thick, emerald-green nectar made of earthly delights of herbs and wildflowers. I was convinced this shampoo would give me the heavenly hair, blown by gusts of angels' wings, that I saw in the commercial. I wanted that shampoo *so bad*. I wanted that angelic, blowing hair *so bad*. (Because of those commercials, Olivia Newton-John, and the Boss, Diana Ross, I still am obsessed with blowing hair, as evidenced by the wind machines employed in almost every photo shoot of me ever.)

Young and culturally isolated, I had no idea how to manage my hair, nor the shame it brought me. I often wonder if my mother ever saw the carelessness that my hair made visible. Was she too preoccupied with her own burdens to notice? Could she not feel the dryness, and the lumps and bumps, of the gnarly tangles in my head? Why couldn't she just sit me down and brush my hair for two hours, the way Marcia Brady did on *The Brady Bunch*? Maybe in her bohemian, sixties-loving ideology she thought I looked free, like an adorable flower child. Maybe she didn't know I felt dirty.

Having one Black and one white parent is complicated, but when you are a little girl with a white mother, largely cut off from other Black women and girls, it can be excruciatingly lonely. And, of course, I had no biracial role models or references. I understand why my mother didn't understand how to manage my hair. When I was a baby, it was, well, baby hair, mostly uniform, soft curls. As I got older it got more complex, with diverse textures arising out of seemingly nowhere. She didn't know what was happening. She was confused and randomly started cutting tragic bangs in my hair (believing bangs would behave in biracial hair is brave).

It was a disaster, and I felt powerless. At seven years old, I really thought maybe if she would just wash my hair with Herbal Essence, a hair fairy would come at night, and I would wake up and poof! I would have perfect hair like my mom or the girls in the commercials.

It took me five hundred hours of beauty school training to know even Marcia Brady's hair wouldn't blow with abandon with just shampoo. It takes professionals, products, and production, *dahling*—conditioners galore, diffusers, precision cuts, special combs, clip-ins, cameras, and, of course, wind machines. It requires a lot of effort to achieve effortless hair.

What I really needed was *any* Black woman, or anyone with some kind of culture, cream, and a comb! But even that wasn't that simple.

One time my father's half sisters staged an intervention of sorts, determined to "do something about that chile's hair." It was going to be an event. I was in the second grade when my father took me to my grandfather and Nana Ruby's house in Queens.

Humor was a tool I used to cope, disarm, and defend myself. I also used it to express my point of view when I had no control. It was a tool I began to sharpen quite early and, to this day, utilize frequently. In the backseat of the car on the long drive to visit my father's family, I overheard Alison, seated up front, grumbling to him about how I was absorbing my mother's quirks and eccentricities (particularly those associated with white privilege). I think she thought I was out in the world "passing" with our white mother (as though a child could make that distinction).

And then, as if I weren't there, she went on a tirade. I continued to stare silently out of the window at the dilapidated neighborhoods we had been driving through to get to Jamaica, Queens, from Long Island. Finally, I couldn't take it any longer. Achieving an (I think) impressive impersonation of my mother, especially for a six-year-old, I groaned sarcastically in her characteristically slow, low, opera diva tone: "I *see* we're taking the *scenic route*!" At which Alison snapped her head toward my father with an exasperated "*See?*" expression on her face. He stiffened, gripped the steering wheel a little tighter, and kept his eyes forward. For effect, I didn't break my bored stare out the window. No one was entertained by my little impersonation. I tried.

Sweet Nana Ruby was my father's father's second wife, with whom he had a whole lotta kids, half aunties and uncles to me, who subsequently produced a gang of cousins, some of whom were around my age. My father and his father, Bob Carey, had a complicated relationship. Bob's mother was from Venezuela, and it is believed his father was Black—mixed with some undocumented lightening factor, as he too was on the fairer side of what was then called the "Negro spectrum."

Until I was about six years old, my father hadn't spoken to his father in years. He was an only child and had a different mother than my grandfather's other children, and as warm and as welcoming as Nana Ruby and her house were—and from what I could see, she showered my father with love—still, she was not his mother, and perhaps he felt like a bit of an outsider with them. I think he made the effort to mend things with his father for the sake of his own children as well as himself. He must have realized how isolated I was, living with just my mother in an all-white community that was becoming increasingly hostile to me. I needed to know *some* family.

And I am forever grateful for it, because that house was a warm place bustling with family life. I loved it there. The whole neighborhood loved my grandpa. He was a regular, fun-loving guy with a hearty laugh, who wore crew socks with his slide sandals. He had a little urban vineyard in his backyard in Queens. He grew sour grapes from which he made sweet homemade wine that he stored in the basement. Nana Ruby and my aunties always had something cooking in the tiny kitchen—chicken, greens—but the standout staple dish was rice and beans. I could eat whole plates of it. There was the clamoring of comforting noises: pots clanging, soul music in the background, the hum of the TV, conversations, giggles, doors opening and closing, feet running up and down the stairs. It was a lighthearted space. There were people just hanging out together, connected to one another. Being there was the closest feeling I had to having a big family, a normal family, a *real* family.

My favorite cousins would come from the Bronx and boy, did we play! We were a creative and mischievous bunch. Sometimes we would hang out the second-story window and drop water-balloon bombs on folks passing underneath. Then we'd duck down out of sight and shake in muffled hysterics. And of course, I loved anything that involved performance. My favorite was reenacting "Mrs. Wiggins" sketches from *The Carol Burnett Show*. Unsurprisingly, I insisted on playing the lead role. I had her signature walk down pat. I stuffed my little booty with a pillow, sticking it way out, acting like I had on a tight pencil skirt. I pranced about on my tippy-toes (maybe this is why I still walk on my toes), taking tiny steps. I'd smack imaginary gum and pretend to file my nails, and speak in the ditsy, nasally voice I had down to perfection. I specialized in character voices very early.

"Oh, Mrs. Uh-Whiggins!" one of my cousins would say in a silly, skewed Swedish accent. I'd snap into character and we'd launch into a full-on improvisation. What I loved most was all the rambunctious laughing with my cousins. I loved the sound of my laughter as a small part in the chorus of other kids who were kinda like me.

Inside the house with my cousins I may have felt a part of something, but outside with kids in the neighborhood was a different story. It's *always* a different story with me. Even though my cousins didn't live on this mostly Black and Hispanic block in Queens, they were known because our grandpa was "that guy" in the neighborhood. When we were outside playing, they'd introduce me to the other kids as their cousin, and some kid would invariably say, "She's not your cousin. She's *white*."

"Yes, she *is* our cousin!" they would snap right back. Who my mother was, who my father was, to whom I belonged, was always in question. But hanging out with my cousins wasn't as heavy. I was part of a group. I was part of *them*, and they defended me. *Yes, she is.* It was that simple. And it was so important. My Black cousins were the only cousins I knew when I was a little girl. Because my mother's side of the family, the white side, had disowned her, I had no way of having a real relationship with any of them as a child.

My cousins were well put together because their mothers were *very* well put together. One auntie in particular was younger, juicy, and just gorgeous. She looked ready to twirl down the *Soul Train* line on TV. Her makeup was consistently impeccable, lips glossed up like glass. She wore funky-chic ensembles, and her hair was always in some superb slick, snatched-back style, so she could feature *face*. She was giving you trendy, sexy, and coordinated at all times, almost as fab as Thelma on *Good Times* (but a little bit thicker). This foxy auntie sold makeup at the department store counter— now *that* was fabulous to me. Once, she gave my favorite girl cousin and me a faux facial evaluation. As she was examining our little faces, she told Cee Cee, "Your lips are good." Then she turned to me with a puzzled look and paused. I was wondering, and worrying, *What's wrong with my face? Me?*

"Mariah, your lips aren't full enough," she said with a sigh.

I didn't know what they weren't full enough for, but I fully accepted her analysis as fact. A few years later, I was about twelve years old and hanging out with a white girlfriend at a department store on Long Island, where they were offering free makeup demos at one of the counters. My friend, by local standards, was a beauty: big blue eyes, a thin nose, and very thin lips. I, no doubt, had on some haphazard ensemble, and who knows what the hair was doing that day. Clearly looking our age, we sat down to have our faces done. Maybe the saleslady thought we had money to buy some makeup, or she was bored, or she simply took pity on us. Whatever the case, she began the process.

As my auntie had done, she studied the contours and angles of both of our faces and reported to me, "*Your* lips are too full on top." *Wait*, I thought. I knew I had a thin upper lip—but not as thin as my white friend, whose lip size was the "standard" at the time. I wanted to say, "Actually, I really want my lips to be bigger"—which I did, ever since the day of my auntie's evaluation—but I held my tongue. Thus I was given two polar opposite professional opinions about my lips as a girl; they were too full for a white beauty standard and not full enough for a Black one. Who was I to believe? It was like my complexes had complexes. And there was no one to tell me, "Mariah, you are *good.*" Period.

And now here we are in a world where white *and* Black women are filling up their butts and lips like water balloons. I guess I should've had my lips injected ages ago, but it's too late. The whole world knows what my real lips look like, so why bother? Why would I do that now, when I can just accentuate them with lip liner, *dahling*?

But I digress. That day at Grandpa and Nana Ruby's house when I was seven, the time had come for my cousins' main event. My aunties had decided it was time to put me together. Some of them were gathered upstairs in Nana Ruby's bedroom, and they summoned me up. My cousins and I went upstairs toward the master bedroom, which was just right of the bathroom. I spent many moments exploring that little bathroom, fascinated with all the *greasings* and *slatherings* it contained. There were endless creams and lotions for the skin, and dressings and pomades for the hair. Imagine: skin lotion and hair grease! In this bathroom every cabinet and free space was filled with mysterious potions and products.

I rarely went into the master bedroom, but it, too, was small, cramped, and comforting. It was humid and smelled like a hot candy store. A large bed, covered with a shiny, quilted white-and-maroon paisley bedspread, with ruffles at the hem, took up most of the room. There was a full-length mirror attached to the back of the door and a low dresser drawer on which my aunties had everything laid out. There was a hot plate cranking.

Upon its sizzling surface was some foreign object that resembled a garden tool, with a dark wooden handle like a hammer, with teeth. Though the metal part was blackened, traces of its original gold color could be seen underneath. This mysterious hammer-fork thing sat menacingly on the plate's surface, getting hotter and hotter. As I crossed the threshold into the bedroom, I felt as though I had entered an alternate universe, a secret chamber—one of Black-girl beauty.

My aunts motioned for me to sit on the side of the bed. I didn't know what kind of ritual was ahead, but I sure was excited. As I settled in on the edge of the bed, feet dangling off the side, I could feel many hands exploring the wild garden of knots, curls, and straight bits that made up my head of hair. My heart was racing. I felt like a long-lost princess sitting in her chambers, hoping this could be it—the moment of coronation, when my hair would finally get *done* and I would be transformed, presented to the world with newfound power and grace.

Finally, I thought, maybe my hair would fit in. Maybe it would fall into sleek and shiny ringlets, and I would look like my cute Black girl cousins and friends who gathered in Queens. Or maybe it would lie down flat and bone straight like the hair of the little white girls I grew up among on Long Island. Either way, I was just thrilled that my hair would at last be cared for by someone who knew what to do.

The action started at the back of my head, with some pulling and separating, and a little sharpness from knots coming undone. The next thing I felt was something I'll never forget. First, there was a heavy tugging and burning sensation near my neck, followed immediately by an alarming searing and sizzling sound and an unfamiliar and vicious smell, like a dirty stuffed animal set on fire. Along with significant smoke, a faint panic began to waft through the room. I couldn't make out much of what was being said, but I certainly heard, "Oh shit!" and "Stop, stop!" several times. And then it did stop. Abruptly. The excitement, the ritual, and the fixing all stopped. I stayed motionless and quiet, a small patch of hair at the nape of my neck still smoldering.

My aunties were apologetic. "Sorry, baby, the hot comb is too strong for your hair," my aunties explained. *Sorry, baby*, and that was the end of it. There would be no rites of passage into Black-girl hair society that day. I didn't emerge transformed into a presentable little girl for Harlem, Queens, or Long Island. I was still a wayward little misfit who wore a disobedient crown on her head—only now with a patch of rough, burned, uneven (and noticeably shorter) hair in the back. I was far from *done*.

On rare occasions, my mother, brother, and I would take a drive to Jones Beach as a family. (Proximity to the beach was one of the few perks of being stranded on Long Island.) One summer morning, the three of us kids, along with one of my brother's buddies, piled into my mother's clunker on wheels and hit the road to the beach. It was a clear, bright day; you could see the ocean in the sky. It was a perfect day for the beach. My mother, sporting a light-blue cotton summer caftan with thin green stripes, was driving. All the windows were rolled down, giving the car a faux convertible feeling; my mother's bell sleeves flapped slightly in the breeze. She had on her signature big sunglasses, and her hair was customarily carefree. My brother sat next to her, shirtless, his big, fluffy Afro bouncing gently.

I sat in the backseat next to my brother's friend, quietly looking out the open window, letting the warm, salty air wash over my face. I was trying to be nonchalant, not to let on I had an enormous crush on this teen-star-looking boy. His silky hair was strawberry blond, with perfect natural highlights, laid out in delicate, feathered layers and parted down the middle. Every dreamy strand rested in its perfect place. The car was quiet as we all enjoyed a rare moment of contentment.

Gradually, though, I became aware that my hair had started to move. But it was not from the wind. Instead, it was from what felt like fingers. There were fingers searching through the wild, tangled bush that was my hair. I didn't dare move or speak. But the boy, he was gently plucking at my hair! Surgically, he worked on the smaller, tighter, matted bits at the ends with the big black plastic comb he kept permanently ensconced in his back pocket. He was using the very same comb that he ran through his field of perfect golden strands on *my* disheveled head! He pulled the comb from scalp to end in small sections. As each portion was released from the weight of its former twisted entrapment, it would float a little bit.

Over the course of the ride, without a single word exchanged between us, he removed all the knots and confusion from my hair. By the time we arrived at the beach, my hair was no longer a burden. It was liberated. I dashed straight to the water—oh, how I love the ocean, a gift from my mother—and as I ran I could feel my hair, buoyant and blowing in the wind for the first time. Hallelujah! My hair was actually blowing like in the commercials!

I dived into the first wave I could and rode it back to shore. When I stood up and touched my hair, it was not the haphazard mix of textures I was accustomed to. Instead I touched orderly, coily, elongated curls! For the first time, my hair felt pretty. *I* felt pretty. I felt soft and light, as if the shame I'd been carrying had been plucked out of me and washed away.

As I stood in the waist-deep water, reveling in the newfound confidence brought by my liberated curls, a sudden wall of ocean appeared, crashing down, pounding against my back. My feet were swept up off the sandy floor and over my head. My tiny body was tossed like a rag doll in the strong waves that had suddenly kicked up. I had no sense of equilibrium or orientation, but I knew I was being pulled down, tumbling in surging, dark water mixed with frothy white foam and grit that was beating against my body like boxing gloves made of sandpaper. Even if I could tell which way was up and how to get there, I knew I was not strong enough to overcome the powerful currents, so I relaxed my body and went with it. I surrendered.

By what I believe to be God's grace, the ocean decided to give me back to the earth. I lay motionless on the grainy, wet sand, winded and salty. When I realized I was alive, I stood up to look for my mother. I spied her and my brother lying on an olive blanket in the distance, shades on, nonchalantly sunbathing. Oblivious. I released a mighty wail, which devolved into hysterical crying, finally catching my mother's attention. Yet another close encounter with death.

To calm my shattered seven-year-old nerves, someone took me up to the boardwalk, to the hot dog stand. I was a wreck—but my hair wasn't. It was still in wavy ringlets. I had achieved perfect beach hair. That day I almost died, but my hair was *done*.

A GIRL'S BEST FRIEND

From the moment I saw her, I felt both awe and identification. I idolized her. She was like a living doll, but neither baby nor Barbie; though she was a real, elegant, grown-up woman, she appeared pure and flawless, as if made of delicate lacquered porcelain. I'd never seen anyone like her—such a radiant, glamorous, vulnerable, yet powerful being. She was supernatural. I stood there staring, fascinated and frozen before the bright screen where she lived.

One evening I had been walking aimlessly down the hall in one of the many houses we lived in. As I passed my mother's dark little bedroom, I casually wandered in. I can't remember whether I saw or heard her first, but I know something carried me into that room. The bedroom was lit only by the washed-out colors of the old TV facing the bed, where my mother was lying in silhouette, watching a special about the life and death of Marilyn Monroe.

I softly pushed open the bedroom door, walking in on the iconic scene from *Gentlemen Prefer Blondes* in which Marilyn sings "Diamonds Are a Girl's Best Friend." She was the most beautiful person I had ever seen.

Her energy was like a fairy's, but she looked like a goddess, swathed in a luxurious electric-pink silk gown and matching opera gloves, with diamonds of every size dripping from her ears and wrapped around her neck and wrists. The only bits of skin exposed were her face, her shoulders, and her arms down to the elbow, yet I remember her flesh seeming so rich and creamy, glistening like homemade ice cream. Her hair was just a few shades lighter, dazzling like finely spun gold. She was voluptuously shaped, with round, curvy hips, a small, cinched waist, proud, purposeful breasts, and arms that stretched wide and hugged close. She was poised, like a dancer, yet her feet didn't seem to move. Instead scores of people danced around *her*: fawning and fanning, kneeling and bowing down to her, conveying her above their heads like Cleopatra. Maybe she was a queen, I thought. The shining queen of movie stars.

I'd never heard the name Marilyn Monroe before that moment. But I was quickly hooked. Not your typical third-grade fare, perhaps, but my childhood was anything but typical. My mother very lovingly supported my fascination with Marilyn. While most girls my age adorned their walls with pictures of Holly Hobbie—the frontier rag doll with freckles and blond yarn braids in a strawberry-print bonnet—I had a poster of Marilyn Monroe dressed as a sensuous showgirl, complete with a black beaded bustier, fishnets, and black patent-leather pumps. I gazed up at Marilyn before I went to sleep and first thing when I woke up.

Later my mother bought me *Marilyn: A Biography*, by Norman Mailer. Though I was way too young for the material, like Marilyn herself I read voraciously. I pored over the large, glossy photos of her, studying all her different moods and looks. She was a shape-shifter—in some photos she was impossibly beautiful and glamorous, in others she seemed shattered and about to disappear. Her hair shifted shapes, too: pin curls, pigtails, sweeping updos, bobs with deep-diving waves. I even detected unruly curls and familiar fuzz underneath the perfect, almost white-blond wave of her hair. There was also something in her physicality, something about her body type, that didn't read as typically Caucasian to me. Not only was she curvy, she had a very particular sensuality, bordering on soulful.

I read a lot about Marilyn, conspiracy theories about her death and about her upbringing. The more I read, the more I connected with her and understood why I was drawn to her. She had a very difficult childhood, moving from one foster home to another. That was close to my story: being uprooted and unprotected, feeling like an outsider. I intimately understood her struggles with poverty and family. Ultimately, what I loved about Marilyn was her ability to come from nothing—to belong to no one—and evolve into a huge icon. I latched onto that. I believed in *that*.

I've heard Marilyn might've even been my mother's inspiration for my name. The first four letters are the same: M-A-R-I. However, my father claimed that my name comes from the Black Maria/Mariah, the infamous police van used to haul people off to prison in the UK. The story *also* goes that I was named after a hit 1950s show tune, "They Call the Wind Maria," from *Paint Your Wagon*, a Broadway show about the California Gold Rush. (Both references use the soft pronunciation, with the second syllable having a *rye* sound.) Perhaps it's a combination of all three: a 1950s starlet, a show tune, and a paddy wagon.

Whatever the origin, when I was younger I didn't like my name. No one else had it, and when you're a kid that's not cool. I always wished I had a regular name like Jennifer or Heather. There were no cute stickers, key chains, or mini license plates with my name on them. But the worst part was hardly anyone could pronounce it. I always dreaded seeing a substitute teacher, knowing roll call would be a Maria/Maya calamity. I wouldn't meet another Mariah until I was about eighteen years old; she was a cool Black girl and we commiserated good-humoredly on the mispronunciations of our childhood. I had no way to imagine that only a few years after that, many people would be naming their children Mariah, after me.

Of all the supposed inspirations for my name, the Marilyn Monroe connection resonates the most with me—self-created and controlled, confident and vulnerable, womanly and childlike, glamorous and humble, adored and alone. Marilyn is a source of inspiration for me, and *Lawd* have I needed that.

When I was in the eighth grade, there was a pack of pretty, mostly Irish girls whom I desperately wanted to befriend. At that time, in that town, most of these girls were considered the pinnacle of physical perfection:

milky skin, silky hair, and blue eyes. They used to have a chant: "Blue eyes rule!" These were not nice girls.

And I felt wholly inferior around them. Compared to them (and in the eighth grade, comparison is the *only* method of measurement) my skin was muddy, my hair was lawless. They called me Fozzie Bear (from the Muppets) because of my unruly hair, and try as I might, I could never flatten it all out to look like theirs, and my eyes were distinctly and undeniably unblue. (I liked my dark eyes, but I never stood up for myself during their weird chant.) Clearly I stood out from their group, but they let me hang with them. Maybe it was because I was the class clown, always quick to crack a joke or snap on somebody and make the whole group laugh. Even if I was only there as entertainment, I was happy to put on a show.

The girl in that clique who was my closest friend (and I use that word liberally) was also the prettiest. I guess now they'd call her a "frenemy." I would tell her I was interested in a boy at school, and, knowing full well I never acted on any of my crushes, she and her big blue eyes would go after him and almost always score. I believe she did this just to push me down, to let me know she had all the power. But what she didn't know was that I didn't ever pursue boys because I wanted to avoid the inevitable humiliation once they learned that half of me was Black and all of me was poor. She also didn't know that I didn't want to get wrapped up in some stupid boy and derail my dreams or, worse, get pregnant like my sister. She didn't know me at all. None of them did.

Some of the girls' parents did know my mother, however. They had a modicum of respect for her because she was also Irish and a professional opera singer—and opera was *classy*. Adult drama works differently than that among teens, but they often intersect. Word got out that the Irish father of the prettiest girl was physically abusing her mother. My mother, who can get really righteous when she wants to, took it upon herself to write him a letter. In that letter I'm pretty sure she disclosed that she had been married to a Black man and that he was the father of her children (of course, I wouldn't learn of the letter until much later).

As I said, these were *not* nice girls, but eventually I was invited to go with some of them, including the prettiest one, to Southampton for a sleepover. One of them had a rich aunt, Barbara, with a fancy house near the beach. *Fancy-schmancy* Southampton? A sleepover with the popular girls? *Of course* I wanted to go. We piled into one of their big cars and took the two-hour-long drive along the lovely Atlantic edge of Long Island to the small village where the wealthy "summer." (Summer was a season for me, not a verb.)

The house was big, airy, and orderly. It even had an all-white room no one was allowed to enter. I was awestruck when we arrived, so busy comparing and craving that I hadn't noticed that the girls had gathered into a cluster by a door.

They called over to me: "Come on, Mariah. Let's go back here."

Without question, I followed. They led me to what I thought would be a playroom or a den (I knew wealthy people had dens). It was a smaller room in the rear of the house, a guest room perhaps. One of them shut the door with a click, and suddenly the mood grew heavy, fast. I thought maybe they'd snuck in some alcohol or something. But there was no excitement, no naughty, girly energy. Instead, all the girls were glaring at me. Suddenly, into the heavy silence, the sister of the prettiest girl spit out her ugly secret for all to hear:

"You're a *nigger*!"

My head began to spin when I realized she was referring to me. Pointing at me. It was *my* secret, *my* shame. I was frozen.

The others quickly joined in. "You're a nigger!" they all shrieked. All together, in unison, they chanted, "You're a nigger!" over and over. I thought it would never end.

The venom and hate with which these girls spewed this new iteration of their usual chant was so strong, it quite literally lifted me out of my body. I had no idea how to handle what was going on. It was all of them against me. They had planned it. They fooled me into thinking they actually liked me. They lured me hours away from home. They isolated me. They trapped me. Then they betrayed me. I exploded into hysterical tears. I was disoriented and terrified, and I thought that maybe, if I held on and just kept crying, surely a grown-up would come and stop the assault. But no one came.

Eventually, I heard another voice whimpering among the mob.

"Why are you doing this?" the small, brave voice asked. It was the older blond one.

The ugly sister of the prettiest shot back, "Because she *is* a nigger."

I don't remember anything else about that day. I don't remember the ride home. I don't remember telling my mother when I got back. How do you tell your all-white mother that your all-white "friends" just dragged you into their big all-white house in all-white Southampton, past an untouchable all-white room, just to corner you and call you the dirtiest thing in their all-white world? *Nigger.*

I was also scared my mother might make a massive public scene and make navigating life at school even more difficult for me. I had no language or coping skills for any of it. It was certainly not the first time I had been degraded by my schoolmates. I'd been singled out on the school bus and spit on. I'd gotten into physical fights. Often, I would clap back; my tongue was sharp, and I could be a real wiseass. Sometimes I even started fights. But for this I had no defense. I was not only outnumbered and isolated, I was bitterly betrayed. This was not your garden-variety school-yard mean-girl scuffle. It was a devious and violent premeditated assault by girls I called my friends. I never spoke of it. I stuffed it inside. I had to find a way to survive those girls, that town, my family, and my pain.

She smiles through a thousand tears
And harbors adolescent fears
She dreams of all
That she can never be
She wades in insecurity
And hides herself inside of me
Don't say she takes it all for granted
I'm well aware of all I have
Don't think that I am disenchanted
Please understand
It seems as though I've always been
Somebody outside looking in

Well here I am for all of them to bleed
But they can't take my heart from me
And they can't bring me to my knees
They'll never know the real me

—"Looking In"

"Mariah only has three shirts and she puts them in rotation!"

The cruel words crashed into the buzzing bustle of the in-between-class traffic of my seventh-grade hallway like a stink bomb. All the pattering of feet, clanging of lockers, chirping of small talk, and little giggles morphed into one giant laughing monster made of kids, sitting in the middle of the hallway pointing at me. My stomach collapsed and my face burst into flames. I thought I might vomit right there on the tile floor.

Middle school is a contact sport, and I was pretty skillful with my own sharp tongue. A lot of kids have to suffer having mean or "funny" names given to them by their peers because of how they look or some embarrassing event, but being teased for being poor felt like a different kind of cruel.

I was severely injured, but I did not let it show. I didn't get sick in front of everybody. I didn't give anyone the satisfaction of seeing me weakened. I showed no emotion and waited patiently for the monster to melt away, as the traffic had to resume and kids had to get to their classes. I understood after that there would be no recovering and no trying to belong. I would survive on the outside with three shirts and no friends in hopes that I would inevitably move again.

In our middle-class community, I was extremely self-conscious of living with a shabby wardrobe in a small dilapidated house; however, by the time I entered high school, I had developed some new survival skills. At that age I didn't have any control over where I lived, but I could do something about what I wore. One of the few advantages of moving so many times was that I got a fresh crop of kids to try to fit in with. One go-round I managed to scrounge together a few girlfriends and convince them we should have a fashion swapping system where we'd exchange our trendiest pieces with one another and coordinate them differently. This gave the illusion that I had a more expansive and up-to-date wardrobe than I could ever afford.

The coolest thing I owned was an oversized red wool and black leather varsity jacket with AVIREX in big letters emblazoned across the back. It was a big deal for me to have a name-brand item, so I made sure I had a signature piece that was adaptable to a variety of looks. I did my best to look the part of a typical cute suburban teen, to fit in with all the other Long Island girls.

By the time I was in the tenth grade I was "going out" with the biggest and scariest dude in town. He was six foot five and had biceps that were thicker than both of my thighs. He was in his early twenties, he had a car, and nobody messed with him. And that's the main reason why I was with him. He was a protector, a force field. The previous boy I had gone out with was volatile; we even got into a physical altercation in front of a group of girls who stood around and watched. After we broke up he proceeded to stalk and harass me—a real charmer. Mr. Six Foot Five caught him verbally attacking me and proceeded to lift him up off the ground and toss him over five parked cars—pow! He actually was pretty cool beyond his brute strength. But high school can be treacherous, especially for an outsider like me, so having the toughest guy in town as *my* guy was good for that moment.

There was a crew of girls who were into a sixties tie-dyed Grateful Dead vibe that I never understood. It was the late eighties, and the street trends were so fresh, I *really* didn't get what they were doing. Why were they harkening back to such a random retro look? Also, they were aggressive and hard, not hippies, Dead Heads, or peace lovers at all. Being the smart aleck I was, I named them the "Peace People." Word got out that I was making fun of them, and they were pissed. Rumblings started circulating that I was going to get my ass kicked. But Mr. Six Foot Five was famous; everyone was afraid of him, so getting at me wasn't that simple.

One morning after completing my routine of going to the Bagel Station to get a bagel with bacon and cheese and coffee, I was walking on the path to "the patio" to finish my coffee and smoke a Newport before homeroom. The patio was a large brick square outside the cafeteria of the school where kids would hang out, smoke, and posture. Several hundred yards before I reached it, suddenly a semicircle of about a dozen white girls closed in around me, and they were all hyped up to fight.

They were screaming at the same time, and the hardest girl of them all broke out from the pack and advanced toward me. I was freaked out but tried not to show how scared I was. The bagel in my stomach had turned into rocket fuel and was going off in my belly, and my head was spinning trying to devise something to say to defuse or derail the situation, because surely *I* was not going to fight. I may have had a tough exterior and a wiseass mouth, but I never wanted to actually fight anyone. I used my wits to survive (plus I was the fastest runner in the school, except for one boy). The crowd had gotten close enough that the heat of their mob mentality was singeing the hairs on my arms. I had to say something, so I opened my mouth and just started yelling—I have no idea what. What I will never forget is seeing their bravado instantly wither into meekness while they slowly edged backward and quickly dispersed. For a quick instant I thought I had really told them off, but then I felt a powerful energy behind me. I turned around, and looking like a fly-girl teen version of a Black Panther protest, there was a big beautiful wall of every style, size, and shade of every Black girl I knew in school. "Oh, we got your back," one of them said, and that was it.

There was no debate over "how Black" I was, or whether I "looked white"—those badass girls just let me know that when it got down to it, they were going to hold me down.

🦋

Years later, after the release of "Vision of Love," I was all over the radio and on TV. My mother was still living on Long Island, and I asked her if we could drive by the house where the prettiest girl and her sisters lived. I stopped the car, got out, and just looked at the modest structure, a symbol of what I had survived. My mother, wrapped in a fur coat I'd given her, got out too. The father of the family (the one who beat the mother) came to the door and, in his dense, twangy Long Island accent, shouted, "Aw, look, Pat's gone Hollywood!" The rest of the family filed out of the house. The prettiest one was stunned. She couldn't believe it had happened.

The mutt-mulatto bitch who lived in the shabby shack down the street had become a star.

The brother called out, "You're a loser!"

That family, that house, that town, that time, that day—suddenly it all looked like nothing to me. It was nothing in nowhere, and *I* had made it out.

As I turned to get back in the car, I heard the blond girl crying after me, "Mariah, I'm so happy for you; I'm so happy for you!" And she became the prettiest sister of them all.

Yes I've been bruised
Grew up confused
Been destitute
I've seen life from many sides
Been stigmatized
Been black and white
Felt inferior inside
Until my saving grace shined on me
Until my saving grace set me free
Giving me peace

—*"My Saving Grace"*

PART II

SING. SING.

A PRELUDE
TO SING SING

Nearing the edge
Oblivious I almost
Fell right over
A part of me
Will never be quite able
To feel stable

—"Close My Eyes"

Even now it's hard to explain, to put into words how I existed in my relationship with Tommy Mottola. It's not that there are no words, it's just that they still get stuck moving up from my gut, or they disappear into the thickness of my anxiety. Tommy's energy was intense, more than overbearing; for me, it was an entire atmosphere. Even before he would enter the room I could sense the air change and my breath grow short. He rolled over me like a fog. His presence felt dense and oppressive. He was like humidity—inescapable.

Never when I was with him did I feel I could breathe easy and fully as myself. His power was pervasive, and with it came an unspeakable unease. In the beginning of our time together I was walking on eggshells. Then it became a bed of nails, and then a minefield. I never knew when or what would make him blow, and the anxiety was relentless. In the eight years we were together I can't recall ten minutes with him when I felt I could be comfortable—when I could simply *be* at all. I felt his grip was steadily choking me off from my essence. I was disappearing in installments.

It felt like he was cutting off my circulation, keeping me from friends and what little "family" I had. I couldn't talk to anyone that wasn't under Tommy's control. I couldn't go out or do anything with anybody. I couldn't move freely in my own house.

Many nights I would lie on my side of our massive bed, under which I would keep my purse filled with essentials just in case I had to make a quick escape—my "to go" bag. I had to wait for him to fall asleep. Keeping my eyes locked on him, I would gradually inch my way to the edge of the bed and surgically roll my hips and swing my legs to the floor. Never breaking my gaze, I'd tiptoe backward toward the door, which seemed a full city block away. Ever so carefully, I'd back out of the door. It was such a victory when I made it out of the room! I'd softly creep down the grand dark-wood staircase like a burglar stealing a little peace of mind, then make my way to somewhere in the manor. Often I just wanted to go to the kitchen for a snack, or to sit at the table and write down some lyrics. But every time, right as I would start to settle into the calm of the quiet dark and begin to find my breath—Beep! Beep! The intercom would go off.

I'd jump up, and the words "Whatcha doin'?" would crackle through the speaker, and I'd gasp and once again lose my own air. Every move I made, everywhere I went, I was monitored—minute by minute, day after day, year after year.

It was as if I was being crushed right out of myself. Everything he felt he didn't create or control was being strangled away. I created the fun and free girl in my videos so that I could watch a version of myself be alive, live vicariously through her—the girl I pretended to be, the girl I wished was me. I would view my videos as evidence that I existed.

I was living my dream but couldn't leave my house. Lonely and trapped, I was held captive in that relationship. Captivity and control come in many forms, but the goal is always the same—to break down the captive's will, to kill any notion of self-worth and erase the person's memory of their own soul. I'm still not sure of the toll it has taken on me, how much of me was permanently destroyed or arrested—perhaps, among other things, my ability to completely trust people or to fully rest.

But thankfully I smuggled myself out bit by bit, through the lyrics of my songs.

I left the worst unsaid
Let it all dissipate
And I tried to forget
As I closed my eyes

I sang some of what I couldn't say. Though I do try, I cannot forget. Sometimes, without warning, I am haunted by a nightmare or flashes of suffocating. Sometimes I still feel the heaviness. Sometimes I have no air.

ALONE IN LOVE

When I was in seventh grade, I had my first professional recording session. I did background vocals on a few original songs, including a cover of the classic R & B ballad "Feel the Fire," originally written and recorded by Peabo Bryson. The session took place in a dinky little home studio, but it was a real job, and I got paid real money. It was also when I began to discover how to create nuances and textures in vocal arrangements and how to use my voice to build layers, like a painter. This was when my romance with the studio began. This was a major moment that began my journey, my drive to succeed.

One session gig led to the next. I was a little big fish in a puddle. The Long Island music scene was pretty small, and word of mouth was the method of marketing yourself. By the time I was fourteen or fifteen, I was writing songs and recording background vocals and jingles for local businesses. I was doing background vocals regularly for these young *Wayne's World* type of guys. They were into wild, loud guitar riffs and stuff, while I was listening to (rather, I was *obsessed with*) contemporary urban radio, which was mostly R & B, hip-hop, and dance music. I lived for the radio. Though our tastes were clearly very different, I liked the work nonetheless. I was making demos for songs and commercials, and learning how to adapt my voice to the task, whatever it was. The studio was my natural habitat. Like being in the ocean, when I was there, I felt weightless, and all my outside concerns fell away. I focused only on the music, and even if I didn't like their songs, I respected the work it took to make them. One day, while we were working on one of their mishmashes of a song, I told them I was a songwriter too. I figured if we could work on their corny stuff, why couldn't we work on my stuff?

Technically, I had been writing since before I was a teenager. I wrote poems and sketches of songs in my diary. Every once in a while I would be alone in the house, or my mother would be asleep, and I would have a moment of lightness in the small, dim living room, sitting on the wooden piano stool at my mother's surprisingly well-kept brown upright Yamaha piano. I would prop my diary on the music shelf, feet dangling. I'd hum a bit of a melody, search for the keys that were the closest to my voice. Then, very quietly—nearly whispering—I'd sing a few words with the melody.

I trusted the music I was hearing in my head. I believed it was akin to the popular songs I heard on the radio. My songs didn't mimic the style or sound of what I heard; rather, I would always search for the *right* sound, the one that felt like *me*. And I believed my sound would fit in with, or even break through, what was on the radio. I really believed that. I knew what I was hearing was advanced for my age, but luckily I was working with two guys who were very collaborative and open to working with such a young and female artist. So it was there in their mother's house, in a sad little slapped-together studio, that I wrote and produced one of my favorite demos, "To Begin" (I still love it, but sadly it's among one of the many lost tapes of little Mariah). I was confident I had a solid song.

They were like, "Why are we listening to this little kid?" Honestly, I just don't think they understood the culture, genres, and tones I was working with. They really were weird little garage-band hippieish-type guys. Indeed, I *was* a little kid, but I also knew where the pulse of the culture was—and that they were not anywhere near it. The discipline of working with them was good for me. But by the time I was fifteen, I had outgrown them.

One of my first regular gigs was with these two sketchy guys who made demos. They liked my sound because I had that young-girl quality that was popular at the time, largely because of Madonna's success. But I was *actually* a young girl, and my vocals could get into that high pitch range naturally. I could emulate the popular Madonna studio technique, but with my voice alone.

I auditioned by singing one of the songs they wrote, and they hired me on the spot. So the sketchy guys began paying me to sing demos. This was the official start of my professional career—and of a never-ending succession of sketchy characters that came with it. I had entered the treacherous territory of the "music industry." Though my journey was just beginning, I would soon be initiated into the complicated dynamics that female artists have to endure. As I now know, most don't make it through.

There were weird vibes from the start because I couldn't really tell if these guys were pervy or not, but I believed nothing crazy would happen because they both had wives who were around all the time. Naïvely, I thought these women might take on big-sister type roles with me. They were all full-blown adults, and I was still just about a child, but unfortunately, my age and talent caused friction. Even though I was a scrawny little teenager (I mean, my body was pretty much a straight line at that age), one of the wives was threatened by me. She was always close by, prancing around in short shorts, giving me evil energy. I didn't understand what was going on. I was too young to get it, and also, I was there to work. Maybe my own short shorts were inappropriate around these older men. I didn't know. I was just a kid getting her first whiff of independence, and besides, a few pairs of cheap shorts and tops were all I owned. I was in a battle of the short shorts, and I didn't even know it.

I continued recording demos of songs for the guys, making a little money. But again, just as with the garage-band dudes, we were putting down *their* songs, though I believed my songs were stronger. And again, I asked if they were open to me writing some songs. Initially, they refused. It was totally frustrating: here I was singing weird, corny songs *again*. Didn't these people even *listen* to the radio? I wondered. Didn't they know what was popular? I studied the music on the radio closely, constantly analyzing what was in heavy rotation. I knew the songs they were writing weren't good. Despite not liking the material, I sang it because it was my job, and I really needed the money. But now that I'd had a taste of making demos, I knew I needed to get my own songs down, and quickly.

Later I was able to make a deal with one of the guys who owned a studio: I would sing demos for him if he would let me work on my own. I brought in one of the songs I had begun at my mother's piano at the shack, called "Alone in Love." I sat in a room alone and began to make my very first demos. My *own*.

Swept me away
But now I'm lost in the dark
Set me on fire
But now I'm left with a spark
Alone you got beyond the haze and
I'm lost inside the maze
I guess I'm all alone in love

—"Alone in Love"

I figured out the setup. I experimented with the songs. I did dance tracks, straight down the line, all different sounds. I learned how to produce under pressure. I was in the studio, doing it. "Alone in Love" was one of the first tracks on my demo. A version of the song eventually made it onto my first album and remains one of my favorites.

You haunt me in my dreams
I'm calling out your name
I watch you fade away
Your love is not the same
I've figured out your style
To quickly drift apart

You held me for a while
Planned it from the start
All alone in love

I was in eleventh grade.

I distinctly remember one night—bleeding into morning. The pink of dawn was seeping through the edges of the deep-purple night sky, and I didn't know where the hell I was, *again*. Somewhere on the Taconic Parkway, or maybe the Cross Bronx Expressway? Clutching the hard-plastic steering wheel of my mother's rickety old Cutlass Supreme, I tried to stay focused on the road and not stress over the needle of the gas gauge that stayed twitching on E.

Every day was a struggle, with me trying to find my way home after work just to grab a few hours of sleep before I had to get to school. I'd recently graduated out of the Long Island music scene. My brother (who was also trying to make a name for himself in the music industry, as a manager or producer—I'm not sure what) had introduced me to a new crop of session musicians and studio engineers in *the city*—New York City. I began commuting to The City to do sessions at night and then would turn right back around and head to The Island to get to school the next morning. So began my first double life (kind of).

Very few of my peers at school knew what I was doing. They didn't know I was driving alone on highways, getting lost at midnight, collapsing on my bed, then dragging myself to school. They didn't know why I was late every day. I didn't talk about it because I knew it would sound crazy—and most people didn't have the ability to really *believe* as hard as I did. Besides, the kids I knew didn't *need* to believe. They were getting new cars, Camaros and Mustangs, for their sixteenth birthdays. They had their paths mapped out and were well financed for generations to come. Most were certain they were going go to college. They had a guaranteed life already planned out for them.

I remember that once, one of the most popular jocks in the school asked me what I was doing after graduation. I usually didn't tell any of the kids around about my dreams, but in this case I did. I told him I was going to be a singer and songwriter. His response was, "Yeah, right; you'll be working at HoJo's in five years." (HoJo's was short for Howard Johnson's, the chain of hotels and restaurants that was still widely popular then.) The degradation was totally intended.

As it turns out, in less than three years, in a simple black dress, with a head full of curls and a stomach full of, yes, butterflies, I walked through a packed stadium among the deafening buzz of tens of thousands of voices. A loud, clear voice cut through the cacophony: "Ladies and gentlemen, please welcome Columbia recording artist Mariah Carey for the singing of 'America the Beautiful.'" The piano track was recorded by Richard T. I held the little mic and sang that big song with everything I had. I hit a really high note on "sea to shining *sea*," and the stadium erupted.

When I finished, the announcer said, "The Palace now has a queen, and the goose bumps will continue." It was Game 1 of the NBA finals, between Detroit and Portland. I knew that the jock who condemned me to HoJo's (no shade on anyone in service work, because I've been there), and everyone who had looked down on me, and millions of Americans were watching. None of the players, none of the fans knew who I was when I walked in, but they would remember me when I walked out. A victory.

Another very early high visibility big breakthrough moment: "Vision of Love" was number one on the R & B charts before it was in the top spot on the pop charts, and so my national television debut was on *The Arsenio Hall Show*. Arsenio was more than a host; he had more than a late night show; it was a cultural *event*, a true Black experience—or, rather, it was a mainstream entertainment show seen through a Black lens. Everyone watched it and talked about it *everywhere*. I will always be grateful and proud that it was on Arsenio's stage that most of America got to see my face, know my name, and hear my song for the first time.

In my teens, living in a constant state of exhaustion and exhilaration became my new normal. But with every mile driven and each dawn met, I was more and more determined. My ambition grew to the level of devotion. And the hard-earned blessings were beginning to come down. My brother did manage to connect me with a reputable producer and writer named Gavin Christopher. Gavin had written big hits for Rufus (the band for which Chaka Khan sang lead) and produced songs for Grandmaster Flash and Afrika Bambaataa. We instantly clicked and began working together to produce one of my first professional demos. I also met his girlfriend, Clarissa, another singer, and we got along well. I liked them both, and I could feel the stirrings of a new life in the city appearing before me.

Making valuable connections in New York City was certainly crucial to my career, but getting out of my mother's house was no longer just a desire, it was a necessity. When I was younger I had no control over our constant moves and my mother's consistently poor choices in men. In my last year of high school she began dating a guy I despised. He was petty and manipulative. On Thanksgiving we all went out to dinner, and he actually insisted that I and my nephew Shawn (who was in middle school), Alison's first son, *pay* for our portions of dinner. He divided up the receipt evenly among the people present and demanded we pay our share. So after I gave him the few pitiful, crumpled-up dollars I had in my pockets, which was just about all the money I had, Shawn and I left and went to the movies to see *Back to the Future II*. No thanks to him.

When my mother decided to marry him, I knew it was my cue to move out. I guess she thought she had struck it rich marrying this guy because he had a boat in the West Seventy-Ninth Street Boat Basin. But that was where he lived before he crashed into the shack, and trust me, his boat was more tugboat than yacht.

Eventually she ended that abominable marriage. The divorce took multiple years and many lawyer fees, which of course I paid for after the success of my first record. Then the jerk even ended up suing me for the rights to some fictitious Mariah Carey doll (if I had a dollar for every deadbeat who sued me, I'd be . . . well, it's been a lot). But I was the polar opposite of rich when I moved out of my mother's house. I was broke and seventeen years old. It was the late 1980s, and I was living completely on my own in New York City.

❦

Fate is a bizarre thing. When I was about seven, we were living in that cramped apartment on top of the deli, and I used to love to hear the sounds of the radio coming up into our windows. I remember swaying, posing, and singing with Odyssey: "*Oh, oh, oh, you're a native New Yorker / You should know the score by now.*" I didn't know what "knowing the score" was, but I wanted that fabulous New York feeling even back then. It took ten more years, but I had finally arrived.

To me, the city had a raw grit and an impossible chicness. It was in perpetual motion: masses of people walking fast, no one looking the same but all moving in sync. The city was crazy messenger bikes whizzing around and countless long yellow cabs zigzagging through the streets like a swarm of rough bumblebees. Something was happening everywhere you looked—huge billboards, flashing neon signs, wild graffiti emblazoned across all kinds of surfaces, covering subway cars, water towers, and vans. It was like one big, funky moving art gallery. The main avenues were grand, crowded catwalks filled with eclectic fashion models, business moguls, street hustlers, and workers of every ilk, all strutting and with no one studyin' each other. Everyone had somewhere to go and something to do. It was a mad and fabulous planet of concrete and crystals populated with misfits, magicians, dreamers, and dealers—I landed right in the middle of it. Hello baby, I was made for this.

MAKE IT HAPPEN

After moving out of my mother's house I crashed at Morgan's empty apartment on top of Charlie Mom Chinese Cuisine in Greenwich Village, while he was in Italy pursuing a modeling career (and Lord knows what else). I fed his two cats, Ninja and Tompkins, and tried my best to feed myself. The first decision of every day was whether I was going to get a bagel from H&H or buy a subway token.

I was surviving on a dollar a day, and something had to give—it was either breakfast or transportation. H&H bagels were sublime: soft, warm, and plump to perfection, a classic NYC morning staple that would keep my stomach occupied until three o'clock (H&H stood for Helmer and Hector, the two Puerto Rican owners, who arguably made the best kosher bagels in the world). But then again, getting around is pretty important, and the New York City subway was the rowdiest but most direct route to anywhere in town. The token was slightly bigger than a dime, a dirty gold disc with "NYC" stamped in the middle and a distinctive slim Y cutout. This was the people's coin, and it could get you anywhere, at any time. But if I could walk to where I needed to go, breakfast would win.

I found a job right away. I didn't have a choice. So I did what every other broke dreamer does when they get to New York City. I grabbed the free newspaper of real New Yorkers, the *Village Voice*, and checked out the job ads. I took what I could get—and what I got was work at a sports bar on Seventy-Seventh and Broadway, cleverly named Sports on Broadway.

I began as a waitress, but as management soon discovered, I was still a teen and couldn't legally serve drinks, so I was moved to the cash register. Boy, was that a disaster. I was a hard worker, but I had spent most of my working time in a recording studio, and working a register isn't like recording background vocals. I wasn't picking it up fast. And this was a neighborhood joint with regulars and no-nonsense waitresses, like "Kiss My Grits" Flo in *Alice* but New York tough. Those broads hated me for messing up their money!

Eventually, I got moved to the coat check. Simple. But while I was hustling, I was also getting hustled: I wasn't allowed to keep my tips, which is pretty much the entire allure of being a coat-check girl. I got a dollar for every coat. I knew it wasn't fair, but I also knew it was temporary. When summertime came around, the coat check was converted into a merchandise booth, and I became the "Sports on Broadway" T-shirt girl. The booth was right at the front door, so the first thing the men would see was me with a welcoming smile, in a white T-shirt with the word "Sports" printed across my boobs. I was grateful for the simplicity of it all: the uniform was the bar's T-shirt and jeans, and since I only had one pair of jeans, it was one less thing for me to struggle to buy.

Not more than three short years ago
I was abandoned and alone
Without a penny to my name
So very young and so afraid
No proper shoes upon my feet
Sometimes I couldn't even eat
I often cried myself to sleep
But still I had to keep on going

—"Make It Happen"

I also only had one pair of shoes, and they were a size and a half too small. They had been my mother's—pitiful flat black leather lace-up ankle boots. They were basic and utilitarian, and I made them work. At some point, the top of the shoe separated from the rubber sole, creating a flap that would slap the unforgiving city pavement as I pounded toward my destiny. The swelling of my feet from standing all day in too-small shoes surely contributed to their demise. Snowy days were the worst; ice would slide into the flap, melt, and seep through my thin socks, and the clammy sensation of wet, cheap leather traveled up my spine. And that year New York had a big, newsworthy snowstorm! But I'd pull myself together, as cute as I could manage, and flash a smile, pleasantly doing my job and just hoping no one would look down at my feet. I had years of training for living through humiliation, but now, I wasn't in school; I was living in The City. I believed in my heart that one day I would make it and have some of the most fancy and well-fitting shoes imaginable.

I had my mighty faith, but I was also blessed with so many signs and acts of kindness from folks along the way. Like Charles, the cook at Sports, who would fry me up a greasy cheeseburger and sneak it to me with a glass of Sambuca. It wasn't glamorous, but I had a meal, an outfit, and a few dollars. Every day that I made it through, I knew I was closer to my dream. I would drop down on my knees each night and thank God for another day when I didn't give up or get taken down.

> *I know life can be so tough*
> *And you feel like giving up*
> *But you must be strong*
> *Baby just hold on*
> *You'll never find the answers if you throw your life away*
> *I used to feel the way you do*
> *Still I had to keep on going.*
>
> —"Make It Happen"

The job at the sports bar was a means, but the studio was the end. Everything went into my demo. One day while I was eating downstairs in the

Chinese restaurant, gratefully savoring the cheap morsels of the day's only meal, I noticed a familiar face. It was Clarissa, the now ex-girlfriend of my brother's producer friend Gavin Christopher. We hugged like old friends. I told her that I had officially relocated to the city. When I gave her the rundown on my chaotic living arrangements, like an angel, she invited me to come live with her.

Though she identified as a "struggling artist," fortunately for me, Clarissa wasn't really struggling that hard. She lived with a gay couple in a huge classic Upper West Side brownstone on Eighty-Fifth Street between Central Park West and Columbus Avenue. I suspected that she was one of those kids who had a trust fund waiting for her once she got over her starving-artist phase. My music was my life. Music was the only plan, ever.

While it was certainly an upgrade from my previous crowded crash pad, living with Clarissa still had its challenges. She had a room (with a whole door, which closed) where there was a loft-style bed set up with recording equipment underneath it. Her room was off to the side of the larger parlor room. My situation was a ragtag loftlike structure built above the kitchen in the communal area that we shared with the couple. To get to my sleeping cranny I had to climb up onto the kitchen counter and hoist myself up into the teeny nook. It was barely more than a crawl space and had just enough room for a twin mattress, outfitted with a single pillow and a blanket (a "house" warming gift from my mother). The space was so shallow and the ceiling was so close that I couldn't fully kneel on the bed without bumping my head (so there, I prayed on my back). It was "decorated" with the only remnants from my life in Long Island: my journals and diaries, my Marilyn Monroe poster, and a handful of books on Marilyn. I still looked up to her.

Connecting with Clarissa proved to be quite the blessing. She helped me find work and covered for me when I couldn't make my share of the five hundred dollars a month rent—a *fortune* to me then. Occasionally she'd take me out to eat. We even did some songwriting in her mini studio. She had a few connections in the music scene from her time with Gavin and would sometimes introduce me to other musicians who also lived on the Upper West Side. On these special occasions, she'd even loan me a little black dress to wear (not dissimilar to what I'm wearing on my first album cover). I certainly didn't have anything of my own that was appropriate for mingling.

Like everything during that time, nothing lasted long. Eventually the addition of some crazy roommates meant that Clarissa and I fled for our lives (I really can't get into the details of *that*) and had to move on and out. We joined my friend Josefin (whom I had met when she was in an open relationship with my brother). She was living with a few other girls from Sweden. So it was five random girls living in a random apartment on top of a club called Rascals, on East Fourteenth Street. I was downgraded to a mattress on the floor, but I was now living "downtown," in the heart of the New York art scene of the late 1980s. It was thrilling, if precarious, and my eyes were always focused upward. I was able to gain a bit of stability and a lot more faith. I knew more than ever that it was going to happen for me.

I once was lost
But now I'm found
I got my feet on solid ground
Thank you, Lord
If you believe within your soul
Just hold on tight
And don't let go
You can make it! Make it happen

—"Make It Happen"

After a few months, the other girls from Sweden moved out, and it was Josefin and I. She helped me get odd jobs, but I was also beginning to pick up more background vocal work. For this work, I'd settled on my young singer ensemble: a little black knit tank dress, black tights, and fat, slouchy socks over a pair of white Reebok Freestyle sneakers (my mother's hand-me-down black shoes having finally been reduced to shreds). Previously, Clarissa had encouraged me to ask my mother to buy me new shoes. My mother then asked Morgan, who, she reported to me, said, "She has to learn to do things by herself." I *was* a teen living on my own in the city, but whatever. Eventually, reluctantly, Morgan did buy me a pair of white Reeboks (why not black, I wondered, which goes with everything—but I was grateful to have shoes that fit and were without involuntary air-conditioning). I wore this outfit to nearly every session; it was like my uniform.

Gavin and I were working on a song together. While we were recording, he introduced me to a producer in the city, Ben Margulies, who was hired as a drummer on the session for our song called "Just Can't Hold It Back." Ben had his own studio, and I had begun working with him occasionally during my singer-student Long Island commuter days. His studio was in Chelsea, on Nineteenth Street between Sixth and Seventh Avenues. Located in the back of his father's cabinet making factory, it was about the size of a pantry. It could've been a chicken coop for all I cared—and it honestly wasn't far from that. What mattered was that it was almost a full recording studio, the place where I belonged. For me, the studio is part sanctuary, part playground, and part laboratory. I loved being there, writing, riffing, singing, dreaming, and taking risks. I've slept many a night on many a studio floor, beginning with this humble yet magical place.

Ben and I worked incessantly over the course of a year or so. Occasionally his partner Chris would be there, helping with the programming. I was coming up with a lot of ideas, and we were recording, but I still felt the guys weren't going fast enough. I was hitting a new stride. I was coming up with all these lyrics and melodies and was frustrated because it seemed to me like it should be going faster. Maybe because I was only seventeen and extremely impatient, but I felt I was differently invested, like I was on a different trajectory than they were. Music was my whole life—so much of my belief system, my *survival*, was entwined in my songs. There was an urgency in my air, in the moment, and in *me*. This was *my* time, and I could feel it. I felt like I was running fast toward something or someone soon, and I was not about to let anyone or anything slow me down.

Ben and I were both excited by the songs we were working on but ultimately our sensibilities and ambitions were incompatible. I think he thought we were going to form a duo, like the Eurythmics, with him as co-lead, the Dave Stewart to my Annie Lennox. I was like, "Um, good luck with that; can we just focus on putting down *my* songs, please?"

We were able to create a full demo that I thought really showcased my songwriting and vocal styles. My most vivid memory of being in that studio is of me sitting by myself on the floor in the corner writing lyrics and melodies, or staring out the window dreaming of the day I would break through. Look, Ben was very committed and I spent a lot of time working with him, and we got a lot done. But I had a vision, even back then, that my career had the capacity to go way beyond what he or most people around me were even capable of imagining.

Ben suggested we have some "security" in place, by way of a formal agreement, so he photocopied a contract out of the book *All You Need to Know About the Music Business* (co-written by Don Passman, who would, ironically enough, several years later become my lawyer). With no parent, legal counsel, manager, or even a good friend, I signed it. I was *maybe* eighteen years old. Obviously I didn't know much about contracts and deals then, but what I *did* know was that there was value in my lyrics and the songs. (I remembered seeing a documentary on the Beatles when I was growing up and being shocked that they didn't have complete ownership of the songs, they'd written—the *Beatles*!) So I knew not to give away all my publishing. Some of the lyrics to songs like "Alone in Love" I had begun writing in early high school.

We started setting up meetings with record companies and things began to move fast. We got an initial offer from a major publishing company for a song called "All in Your Mind" to be placed in a movie. I remember they offered me five thousand dollars for the publishing.

Come closer
You seem so far away
There's something I know you need to say
I feel your emotions
When I look in your eyes
Your silence
Whispering misunderstandings

There's so much you need to realize
You'll feel my emotions
If you look in my eyes
Hey darlin'
I know you think my love is slipping away
But, baby, it's all in your mind

—"All in Your Mind"

I refused, even though back then five thousand dollars seemed like a million (which was how much I got for my first *real* publishing administration deal). Thank God I had a cautionary Beatles tale fresh in my mind. I didn't sell because I believed my songs came from somewhere special inside of me, and that selling them would be selling a piece of *me*.

The music business is designed to confuse and control the artist. Later, seasoned music executives told me that Ben's deal was truly a golden ticket. I was trying to be loyal to someone who believed in me at a crucial time, but in my naïveté, I didn't realize the enormity of what I had signed away. I was informed, and what I remember, was that he got 50 percent of the publishing on all songs we worked on together for my first album. Okay *fine*. But additionally, he received 50 percent of my *artist's* royalties for the first album, 40 percent for the second album, 30 percent for the third, and so on. It went on that way from 1990 until about 1999. Even though Ben didn't write one word or note with me after the first album. Out of loyalty to him and the hard work we put in together in that little studio, I never looked back and tried to reset or recoup.

So yeah, a photocopy: that's the unceremonious origin of my first "official deal." What a welcome to the music business! Which I was so eager to get into, but I soon came to believe that my first signature was on a pretty shady piece of paper—and one that would be hard to get out of. But it certainly wouldn't be the last. A whole forest full of shade was yet to come.

One must pick one's battles wisely, and I wasn't about to come for someone who I had already left behind. I was on my way. I'll be eternally grateful, and I wish him well.

At least we made The Demo.

That demo stayed in my Walkman, which stayed on my hip, and the music stayed in my ears. Aside from the radio, the songs we laid down were all I listened to. And the offers from the major publishing houses gave me confidence that things were going to happen. I just had to keep the faith and keep working. I didn't stop. I kept going to more sessions, doing more connecting, and getting more background vocal work. I began doing vocals for the musician and producer T. M. Stevens, who'd written with Narada Michael Walden and played bass with James Brown, Cyndi Lauper, Joe Cocker, and other major artists. It was through him that I had the good fortune to meet the amazing Cindy Mizelle at a session.

Since that first background gig at twelve years old, I'd gained a respect for the specific skill and talent it takes to be a good background vocalist. I would listen specifically to background on the radio. I'd study the liner notes on albums and CD jackets to learn who was doing the background vocals (especially on dance records, as I believe backgrounds are what make those songs). I became familiar with all those exceptional singers, like Audrey Wheeler and Lisa Fischer . . . and *Cindy*. To me, she was one of the absolute greatest. Cindy Mizelle was *the* background singer. She sang with the most gifted vocalists of all time—Barbra Streisand, Whitney Houston, Luther Vandross, and the Rolling Stones. She was a real singer's singer. Cindy was *that* girl to me. I looked up to her so much.

I remember in the beginning of the session, we were at the microphone, doing a part that I was having a difficult time getting right. Cindy's such a perfectionist (as I am now), but she had patience with me. When you first learn how to do background vocals—different tones and styles—it's not easy. Producers liked my tone, but I had to learn how to really get in the pocket, to get it exactly how they wanted it. Precision takes practice. Cindy had a new gig practically every day; she was a master. When I first started singing alongside her, I had to work hard to keep up. Now, background vocals are one of my favorite elements in building a song. I love the textures and layers and how lush they can make a song; backgrounds get into your bones.

Once, while Cindy and I were recording and standing very close to each other at the microphone, she could hear my stomach rumbling. She looked down and saw the sad shoes I was wearing, scanned my crumpled outfit, and then looked up at me with pity and recognition. I was too excited to be self-conscious—at that point in life, my ambition was stronger than my shame. Who cared if I arrived a little hungry and a little shabby? I was finally singing for a living, right next to a consummate professional.

Cindy gave me her number that night and told me if I ever needed anything, I could call her. I didn't know what to do with that. She'd sung with huge acts all around the world—what business did I have calling her? What would I say? I didn't call, and the next time I saw her she called me out on it. It wasn't easy for me to ask for help. I didn't want to bother or burden her, I explained. Cindy looked me in the eye and said, "Mariah, you *need* to call me."

Suddenly it struck me. *Oh, I get it.* I was *supposed* to call her. I hadn't understood right away that this was part of the process: the initiation, the mentoring, the nurturing, the entry into a society of sister-singers. These rituals were all new to me. And I was unfamiliar with being welcomed into a family of artists—into a family of any kind.

Once I had broken into the inner circle of elite background vocalists, recommendations started to come in. Background vocalists are hired by word of mouth—one singer will recommend another, and good singers like to work together. If the squad is strong, the session is strong, and if the sessions are strong, the money is good and steady. I was now in the tight and talented community of working musicians in New York City. Though I was invariably the youngest in the crowd, I also often hung out with some of them outside of work hours, mostly on Manhattan's Upper West Side. I wasn't into drinking or hooking up at all; the hang, to me, was about networking—emphasis on *work*. It paid off.

I got an offer to do a demo session for a group called Maggie's Dream. When I got to the gig I was told I would be singing for a male vocalist. In walked this sexy, serene, toasted-almond-colored artsy young man—he just looked like the *definition* of an artist. His thick, dark hair was just in the beginning phases of dreadlocks. He had a perfect five o'clock shadow, with a thick stripe of goatee down the center of his chin. He was dressed rock star casual: heavy black leather vintage motorcycle jacket, black jeans, black T-shirt. He had a thin ring in his nose and smelled how I imagined ancient Egyptian oils would smell. His face was kind and fine, with a boyish smile. He went by the name of Romeo Blue. His friends called him Lenny. And about a year later, the world would know him as Lenny Kravitz.

Maggie's Dream had a drummer named Tony, who was also the drummer for the band of a singer named Brenda K. Starr. Brenda had a big R & B pop hit out called "I Still Believe," which the record company was looking to rework. There was an opening for background singers, and Tony got me a slot at the audition. I was excited because Brenda had a big song on the *radio*—and you know how much I loved the radio. At the audition, we were asked to sing Brenda's song right in front of the table where she sat. I gave it my all.

I sang for my life. I did all kinds of runs and belted out the last note. When I was finished, I stood perfectly still, returning back to Earth, heart on fire. Brenda gave me a long, flat stare, then suddenly broke into a mischievous little giggle. In her clipped, nasally accent, she said, "You trying to steal my job?" I didn't move. But her giggle turned into hearty laughter. I didn't realize you weren't supposed to outsing the singer who could hire you!

"Mariah is my new best friend," she said, breaking my trance. Wait. She knew my name! I couldn't believe someone who had a major song on the radio now knew *my* name. Immediately after the audition, Brenda had to fly somewhere to perform, but as soon as she returned, I was hired. She kept saying, "I told everybody about this girl Mariah!"

Brenda was a spicy mix, in the true meaning of the word. She grew up in the projects on Ninetieth and Amsterdam Avenue, and the culture of the projects grew in her. She told me her mother was Puerto Rican and Hawaiian and her father, Harvey Kaplan, was Jewish and in a band called the Spiral Starecase. They had a hit song: "More Today Than Yesterday." Brenda was a bit older and more street savvy than I was and had an effortless and silly sense of humor. It was easy to become friends.

My life as a professional singer was moving swiftly, but at the same time, I was still a teenager. One time I was hanging out with the guys from Maggie's Dream, and one of them started teasing me because I was a virgin. (Apparently, Clarissa had told them I was.) Everybody was laughing, but I didn't get why it was funny. I was a kid. I was always the youngest and clearly the most idealistic, so I had to suffer through some of the more crass amusements of adult musicians.

I may have been young and naïve, but Brenda knew my songs were good, and wise beyond their years. When I let her listen to my demo, she said, "Oooh, Mariah, I wanna do this on my next album." She currently had a song that was still in active rotation on the radio, and every time we were together and I heard it play, it was mind blowing. I couldn't believe I was working with her and she was my friend, not to mention that she had given me my biggest gig to date.

Yet I said, "I know I don't have anything big going on yet, but I'm sorry, I have to keep these songs. These songs are the ones I wrote for me."

I may have been insecure about my money, my clothes, my family, and a whole host of other things, but I knew my songs were valuable. I was really excited to finally be in the company of young and some struggling current musicians and artists, but the truth was that I had always believed this would happen to me. Brenda never pushed me to use my songs after that.

Singing background with Brenda while she toured with her big song was big fun. Once, we went to Los Angeles to appear at a popular radio station's concert. It was the first time I'd ever been to LA and one of the few times I'd ever set foot on a plane. Now, I was boarding a plane as a professional singer, going to do a big outdoor radio-sponsored concert in LA! To me, being on the radio *was* being famous. For the show, Brenda was set to sing "I Still Believe," with me as one of the background vocalists. Will Smith was there too, to perform "Parents Just Don't Understand."

Jeffrey Osborne (from the group L.T.D.) was also there; he did "You Should Be Mine (The Woo Woo Song)" as part of his set. I was in the audience, watching. Jeffrey, the veteran among us, began singing the chorus to his song with his seasoned, smooth voice: "And you woo-woo-woo," he started off. The crowd joined in. After a few rounds he offered his microphone out into the audience.

"Pass it to her! Pass it to her!" Brenda chirped, wagging her finger at me like a happy puppy's tail.

I took the mic and gave that "woo-woo" a special Mariah remix, with all kinds of vocal flourishes, and in the end I took the last "woo" way up into my high register, and the whole crowd broke out in wild claps. That was the day Will Smith and I became friends.

Will and I were both really young, and looked it. Above my signature blown-out bangs, I had gathered the top portion of my unruly, crinkly hair into a yellow scrunchie, hair fanning out of it like a furry fountain, and let water and nature do their own thing with the back half of my 'do. I was wearing a little bubble-gum-pink tank dress I had borrowed from Josefin. Will was tall and lanky, dressed as if he expected a pickup game of hoops could break out at any moment. He was incredibly friendly and funny, as was his charismatic friend, Charlie Mack. Immediately I could tell that he was not only super talented but really bright and laser-focused. I loved "Parents Just Don't Understand" and was very impressed with what he had accomplished.

Will and I would sometimes hang out at Rascals, below the apartment I shared with Josefin. He was an uncomplicated friend. Both of us were absolutely ambitious and still maintained a childlike wonder and curiosity about the world. Our relationship was always platonic and never got weird.

After he heard me sing, Will believed in my talent. He took me with him to Def Jam Recordings, the hottest new hip-hop label at the time, where he was signed. As we walked down the street on our way to Def Jam, we saw this tall, thin white man approaching us. He stood out because he was kind of dancing and bopping, with headphones on that were blasting music so loud you could hear it: "It takes two to make a thing go right!"

I later found out it was Lyor Cohen, who managed Run-DMC and LL Cool J and signed Eric B. & Rakim and DJ Jazzy Jeff & the Fresh Prince. It was a curious scene to me: this sinewy grown man, dressed kinda cool, singing aloud, "I wanna rock right now!" I was thinking, *How does he even know this song?*

The Def Jam offices had a very "downtown" vibe. This was the label of many hot male hip-hop artists, so obviously there were a million girls going in and out. Most people probably just assumed that I was a groupie, strolling in on the arm of the Fresh Prince. Will had never heard my demo; he'd only heard me sing at the concert, but that was enough for him, I guess. Upstairs we found ourselves with a junior executive who wanted me to sing. Once again, I may have looked a little shabby and young, but I was discerning enough to understand: I wasn't going to sing for this random guy. I was grateful for Will's confidence, but I had my sights on a major label with a legacy of artists more in alignment with my singer-songwriter ambitions—somewhere huge, like Warner or Columbia Records. That's where I knew I belonged, and that's where I believed I was going to be.

My faith and focus were strong, but there was also evidence of my hard work, like a possible deal moving at Atlantic Records. During this time the majors were reaping the benefits of their teen stars—the Tiffanys and Debbie Gibsons of the world. As the story goes, Doug Morris, the head of Atlantic, responded to my demo by saying, "We already have our teen girl," referring to Gibson.

Clearly, he didn't really get it. For that matter, most labels didn't really get *me*. They really didn't know where I fit. They didn't understand my sound; the demo had songs that didn't fit neatly into an existing genre. Though really young, I was definitely not teen pop. There was a bit of soul, R & B, and gospel infused into my music, *and* I had a hip-hop sensibility. My demo was more diverse than the music industry at the time.

Then, of course, there was always the blondish biracial elephant in the room. Executives at Motown supposedly reacted to my demo by saying, "Oh, no, we don't want to deal with a Teena Marie situation again"— meaning they didn't want to force the general public to grapple with wondering if I was Black or white or what. They didn't know how to market me. Most record executives just didn't know how they would work my record. They weren't sure it could "cross over." But for the record, Teena Marie never cared about crossing over. And I didn't want to cross over either.

I wanted to transcend.

CHERCHEZ LA FEMME

One night Brenda announced, "I'm going to take you to this party, and you're going to meet a big record executive, Jerry Greenberg, and it's going to be great."

Sure, why not? I thought. I was feeling enough professional confidence to let her drag me to an industry party. I was doing sessions and had a deal brewing at Warners for one of my songs to be used in a movie. I wasn't too invested in this party being *the* party. While she had a generous heart, Brenda could also be pretty zany, so I sometimes took a lot of what she said with a grain of salt.

We were going to get dressed at her house in Jersey, since she had all the clothes, makeup, and accessories from being on tour and having some money. She was supposed to pick me up from my apartment. I waited in my cramped vestibule, slumped on the tile floor, for over an hour (mind you, there was no texting back then). Finally, she appeared, revved up, full of energy, and ready to party. Her excitement was infectious.

We started our going-out ritual in her large bathroom. Brenda had all the mousse, hair spray, combs, and curlers you could imagine. With her mixed Puerto Rican and Jewish heritage, I could certainly work with what she had. I attempted to create one long, uniform coil all around my head by twisting sections of hair around the rod of a curling wand. I finished it off with a straight bang. I borrowed a little black dress from her (what else!). I had brought a pair of my own opaque black tights, but I couldn't fit into her shoes; they were too small. So I layered my black Vans sneakers with ribbed slouchy socks. I topped off the ensemble with my one statement piece—that Avirex jacket from high school.

I really tried with my look, and it was all right. Brenda told me the party was to celebrate a new record label, but since, by this time, I was interested in the big labels with the big boys and big artists, I didn't have high expectations about who would be in attendance. The new label was the collaboration of three well-known industry guys who had come together to form their own label, WTG Records. "WTG" stood for Walter, Tommy, and Gerald. It sounded like a tire business to me; I didn't really know who anybody was yet. But Brenda knew Jerry (Gerald Greenberg), who she told me was a big shot in the industry (in 1974, at thirty-two, he became the youngest-ever president of Atlantic Records). When she explained this, the party started to get a bit more interesting.

I now understood why Brenda wanted me to bring my demo with me (not that I ever went *anywhere* without it)—she'd brought me there to meet a guy from Atlantic Records. When we got to the party, I was surrounded by "industry people," though I still had no clue what that meant. As I walked around, I took in the scene. Some handlers were traipsing a female artist around, like a show horse. She was very blond, very pretty, very white, and very dolled up and coiffed, with a flurry of label folks forming a tight, buzzing cloud around her. There were large blown-up pictures of her all over the room. I guessed we were supposed to ooh and ahh in her presence. But I wasn't interested in her. I was just thinking, *Who is she, why should I be excited?* To me she was just someone they were toting around. Frankly, I was unimpressed by the whole scene.

Brenda and I sat down at a table. We were trying to have a good time in the room full of suits, but all I could think was that I could be at the studio working on songs or something. That was where I always wanted to be. We got up to go to the bathroom, making our way through the crowd to get to the staircase that led to where the restrooms were.

As we bounced up the stairs, I saw him.

He wasn't anyone I would have normally noticed: not particularly tall or short, not stylish or tacky. I'm pretty sure he had on a suit. He would've been totally forgettable if it weren't for his eyes. Our eyes locked, and an energy instantly rushed between us, like a mild electric shock. He had a piercing stare.

He looked *into* me, not at me. I was a little shook—not in a bad way, but not in a love at first sight way, either. I kept going up the stairs, this time at a slower pace, as I adjusted to what had just happened. When I closed the bathroom door, the odd sensation was still pulsing through me. What had happened? I didn't know who he was, but I recognized him somehow. I knew it wasn't from TV or anything like that. It wasn't his face; it was something else. I recognized his energy, and I think he recognized mine.

Brenda was all excited. "Did you see how Tommy Mottola *looked* at you? *I* did!" she said, her eyes wide.

"Who's Tommy Mottola?" I asked.

"*Girl.*" She looked at me quizzically, a sense of seriousness about her. "'Who's Tommy Mottola?'!" She began to sing a familiar refrain: "*Tommy Mottola lives on the road* . . . You don't know who that is; you don't know that song?" I shook my head. She sang a little bit more: "*Oh, oh, oh, oh, oh cherchez, cherchez—*"

It hit me. "Oh! Yeah, I know that song!" I joined in: "*Oh, oh, oh, oh, oh, cherchez, cherchez.*" It was "Cherchez la Femme / Se Si Bon," by Dr. Buzzard's Original Savannah Band.

I let her know that I used to like that song when I was a little girl.

Brenda said, "*That* is the Tommy from that song. He's one of the biggest record guys, *ever.*" Brenda and I headed over to the spot where they were all standing.

I was standing by wondering, if he was such a big shot, what did he want with me? The party was filled with prettier girls, with professional makeup and far better footwear. Tommy said to Brenda, "Who's your friend?"—the most intense three words I'd ever heard.

Brenda directed her answer to Jerry. "She's eighteen years old; her name is *Mariah*. You gotta listen to this!" Just as she went to hand Jerry my demo tape, Tommy's hand swiftly cut her off mid-extension. He snatched the tape, got up, left the table, and left the party. It was bizarre and bewildering. I was like, *What kinda shit is that?*

That was an important demo. It had some of my best songs—"All in Your Mind," "Someday," and "Alone in Love." Had this Tommy guy just taken all that work (and money!)? I wasn't sitting there thinking, *Yay, I just gave my demo to a big-time record executive.* I was focused more on the fact that I was out one more copy of my demo. *I know this Tommy guy's never going to listen to it*, I thought.

The popular story goes that Tommy left the party to get in his limo, where he could immediately listen to the demo. I didn't know what was the reason he left the party so abruptly. But after he did, I was ready to leave too. So I did.

Eventually Tommy came back looking for me, apparently not believing what he had just heard had come from that same girl on the stairs, the innocent-looking kid in Vans and slouchy socks. All those dressed-up girls in high heels were working so hard to get the attention of W, T, or G—and T came back looking for *me*.

Tommy was already the president of Sony Music, so getting my phone number was nothing. He called me and left a message on my answering machine.

Josefin and I made performance art out of goofing around and doing silly voices on that answering machine. I'd come in from the studio at five in the morning, and we'd make these crazy messages. In the one Tommy heard, I was mimicking her Swedish accent: "If this is the super, we need some help here! We have flies in our cats' tails. There's no hot water"— followed by hysterical laughter. It was funny to us, but it was also the truth. The conditions in our apartment were pretty gross. We had sticky flypaper hanging from the ceiling and on the walls, which our cats would brush up against. We really didn't have hot water either; it was a mess. But we were young, giddy girls, and we made a joke out of our circumstances.

The first time Tommy called, he hung up. But he didn't give up. He called back and this time left a curt and serious-sounding message: "Tommy Mottola. CBS. Sony Records." He left a number. "Call me back."

I couldn't believe it. I immediately called Brenda, who confirmed that indeed, Tommy's office had called her manager, and he wanted to sign me. This was the first of what would be a strange and fantastical series of Cinderella stories in my life. But I was not swept off my feet, and trust and believe me, Tommy Mottola was no Prince Charming.

PRINCESS. PRISONER.

Once, I was a prisoner
Lost inside myself
With the world surrounding me

—"I Am Free"

Once upon a time, I lived in a very big house named Storybook Manor. And in it were big diamonds and big closets full of the most spectacular gowns and bejeweled slippers. But also within its walls was an inescapable emptiness, bigger than everything else inside, that almost swallowed me whole. This was no place for Cinderella.

If there were a fairy tale that could come close to describing my life, it would be "The Three Little Pigs." My childhood was a series of fragile, unstable houses, one after the other, where inevitably the Big Bad Wolf, my troubled brother, would huff and puff and blow it all down. I never felt safe. I never *was* safe. His rage was unpredictable; I never knew when it would come, or who or what it would devour. What I did know was that I was truly on my own, out there in the wild woods of the world. I knew that if I was ever going to find a safe place, I would have to make it myself.

I remember the very first time I ever felt I was in something like a safe place. I was living on my own in New York City, in a one-room studio apartment on the tenth floor with a spectacular view. The building was called Chelsea Court. I loved the name of that building: it had such a regal ring to it. I could see the Empire State Building from my apartment window. *My* little apartment—the first that was all mine.

I had just gotten my very first artist advance. It was five thousand dollars, which is a number I'll never forget. Five thousand dollars was more money than I'd ever seen at once, let alone had to call my own and spend as I wished. As soon as I got that advance, I got my own apartment. I could finally pay my own rent! No more living in nooks and crannies, no more sleeping on floors or sharing cramped bathrooms with four or five other girls.

The first thing I did was buy my own new little couch with four stable legs. Sometimes I would just stroke the fabric on the arm of my new little couch as if it were a baby. It was that major for me. I upgraded from a mattress on the floor to my own bed. I had a little kitchen. I had the two cats, Tompkins and Ninja. I had a little peace. I was having a moment, and I felt like I could toss my raspberry beret in the air and do a twirl in the street with my laundry bag—because I had survived. I survived the danger. I survived the hunger. I survived the uncertainty and instability, and now here I was, every day coming closer and closer to my destiny. I was independent in New York City, in my own apartment filled with my own furniture, working on my own album, filled with all of my own songs. I could have my own friends over. It was my first taste of autonomy, and it was divine. But it would not last long.

In the beginning, Tommy protected me. Even though I was breathing a bit easier, with some early breaks and a clear path to success, the traumas and insecurities of my childhood—and pressure from my brother and other people trying to take advantage of me—were still right at my back, haunting my every move. I never stopped looking over my shoulder. Tommy shielded me from all the people who thought I owed them something or who wanted to use me. That meant Tommy also protected me from my own family.

I was nineteen years old and had already lived a lifetime of chaos, surviving only by my own scrappy determination. Then this powerful man suddenly came along, parting the seas to make room for my dream. He truly believed in me.

With all due respect, Tommy Mottola was *just* the bitter pill I needed to swallow at a pivotal period in my life. And there *is* a lot of respect due to him. He was a visionary music executive who fearlessly and ferociously dragged his visions into reality. He believed in me, ruthlessly.

"You're the most talented person I've ever met," he would say to me. "You can be as big as Michael Jackson."

I heard music in the way he said that name: *Michael. Jackson.* Here was a man who had played a large role in advancing the careers of some of the biggest names in the industry, and he saw *me* sharing the same rare air as the most influential artist and entertainer in modern history. *Respect.*

And it wasn't a sales pitch or a cheap come-on. It was *real.* We didn't play when it came to the work. My career as an artist was the most important thing to me—it was the *only* thing. It validated my very existence, and Tommy understood the power of my commitment. I was serious and ambitious. He knew my vocals were unique and strong, but he was most impressed with how I created songs: the structure of my melodies, the *music.* I became his new star just as he was beginning a huge position at a new label, so he had the influence to clear the runway for my ascension into the sky. He was willing to move heaven and earth to make me successful. I recognized and respected that power. Despite having been around some of the biggest names in the music industry, Tommy told me I was *the* most talented person he had ever met. He was for real, and I really believed him.

Soon after we met, Tommy started making romantic overtures. At first, they were a bit awkward and adolescent, like sending me expensive Gund teddy bears. Yet his persistent gestures and constant attention also gave me a sense of safety. Tommy had a brazen confidence I had never seen up close. He impressed me, and I saw him as a truly empowered person, which I found very attractive. Underneath the shine, however, I had some inkling that there was a darker energy that came with him—a price to pay for his protection. But at nineteen, I was willing to pay it. For me, Tommy was a potent combination of father figure, Svengali, business partner, confidant, and companion. There was never really a strong sexual or physical attraction there, but at the time, I needed safety and stability—a sense of home—more than I needed a boyfriend. Tommy understood that, and he provided. I gave him my work and my trust. I gave him my conviction and the combination to my moral code.

The relationship was intense and all-encompassing—after all, we already worked together, which was how we spent most of our time. When we weren't working, we were dining at high-end steakhouses or infamous Italian restaurants or attending industry events together. I was spending less and less time at my Chelsea apartment and began spending most nights with him.

Soon, I felt pressure from Tommy to give up my place, and against my better instincts, I gave in. Little did I know, that relinquishment would mark the beginning of a slow and steady march into captivity. Little did I know, giving in to Tommy's demands would gradually swallow my privacy and begin to erase my identity.

On weekends, we drove up to Tommy's farmhouse in Hillsdale, New York, which I eventually "affectionately" came to call "Hillsjail." On the night I got my first publishing advance, for a million dollars (a *million* dollars buys a lot of H&H bagels!) Tommy drove us up the Taconic Parkway and pulled up before a gorgeous piece of land. He stopped the car and told me to get out. I looked at the sprawling expanse, shivering in the autumn breeze—it really was stunning.

"Let's build a house here!" Tommy proclaimed. I knew what this translated to: this *is* where we are building our house. I had no idea the scope of what I was getting myself into.

Now, this was no Hillsjail. It was impressive and majestic: fifty acres of fertile green land adjacent to a nature preserve in Bedford, New York. It was sandwiched between properties belonging to Ralph Lauren and a very prominent billionaire, an area guaranteed to be secure. But, as I would soon discover, the concept of security was about to turn on me.

I hadn't ever wanted to leave the city, but that's what we were doing. Outside of the recording studio, I wondered, when would I ever be back in my beloved Manhattan? Certainly, building a new house would be a monumental undertaking, but it did have a strong appeal to me, creatively and emotionally.

After a childhood of being uprooted and plopped into all kinds of precarious living arrangements, I finally had the chance to build my own, from the foundation. I got excited. I got into it.

I insisted on being fully involved in all aspects of the design, and I also insisted on paying half of all the costs. I wanted it to be *my* house. I had fresh memories of witnessing my mother go through the humiliation of a boyfriend shouting, "Get out of my house!" I told myself that no man would ever do that to me. *Ever.*

Much of what I learned from my mother and older sister was what I *wasn't* going to do when I grew up. I had very little guidance in what *to* do as a woman, though I'd been forced into adult situations when I was still quite young. Tommy was twenty-one years older than me; he could have been my father. He was also the head of my label. There was no wise woman around me to point out that the power dynamic in our relationship was nowhere near fifty-fifty, so maybe I should think twice about going in fifty-fifty with him on an expensive piece of property. To top it all off, we were not yet married.

But I was young, and I was all the way in with Tommy. I was proud of making my own money (though I had no real concept of money). I'd recently received an enormous royalty check from sales of my debut album, so I thought I was set for life. Building a dream house with Tommy did not seem like a risk. I was selling millions of records by then. But I didn't know that our dream mansion would come with an unfathomable thirty-million-dollar price tag. And as it turned out, my time in that house with Tommy would end up costing me so much more than money.

I did love the process of building that grand manor in Bedford. It opened up a new area of passion in me. I was finally able to give life to my childhood obsession with old Hollywood movies. Ironically, I was especially influenced by *How to Marry a Millionaire*, starring Betty Grable,

Lauren Bacall, and Marilyn Monroe (of course). The images of palatial arched windows and glamorous, glossy floors were seared into my little-girl imagination. I made sure every room in our house was pristine and spacious, filled with air and sparkling with light. We worked closely with the designers and architects; we went over every detail together. I taught myself a lot about the styles of moldings and tiles. I became an expert in sconces—*sconces*, dahling! I also learned a lot about materials and would often visit various rock quarries. Though by no stretch do I like a rustic look, I do have a preference for tumbled marble on my kitchen floors. I was very particular and confident about what I liked.

Naïve as I was at the time, I decided I was going to build a great house. I had come from far too little to complain, "Oh, poor me; I have to build a mansion!" I was into it. After all, I sincerely thought I would be with Tommy forever and that the home we would make together would be just as timeless, everlasting, and spectacular as the music we were creating—behind which, of course, I was also the creative force.

And spectacular it was. We even had a ballroom. I was in my early twenties, with my own ballroom! I built a grand closet inspired by Coco Chanel's closet in her 31 rue Cambon flat in Paris, full of opulent mirrors and a spiral staircase that led to its own shoe section. I had acquired so many shoes through all my photo and video shoots that I had to build entire walls of shelving for them. It was staggering to think that just a few short years before, I had been walking in my mother's too-small, beat-up shoes, snow pouring in through cracks in the soles. I kept those dismal ankle boots for a while, with the intention to bronze them like baby boo-ties, so I would never forget where I came from (as if that were even an option). In such a short time, I had gone from raggedy hand-me-downs to my own manor, complete with walls custom-built for an entire footwear collection. My faith and my fans blessed me with unimaginable riches. I was immensely grateful. But, despite that huge accomplishment, I had yet to learn that in reality, I'd just provided the design inspiration, and put up half the money, to build my own prison.

The magnificent compound I built in Bedford was just over ten miles from the village of Ossining, another quaint, wooded Westchester town, home to the most famous maximum-security prison in New York State, and possibly in the country: Sing Sing. A complex of grim stone and brick on 130 acres, landscaped with grand elm trees, Sing Sing sits formidably on the eastern bank of the Hudson River. The roller coaster–like arches of the Tappan Zee Bridge can be seen from the watchtower. In autumn, the views are breathtaking; the trees burn fiery orange, gold, and red.

Sing Sing confines about two thousand human beings. The popular terms for being locked up—being "upstate" or "up the River" or in "the Big House"—were coined at Sing Sing.

No matter how prime the real estate, how grandiose the structure, if it's designed to monitor movement and contain the human spirit, it will serve only to diminish and demoralize those held inside. None of the irony of my proximity to the infamous prison, nor that of its peculiar name, was lost on me: jokingly, I referred to the Bedford estate as Sing Sing. It was fully staffed with armed guards, security cameras were installed in most rooms, and Tommy was in control.

🦋

While I was building Sing Sing, I thought it would be a healthy idea to have my mother and my nephews, Mike and Shawn, live closer to me. I loved the process of designing and creating a gorgeous home. While I had little freedom at Sing Sing, Tommy did support me buying a house nearby for my mother. It became a big thing for us to talk about, and he eventually understood how important it was to me to try and create something stable for my family. I later found out he secretly had security follow me around whenever I went to look at houses or run errands, but I was grateful for the small window of ignorance.

That child in me, deep down, still dreamed of a family that wasn't fractured. I had begun to make my career dreams come true, and I thought maybe I could make us a family home—a home base, where everyone was always welcome—and I'd make my mother the head of it. I got excited about the idea of buying a home my mother would love, and I could finally afford to do it in style. Finding the perfect house for her was my new project. Just like I wanted every bit of my house to reflect me, I was determined to put that attention to detail into the house for my mother. I wanted her to love where she was going to live.

We recruited friends of Tommy's in real estate to help me find a place nearby. They showed me several lovely homes, but I was holding out for the right thing, for *her*. My taste leaned more Old Hollywood, and hers was more "Old Woodstock."

After an extensive search within a twenty-minute radius of our estate, we finally rolled up on a deeply wooded property with a house set far back from the road. It wasn't meticulously manicured, which was typical of that section of upper Westchester; rather, the landscaping was intention- ally organic. The six green acres were filled with splendid old oak trees. And the house blended into the nature around it beautifully. The interior was both spacious and cozy, with warm wood tones and soothing light streaming through gracious windows. Once inside, you couldn't hear or see the outside world.

I had found the only hippie-opera-singer-dream-cabin-in-the-woods in Westchester! It was perfection, and I knew exactly what to do to bring it to life. I took it on like I was an interior designer on one of those make- over shows. I picked out and paid for every piece of brand-new furniture, all the knickknacks and accouterments. I chose every detail, from light fixtures to paint colors, all in "Pat's palette." I hung wooden flower boxes outside and filled them with romantic wildflowers. I got photo prints made of her Irish family members and Irish crests, had them mounted and framed, and hung them ascending the wall along the staircase. And I managed to keep it secret from her.

The biggest challenge was getting her piano in without her knowing. I knew it was important that it was her old blond-wood Yamaha upright that would be in the living room, not a shiny new model. Her piano held memories in its keys; it was a symbol because it was a significant, sta- ble object she provided during my turbulent childhood. I made up some story that I was going to get it tuned or something before it went into storage; I even had her sign fake moving documents so it could be taken away without suspicion. Her old piano would be the pièce de résistance in her cabin in the Westchester woods.

One of the details that sold me on the property was a wooden sign that had the words "Cabin in the Woods" carved into it. The sellers didn't want to part with it, but I fought tooth and nail because I just knew my mother would *love* it. I got so much joy from making plans, keeping the secret, and working to make everything just so. Growing up, I had always wanted a family house where I wouldn't be embarrassed to bring my friends. Creating a place where my mother could live comfortably and the whole family could gather was so special—healing, even. It was like preparing a spectacular Christmas for my mother and family.

I was giddy with excitement when it was time to present the house I had created to my mother. I was proud of the work that I had done. To me, this house was also testimony to my ability to hold on to childhood desires, proof that the trauma and danger I had faced hadn't destroyed my hope. My mother thought she was coming up to Sing Sing for one of our semiregular dinners. When I picked her up, I told her I had to swing by Tommy's friend Carol's house, which was nearby. When the wrought-iron gates I had installed swung open like welcoming arms from the stone pillars and we entered the property, I felt my mother go still, then heard her take a deep breath. Trees will do that: make you stop and breathe. She moved out of the car as if the fresh air was making her slow down.

She looked up at the house in all its beauty. I watched her take in the grace of the flower boxes. And as Carol opened the front door, the aroma of rich coffee and hot cinnamon buns drifted past us. (I had orchestrated it to be brewing and baking when we arrived, as I wanted those details to set the mood.) My mother stood in the doorway and softly said, "Oh, Carol, your house is *beautiful.*" Playing right along, Carol offered to show her around, and I followed behind. When we got to the staircase my mother paused at the photos, but I could tell it didn't quite register. So I broke her trance. "Mom, look at who's in the pictures." She was struck with utter confusion as she noticed *her* family on Carol's wall. Faintly, she replied, "I . . . don't understand."

"This is all for you. This is where you live now," I said. She was speechless. And I was the proudest I'd ever been.

Mike, who I completely treasure, was still quite little then. He went tearing through the house and out to the backyard, running along the plush grass, squealing with delight. He was full of such pure joy (and is still such a source of joy to me). He was free. A little boy playing in the afternoon breeze with no filth, just *free*. We had come full circle from swinging over trash heaps or being thrown out like garbage—or so I thought.

Along with the ballroom and couture shoe closets of Sing Sing, I built a fantastic state-of-the-art recording studio. Adjacent to the studio was a huge Roman-style swimming pool of white marble inside of a grand parlor. In these two places I found solace and solitude. They were a temporary reprieve and a chance to feel weightless—in the recording studio and in the water. But the studio, the pool, and I were all still confined, enclosed within the bounds of Sing Sing's fortress.

Under ordinary circumstances, the chance to have my own studio—custom-made to my exact specifications and at my disposal at any time—would have been liberating. In the early days of my career, I was at the mercy of other people to get studio time, grateful to be in grim little spaces, singing songs I didn't like, bartering, doing whatever it took to get my songs recorded. And now, I had my own fully equipped, gorgeous recording studio. I imagined I could have my own sessions when I wanted to and call in the artists I wanted to work with, like Prince did. Sing Sing wasn't Paisley Park, but it was fabulous, and it was mine. Well, *half* mine. There was a studio with sophisticated recording equipment, but there was also very sophisticated security equipment outfitted throughout the house—listening devices, motion-detecting cameras—recording my every move.

A FAMILY

So when you feel like hope is gone
Look inside you and be strong
And you'll finally see the truth
That a hero lies in you

—"Hero"

I t was the middle of July 1993, and I was headed to Schenectady, New York, to record a Thanksgiving special for NBC. It was the first event to kick off promotion for my soon-to-be-released third studio album, *Music Box.* The first single, "Dreamlover," would be dropping in a week, and the full album would be released on the last day of August. Schenectady, a typical industrial city in eastern New York, was largely made up of Eastern European immigrants and Black folks who had come from the South to work in the town's cotton mill. It's a straight shot north along the Hudson River from Hillsjail.

The concert was to be taped in Proctors Theatre, a former vaudeville house complete with a red carpet, gold leaf galore, Corinthian columns, chandeliers, and Louis XV couches in the balcony promenade—the whole nine yards. Even though it was a beautiful, classic theater, it was not the setting I would have chosen, to be sure; nor would most twenty-year-olds in the early 1990s. But I made few decisions about my whereabouts then. Outside of the recording studio, every aspect of my life was decided by a committee in those days, with Tommy acting as chairman of the board. (Oddly enough, I was never invited to the meetings.)

As we pulled up to the center of town, the streets seemed to be increasingly empty, and I began to notice a lot of police officers. Several streets were blocked off near the theater, patrolled by clusters of men in dark uniforms, outfitted with shiny shoes and black guns. The limo slowed to a crawl as I stared out the window, the eerily quiet streets rolling by. A familiar anxiety was rising inside, which I fought mightily to contain. I had to mentally prepare to present new songs in front of new people, a performance that would be televised to millions on a major network. I knew I couldn't let my anxiety develop into fear. With the exception of the cops—who had called all these cops? I had my own security with me; in fact, I *always* had security with me—the street behind the theater, where the backstage door was located, was desolate.

Before I was quickly whisked into my gilded dressing room, I caught a glimpse of crowds of people behind barricades. Though I now had a moment to settle in, I still felt anxious. Eventually I asked why the streets were blocked off and full of police. What in the world was happening in downtown Schenectady on this hot midsummer day?

"Miss Carey," they told me, "it's for you. It's because you were coming to do the show."

Apparently, masses of young fans were crowding the streets, hoping to catch a glimpse of *me*. At first, I couldn't fully digest this response. What did they mean? The barricades, the squads of police, the emptied streets were because of *me*? My first album, *Mariah Carey*, had come out three years prior hitting and holding the number-one spot on the *Billboard* 200 chart for 11 consecutive weeks, remaining on the list for 113 weeks in total, with four singles going number one back-to-back. I had won Grammys for Best New Artist and the best female pop vocal performance, and received nominations for both Song of the Year and Record of the Year for "Vision of Love," which I performed on *The Arsenio Hall Show, Good Morning America, The Tonight Show*, and *The Oprah Winfrey Show*. The album would go on to sell nine million copies in the United States alone and was still selling all over the world (it would go on to sell more than fifteen million copies). My second album, *Emotions*, had been released just the year before. I particularly adored working with David

Cole (one half of the fab C + C Music Factory). He was a church kid who loved dance music (as evidenced on "Make It Happen"). As a producer, he pushed me as a singer, because he was one too. I released an EP with live versions of songs from my first two albums for the wildly popular show *MTV Unplugged*. It included a remake of the classic Jackson Five hit "I'll Be There," featuring my background singer and friend Trey Lorenz. The song quickly shot to number one after the show, making it my fifth number-one single and the second time "I'll Be There" held the coveted spot. I performed "Emotions" at the MTV Video Music Awards and the Soul Train Music Awards. And here I was again, about to hit another stage, and somehow I had no clue that I was famous.

For four solid years of my life, I was writing, singing, producing, and doing photo shoots, video shoots, press junkets, and promotional tours. All the awards and accolades I received were handed out in highly coordinated industry settings. It just seemed to be part of the work. If I had any "free" time I was sequestered in an old farmhouse up in the Hudson Valley. Tommy orchestrated all of it. I was in my early twenties.

Because I was never alone, I had no comprehension of the impact my music and I were making on the outside world. I never had time to think or reflect. I now believe that this was completely by design. Did Tommy know I would be easier to control if I were kept ignorant of the full scope of my power?

I'm told that in the *Music Box* era, as a gift to me, my then makeup artist Billy B and hairstylist Syd Curry made a thoughtful scrapbook for me, in which they gathered little notes of love and appreciation from other artists or celebrities they worked with or saw in their travels. Joey Lawrence (remember Joey from *Blossom*?), who was such a heartthrob at the time, apparently left a significantly sweet message. Well, Tommy saw the lovefest of a book, ripped it up, and burned it in the fireplace before I was able to see it—a childish act of cruelty, especially to Billy and Syd, who went through all that effort to prove to me how big I was even among the stars.

With no parental or familial management or protection, I was easy to manipulate, but the dynamic of my relationship with Tommy was complex. In many ways, Tommy protected me from my dysfunctional family, but he went to the extreme: he controlled and patrolled me. Yet his control also meant that in these early years, all my focus, all my energy, and all my passion went into writing, producing, and singing my songs. Tommy and his stranglehold on my movements seemed a fair price to pay for getting to do the work I had always dreamed of. He had my life, but I had my music. It wasn't until that moment in Schenectady that I began to realize the degree of my popularity. I had *fans*! And soon they would become another source of my strength.

In the dressing room, where I sat in a chair having my hair first straightened, then curled and sprayed, the magnitude of what I had just learned began to sink in. The police were not around because of some violent or dangerous incident—they were there to make a clear way for *me*. My family may not have provided me safety, my relationship may not have given me security, but realizing that there was a multitude of people showing up and pouring out love for me gave me a new kind of confidence. Because Tommy never allowed me to experience the glamorous privileges granted to the young, rich, and popular, the fame I discovered was solely defined through my relationship to my fans and their relationship to my music. I decided that day that I was prepared to be devoted to them forever.

The Thanksgiving special was titled *Here Is Mariah Carey*, and I was going to debut three new songs from *Music Box*: "Dreamlover," "Anytime You Need a Friend," and "Hero," along with some of my known hits— "Emotions," "Make It Happen," and of course, "Vision of Love." I had always written songs from an honest place, using my own lived experiences and dreams as a source. I also pushed my vocals to their extreme. I was also going to debut "Hero." It's always a risk to debut songs at a live show that people have not had the opportunity to connect with through radio repetition. Even though I wrote "Hero," it wasn't originally intended for me to perform.

🦋

I was asked to write something for the movie *Hero*, starring Dustin Hoffman and Geena Davis. Tommy had agreed I would submit a song for the film, to be sung by Gloria Estefan, who was on Epic Records (Sony,

Tommy's label, was the parent company). I knew that Luther Vandross was also writing a song for the soundtrack, so I would be in great company. I hunkered down in Right Track, or the Hit Factory—one of the major studios where I had spent a major fortune. I was there that day with Walter Afanasieff.

The plot of the film was explained to everyone in the studio in five minutes: a pilot goes around and rescues people. That's about all I absorbed. Shortly after, I got up to go to the bathroom, one of the few activities I did unaccompanied by someone on Tommy's payroll. I lingered in the stall to luxuriate in my fleeting moment of peace. Savoring my time, I slowly walked down the hall to return to the studio. As I walked, a melody and some words came clearly into my mind. As soon as I got back into the room, I sat right down at the piano and said to Walter, "This is how it goes." I hummed the tune and some of the lyrics. As Walter worked to find the basic chords, I began to sing, "*and then a hero comes along.*" I guided him through what I had heard so vividly in my head.

"Hero" was created for a mainstream movie, to be sung by a singer with a very different style and range than my own. Honestly, though I felt the message and the melody were fairly generic, I also thought it fit the bill. We recorded a rough demo, which I found a bit schmaltzy.

But Tommy heard the potential for a classic. He insisted not only that we keep the song but that it was going on my new album. I was like, *Okay. I'm glad he likes it.* I finessed the song and made changes to the lyrics to make it more personal. For that, I went to the well of my memories and dipped into that moment when Nana Reese had told me to hold on to my dreams. I did my best to reclaim it, but it was a gift no matter who it was for.

By the time of the Schenectady show, "Hero" had lost its simplicity and gained some depth. The initial trepidation I felt about singing it live for the first time in front of an audience was melting away as I thought about all the people who had lined the streets and packed the theater to see me that night. I decided that this song did not actually belong to Gloria Estefan, a movie, Tommy, or me. "Hero" belonged to my fans, and I was going to deliver it to them with all I had.

The Thanksgiving special included inner-city kids from a local community organization. I saw the kids backstage, brimming with both promise and fear, and in them, I saw me. I would sing this song for them too. The concert opened with my latest hit, "Emotions"—upbeat and embellished with lots of my signature super-high notes. As I was singing "Emotions," and through the several stops and retakes required (singing live for TV recording is tedious work), I was able to really look at the people in the crowd. This was Schenectady, and these were real folks—not paid seat fillers or trendily dressed extras but authentic, mostly young people with that unmistakable hunger and adoration in their eyes. I saw them for who they were, and they were *me*. I closed my eyes and said a prayer. As the first few chords of the piano intro played, I started to hum from my heart. When I opened my mouth, "Hero" was released into the world.

Some of us need to be rescued, but everyone wants to be seen. I sang "Hero" directly to the faces I could see from the stage. I saw tears well up in their eyes and hope rise up in their spirits. Whatever cynicism I had about that song was gone after that night. But Tommy, too, had noticed the size of its impact.

Later that year, on December 10, 1993, when I performed "Hero" at Madison Square Garden, I announced that all stateside sales proceeds would be donated to the families of victims of the Long Island Railroad shooting, which had happened three days prior. On a train—a route I'd ridden before—a man pulled out a 9-mm pistol and opened fire, killing six people and wounding nineteen. Three brave men, Kevin Blum, Mark McEntee, and Michael O'Connor, subdued him, thus preventing more slaughter. They were heroes, and so I dedicated "Hero" to them that night. Just ten days after the September 11 attacks, I sang the song as part of the *America: A Tribute to Heroes* telethon. And on January 20, 2009, I had the unthinkable, unparalleled honor of singing it at the Inaugural Ball of the first African American president of the United States of America. To this day, "Hero" is one of my most performed songs. *Music Box* would go on to reach diamond status in the United States and is one of the highest-selling albums of all time.

And here's a side note with a side eye: A couple of people have come for "Hero," and for me, with both royalties and plagiarism claims. Three times I have been to court, and three times the cases have been thrown out. The first time, the poor fool going after me had to pay a fine. Initially I felt victimized, knowing how purely the song came to me, but after a while I almost began to expect lies and lawsuits to come with my success—from strangers and my own family and friends. And they won't stop.

The taping that night in Schenectady took several hours. A television show has so many technical needs—multiple cameras, close-ups, far and cutaway shots, costume changes, hair and makeup touch-ups, extras, audience reactions—it's a *production*. When we finally wrapped, I said all my thank-yous to the kids, the choir, the orchestra, and the crew. Then, just as I had come in, I was whisked out the backstage door, which seemed to lead not to the street but straight into the limo.

I plopped into the backseat, buzzing from a contradictory cocktail of exhaustion and exhilaration. As we pulled out into the street, I noticed that where there was once emptiness and a scattering of barricades, there were now crowds of people swelling over the flimsy metal partitions, screaming my name and "We love you!" I noticed the cops too, standing there, unfazed, in the pulsing midst of the energy and excitement. It was one thing to be informed, but quite another to see with my own eyes, hear with my own ears, and feel in my soul the reaction from real people to me and my music. What I felt that night in Schenectady was not idol worship, it was *love*. It was the kind of love that comes from honest connection and recognition. I was mesmerized as I looked out the window, watching all these people shower me with such love. Not just fans. A *family*.

As the crowd faded from sight and we neared the outskirts of town, approaching the highway, my high began to wear off. And by the time the wheels touched the tar of the Taconic Parkway, the mood in the car had returned to its routine gloom. Most Thursday evenings Tommy and I would ride up the southern stretch of this highway, leaving glamorous Manhattan behind to spend the weekend in Hillsdale. As the lights and high-rises shrank in the rearview mirror and the magnetic pull of the city dimmed, a part of my life force grew faint as well.

When the car radio, which stayed locked on Hot 97 (their then slogan: "blazing hip-hop and R & B"), would begin to break up, muffled by static, I knew my life as a Grammy award–winning singer-songwriter twenty-something was over. Every weekend, Tommy would turn off the radio that was my lifeline and take a moment of silence before popping in one of his beloved Frank Sinatra CDs. What a tragic metaphor, listening to Tommy hum "My Way" as he drove us back to my captivity.

I was conditioned to either talk shop or go silent on our bleak commute. Mostly, though, I just stared out the window at the grand Hudson River, preparing for my first major role: contented wife-to-be. This was the only acting job Tommy ever encouraged. Taking acting classes or accepting roles in movies or on TV was strictly forbidden.

On the ride back from Schenectady, I don't recall Tommy and me discussing what had just happened. Perhaps he knew that I saw the purity and power of the fans—that I'd discovered how their love couldn't be controlled. It is fans who create a phenomenon, not record-company executives. Tommy was smart. He knew. But I don't know if he realized that after that moment, I finally did too.

We arrived at the farmhouse, and all I wanted to do was take a bath. Being a performer is a production. You build up and put on, you strategize, manipulate, accommodate, and shape-shift. It requires rituals (sometimes in the form of bad habits) to return yourself back to yourself. My ritual was to wash the performer off. The addition of a large tub facing an expansive picture window was one of the few contributions I got to make to Hillsjail. The bathroom was my refuge, since putting a camera or intercom in there would've been a bit much, even for Tommy. The cool marble tile sent a soothing sensation through my bare feet, which had been hoisted up in heels all night. I lazily peeled off my ensemble, thankful that the sound of the water running was the only one I heard. I lowered the overhead lights and ceremoniously lit a few white candles. The water was welcoming, and I surrendered. As if being baptized, I submerged my head and lingered in the warm, dark quiet. I gently rose up, tilted my head back, and propped my arms along the edge of the massive basin, eyelids still shut, savoring every moment of this calm solitude. Slowly I opened my eyes to a radiant full moon, glowing against a clear, blue-black sky. Softly I began to sing: "*Da, da, da, da, da . . .*"

Images of the scene I had just left—adoring fans screaming and crying—flashed through my mind, blending with painful recollections of my brother screaming and my mother crying, of myself as a lonely little girl in a neglected dress. I was floating in a tub that was larger than the size of my entire living area just five years before, in a room bigger than all of the living rooms in all of the thirteen places I lived with my mother growing up. The enormity, complexity, and instability of the road I had traveled to get into this bath hit me. It was the first time I felt safe enough to go back and peek in on Mariah, the little one, and recognize what she had survived. And suddenly, the first verse and chorus of "Close My Eyes" came to me:

I was a wayward child
With the weight of the world
That I held deep inside.
Life was a winding road
And I learned many things
Little ones shouldn't know

But I closed my eyes
Steadied my feet on the ground
Raised my head to the sky
And the times rolled by
Still I feel like a child
As I look at the moon
Maybe I grew up
A little too soon.

It would take me years to finish this song—years of anguish and survival.

MY BIG FAT SONY WEDDING
(AND LITTLE SKINNY
HONEYMOON)

To announce our engagement, Tommy and I took my mother to a swanky dinner in midtown Manhattan. As we walked outside after the meal, the city was all dressed up in its evening wear of bright lights and flashing billboards, and I showed her the engagement ring, a Cartier tricolor gold band with an immaculate, modest-sized diamond. It was understated, but it was also *Cartier*. My mother looked at the delicate, dazzling ring on my slender (and very young) finger and quietly said, "You deserve it."

That was it. She got into the limo I had waiting for her and rode away. I never really knew what she meant by that. But that was all that was left between us. There was no womanly advice or girlish giggles—which, honestly, I didn't expect, but I did think the occasion called for more than a one-liner.

Many reasonable people have questioned why I married Tommy. But none of them questioned the decision more than I did. I knew I would lose more power as a person, and I was already completely suffocating emotionally in the relationship. We were equally yoked to each other through the music and the business. However, the personal power dynamic between us was *never* equal. He convinced me that everything would be better if we were married, that things would be different. But what I really hoped was that *he* would be different—that if I gave him this thing he so adamantly wanted, this marriage that I believed he thought would legitimize him, or quell chatter about him having an affair with an artist on the label, it would change him. I was never completely sure why he wanted to get married so badly. I prayed that in doing so he would calm down and loosen his vise grip on my life. I hoped maybe he would trust his "wife" and let her breathe.

I was in my early twenties, just a few years removed from the shack, and the concept of a life that included *both* personal and professional fulfillment was unfathomable to me. I truly believed that I was not worthy of both happiness *and* success. I was accustomed to making all my life choices based on survival.

Back then, I didn't choose what glamorous outfit to wear each morning; I chose what survival mechanism I needed to arm myself with that day. More than my personal happiness, I needed my career as an artist to survive. Happiness was secondary. Happiness was a fleeting bonus. I married Tommy because I thought it was the only way for me to survive in that relationship. I saw the power he could put behind my music, and he saw the power my music could give him. Our holy matrimony was built on creativity and vulnerability. I respected Tommy as a partner. If only he had known how to give me the respect I was due as a human being.

❦

At the first real wedding I ever attended I was the bride. I never dreamed of getting married when I was young. I hadn't really wanted to. In high school, girls fantasized about big, poofy dresses and Long Island weddings while I visualized a dream of becoming a successful musician and actress. That's all I cared about, so it was pretty ironic that I ended up having one of the decade's most lavish New York weddings in one of the decade's most dramatic, voluminous gowns.

Apart from the ambition, Tommy and I were completely different, and the Black part of myself caused him confusion. From the moment Tommy signed me, he tried to wash the "urban" (translation: Black) off of me. And it was no different when it came to the music. The songs on my very first demo, which would become my first smash album, were much more soulful, raw, and modern in their original state. Just as he did with my appearance, Tommy smoothed out the songs for Sony, trying to make them more general, more "universal," more ambiguous. I always felt like he wanted to convert me into what he understood—a "mainstream" (meaning white) artist. For instance, he never wanted me to wear my hair straight. I think to him it didn't look naturally straight, it looked *straightened*. He thought it made me look too "urban" (translation: Black) or R & B, like Faith Evans. Instead, he insisted that I always wear my loose and bouncy curls, which I think he thought made me look almost like an Italian girl (though, ironically, my curls are a direct result of my Black DNA, assisted by a good small-barrel curling wand to integrate the frizz).

My curls had certainly crisscrossed with Italian culture before I met Tommy. (I *did* live in more than a dozen places on Long Island.) In the eleventh grade I attended a beauty tech school. I was there mostly to kill time before I became a star (my only career goal). It was more creative, entertaining, and practical than regular high school. I'd always struggled with pulling a cohesive look together—there weren't any of the tools or potions at home for me to play with, and I certainly didn't have a consistent crew of girls to go through the passage from girl to teen with. There was a real allure to gaining more refined beauty skills. Also, I was a huge fan of the musical film *Grease* growing up; I thought I could have my own Pink Ladies moment. And I kinda did.

My beauty school class was made up of mostly Italian girls. There were mean girls, there were shy girls, there were regular girls, and then there were *the girls*. They were a clique of about three or four fabulous ones, who comparatively, of all the girls I'd ever seen on Long Island, were the most glamorous—or rather, they seemed to be having the most fun with it. But they were *so* serious about their look.

Subtlety, to these girls, was a waste of time and flavor. They were terminally tanned. Their heavily highlighted hair was *coiffed* within an inch of its life, every ringlet, puff, and bang sprayed into obedience. Their makeup was bright, flashy, and perfectly applied. They wore their fingernails long and *did*. Some even had nail art: a line of tiny gold studs, or their initials in crystals on a perfect, thick, bright white "French"—*major*.

We all had to wear a uniform of a drab maroon button-up smock with white pants and hideous, chunky white nurse shoes. But these girls would not have their flamboyance hidden. They wore their smocks open, revealing the leggings and boys' ribbed white tank tops with fancy, lacy bras they featured underneath. And, of course, there was the jewelry: thick and thin gold link chains in flat, herringbone, and rope styles with Italian horns, crosses, and initial pendants dangling from them layered on their necks, hoops in their ears, and delicate gold and diamond rings on every finger.

They were so adult to me. They were obviously already having sex—obviously not only because they carried their bodies in a particular way but because they let everybody know it. They talked easily and openly about sex (which was secretly shocking to me). They called themselves "Guidettes," and I had no idea what that meant, but I thought it was cool they had a name, like a singing group or something.

They would roll up to the beauty school in flashy cars, bumping WBLS, the urban dance radio station—ooh, if they only knew we called it the "Black Liberation Station"—*loud*. And of course I knew every song, and I would *sing* them—like Jocelyn Brown's "Somebody Else's Guy" (I quite enjoyed laying into the big, slow vocals at the beginning) or "Ain't Nothin' Goin On But the Rent" by Gwen Guthrie. The girls loved it, and my teacher hated it, because I was *always* singing, blowing out notes rather than doing blowouts.

It was my singing and constant popping of jokes that won these flashy teen princesses over, because I was from another school, and I hadn't formed my own confident look—I was not quite cool clique material. We did manage to do each other's hair. Surprisingly, no one ever questioned me about my mixed texture, the thickness (or thinness) of my lips, or any of my features. I learned a lot from those girls. They helped me bring more volume and energy to my hair and more gloss to my lips.

We had more in common than one would imagine. There's always been an underground relationship between hip-hop and the mob in pop culture. We especially loved the style and swag of movies like

The Godfather and *Scarface*. Later, I re-created the hot tub scene with Jay-Z for the "Heartbreaker" video. That video will always be one of my favorites. I enjoyed paying homage to Elvira, Michelle Pfeiffer's character, the tortured and trapped wife, who had a spectacular home and sexy designer clothes (I could *relate*).

Though I did try, it turned out that I was bound to be a beauty school dropout. Most of the girls in my class were really focused and had talent for the field. They were destined to do hair. Thankfully, I had another sweet destiny waiting for me, because I certainly would never be crowned queen of finger waves.

I could have never imagined just a few years after my five hundred hours with the Guidettes, I'd be at the altar with one of the most powerful men in the music industry—an Italian, no less. I hadn't been looking for anyone romantically. I certainly wasn't looking for a husband. And I most definitely wasn't looking to marry Tommy, but it happened anyway. And what a *happening* it was. Once I said yes to the marriage, I thought, *Hey, we might as well make it an event—an EXTRAVAGANZA!* As with any project or production I'm involved with, I wanted to bring as much optimism and festiveness to it as possible. Tommy was also enthusiastic about the potential pomp and circumstance we could create. He focused on curating the most influential and impressive audience—I mean, guest list—he could.

Clearly, there was no family or mother of the bride running the show here. Lord knows this task was way beyond anything my mother could ever comprehend. Besides, this wedding was designed to be an entertainment-industry spectacle; even a capable mother or sister couldn't manage the production we were going to put on. The wife of one of Tommy's colleagues, who was a socially well-connected middle-aged woman, was given the role of production coordinator. She helped me with all the major details, such as the dress.

That dress was an event unto itself. My coordinator was friends with one of the most prominent female fashion designers of the era, whose specialty was bridal. It seemed like I spent as much time in her showroom for fittings as I did in the studio for an entire album. There were at least ten fittings—crazy for a girl who, not so long before, had only had three shirts in rotation.

Of course, I was inspired by Princess Diana. Who wasn't? She was an inspiring figure! I loved that wedding, and really it was my only reference point for how a wedding should look. I didn't grow up looking at bridal magazines, and besides, the royals know how to throw a good wedding—obviously. In the end, nearly every princess element or symbol imaginable could be found in that dress. The crème silk fabric was so fine, it seemed to glow. The sweetheart neckline swooped gracefully off the shoulder before blooming into exaggerated poof sleeves. The structured bodice was intricately encrusted with crystals and beads exploding into an enormous ball gown skirt, kept afloat by layers upon layers of crinolines. But the most notable feature was the ultra-dramatic twenty-seven-foot train, which required its own team of handlers. Affixed to a diamond tiara was an equally long veil. Syd Curry twirled my curls to tumble down like Rapunzel's, and Billy B did my face, serving up both glamorous ingenue and Belle of the Ball. I had come a long way from Cinderella of the Shack. The bouquet was unforgettable: a cascade of roses and orchids, studded with various all-white blossoms romantically tangled with vines of ivy. A small troupe of little girls threw white petals at my feet.

Tommy did not disappoint on his assignment either—the casting was impressive. The guest list included heavy hitters from Barbra Streisand to Bruce Springsteen, Billy Joel and Christie Brinkley—even Ozzy Osbourne and Dick Clark! To top it all off, his best man was Robert De Niro! Though my bridesmaids included my longtime and trusted friends Josefin and Clarissa, they brought me no comfort. No one could. I was deathly afraid.

I hardly remember the ceremony at the majestic Saint Thomas Church (we needed a venue that could accommodate the drama of the dress, after all).

I remember our song was "You and I (We Can Conquer the World)" by Stevie Wonder, because I chose it, of course. I recall my face shaking involuntarily at the altar. But the moment those church doors opened up onto Fifth Avenue, I heard the roar of screams and saw the hordes of fans flooding every inch of sidewalk as far as the eye could see, camera flashes popping like fireworks. I walked down the stairs and smiled at *them*. For me, my wedding wasn't for all those rich and famous people I barely knew. It wasn't for my distant, dysfunctional family (though I do fondly remember my grandfather, by then in the grips of dementia, lovingly yelling my name like he was on the block: "Mariah! Mariah!") To me, the wedding spectacle was mostly for the fans, and we gave them the fabulous moment *they* deserved.

There was a star-studded reception at the Metropolitan Club (I liked the venue because it had "MC" monogrammed everywhere, but we didn't mention that to TM) that I barely remember. I was *exhausted*. It had taken so much energy just to plan the thing and then get through it.

The night before I'd had a girls-only sleepover at the Mark Hotel. I was clearly conflicted. My friends knew I didn't even really believe in the institution of marriage, and yet here I was about to put on this major show with a man who was already showing dangerous signs, professionally and personally. He would become my next of kin; the stifling hot mess of a relationship that I was already in with him would only become more foul and imbalanced.

"You don't have to do this," they all said. But I truly believed I had to. I saw no way out. I didn't know what else to do. I'd learned how to endure disappointment and carry on, to make the best of things and keep working. I certainly knew how to live with fear. I didn't know life without fear.

Tommy and I pulled off the wedding. The next day we flew to Hawaii. I can't, in good conscience, refer to what we did as a "honeymoon." It was not sweet. It was not dreamy. At. All. We were staying at someone's house, which was already pretty lackluster. I didn't really care that much, since my relationship with Tommy was never about romance, but still, it was technically my "honey moon-ish" . . .

Thankfully, the house was on the beach, and being near the ocean is always a comfort to me. The next day I had gone to the bathroom to change into a swimsuit when I heard Tommy ranting on speakerphone. I could tell he was arguing. *Great.*

"What's the matter?" I asked. He was on the phone with his very high-powered publicist, who was going ballistic, screaming and cursing because he didn't want our wedding photos on the cover of *People*, as we'd planned. The publicist was telling Tommy that it wasn't appropriate for his executive image. *His* image? I mean, why go through all of that grandiosity for some little corner picture, as the publicist was urging? I shared this opinion with him and Tommy. The publicist exploded.

"Are you fucking kidding me?!" he yelled at me.

Tommy didn't come to my defense. So here I was, twentyish, on my honeymoon-ish with a fiftyish-year-old man screaming and cursing at me over the phone while my fortyish *husband* sat there, not doing a damned thing about it. And to top it all off, I was right! Of *course* our wedding should have been a big cover story. It was planned that way—this was show business!

While the two angry men yelled at each other and me like children, I broke out crying and broke out of that house. I just started running aimlessly down the beach, tears streaming down my face. We hadn't even digested the wedding cake, and here we were again, back to bickering, back to raging, back to me being dismissed and outpowered. Nothing had changed or calmed down. I just ran, not knowing where I was going. Eventually I came upon a hotel with a beachside bar. *Perfect*, I thought, *I could use a drink.*

But when I sat down I realized that I had left empty-handed. I didn't have a phone or a purse, no cash, no card, no ID. I couldn't even get myself a sympathy drink to cry into. With my hair bunched up in a topknot, wearing nothing but a bikini and a sarong, I looked like a thousand lonely young women on the beach, not like a famous pop star who had sold millions of records worldwide. I most certainly didn't look like a honeymooning bride. If anyone did recognize me, they left me alone—and no one could imagine how alone I felt.

I asked to use the phone and made a collect call to my manager (remember when you had to memorize important phone numbers?). I asked him to give the bartender a credit card number so I could at least get a drink. I ordered some sweet and sorry frozen daiquiri. I sipped on it and listened to the waves crashing on the shore as the reality of the situation began to sink in.

Eventually I made my way back down the beach and to the house. But I knew the drill. Once again Tommy and I would sit in silence, after all was said and done. The little bit of hope I'd had that getting married would change him washed away like footprints in the sand. That was the day I began to hold my breath and resist the undertow of Tommy.

THANKSGIVING
IS CANCELLED!

And I missed a lot of life, but I'll recover
Though I know you really like to see me suffer
Still I wish that you and I'd forgive each other
'Cause I miss you, Valentine, and really loved you

—"Petals"

I called him T. D. Valentine. That was his stage name back in the day when he fancied himself a musician. He loved music, that much is true, and he found a way to have a lifelong affair with it. As I've said, our mutual love of music, ambition, and power was completely inter- twined with our personal relationship. Music *was* the relationship, but try as we might, that couldn't make it a marriage. I sincerely believed in my heart I would be with Tommy *forever*. But my sanity and soul would not surrender to my heart, and the marriage swiftly began to harm me on an emotional and spiritual level.

There was a popular mythology that I was some sophisticated gold digger who bagged a big-time hit maker who was now bankrolling my princess lifestyle—that I was just sitting pretty on a throne in my thirty- million-dollar mansion. The wedding certainly gave that illusion, and that's all it was, an illusion. If there was any perception of a fairy-tale mar- riage or life, it was absolutely smoke and mirrors. The ironclad safety that Tommy provided from my family turned into an ironclad dungeon.

The control and imbalance of power in our relationship accelerated. My manager was a childhood friend of his. His preferred security was the tough guy he idolized from his school days (even though I towered over him when in heels). Everyone whose job it was to look after me had deep connections to *him*. I was very young and inexperienced when Tommy met me; he knew so much more about a lot of things, especially the music business. But I knew some things he didn't know too, particularly when it came to trends and popular culture, which I suspect made him feel threatened. He seemed threatened by anything he couldn't control.

Even the *idea* of me doing something he couldn't control would send him into an irrational tailspin. One prime, ridiculous example: once, there was a copy of *Entertainment Weekly* on our kitchen table in Sing Sing. In it was a short piece wherein a writer mused about the idea of a modern remake of *All About Eve* starring Diana Ross as Margo Channing and me as Eve Harrington—genius! Of course, I adored the original movie, not only for the glamour and the iconic performances but also because Marilyn Monroe had a small but delicious part as Miss Casswell, a gorgeous, ambitious actress.

Tommy read the article and got pissed—at *me*! Somehow he found a way to blame me for someone else's fantasy of casting me in a movie (which didn't even have a love scene, for God's sake!). As if he were an overbearing father or warden, his anger would permeate the house and rattle my whole being. I got in trouble (yes, "trouble," because I felt so infantilized by him) for the mere suggestion, made by *someone else*, of me doing something beyond his control.

The gap between our tastes and instincts in music and pop culture was more divisive than the gap between our ages. In the late eighties and through the midnineties, Uptown Records, led by the late and legendary Andre Harrell, was *the* label for R & B, hip-hop, and the hybrid that would become known as New Jack Swing. Uptown had Heavy D & the Boyz, Guy (featuring Teddy Riley), Jodeci, Mary J. Blige, and Father MC. Father MC's album was one of my favorites. Mary J. Blige was doing background vocals and hooks for him and he would also feature Jodeci-*love*. I would listen to them all the time. Tommy would watch me listening. He knew to pay attention to what I was interested in because he knew my ear and instincts were sharp. But I knew he couldn't *feel* it. He couldn't fully grasp its cutting edge. He never really believed in the enduring cultural power of hip-hop because he couldn't fully understand it. He thought it was a passing fad or trend.

One night, Tommy and I were out with a group of friends and major music executives, in a beautifully lit dining room in an Italian restaurant that served unforgettable warm focaccia and was frequented by music industry illuminati. We were all seated around a big table. My friend Josefin was in from Sweden, and she and her new husband were among the guests, so it wasn't completely a work dinner, but at this point my work, social, and personal lives were pretty much one and the same. Even our home had been largely designed for conducting business and impressing partners (though *my* contemporaries' main concern was where they could chill and smoke a spliff—of all the lavish rooms available, no surprise, we preferred the studio). We would sometimes host big, festive dinners there, some of which were both fun and fabulous, but they never felt like *family*. Nothing feels like family when you are under surveillance, which I always was.

The midnineties were an exciting era in music, and I was part of a pioneering generation of innovative young artists, songwriters, producers, and executives. We were intent on making a new kind of sound, based in R & B and rap but unrestricted by old formats and formulas. We were playing with new technologies and irreverently blending fluid melodies with gritty hip-hop aesthetics and energy. The music we were making was raw and smooth at the same time, and we were the only ones who knew how to make it work. It was our sound, a reflection of our time and our sensibilities.

My former manager was also with us at the restaurant. The conversation drifted to Puffy aka Sean aka P. Diddy, who had recently left Uptown Records, where he'd started as an intern, eventually becoming head of A&R. Now he already had his own record label, Bad Boy, and his star artist, the Notorious B.I.G., was all over the radio and beginning to spread all over a generation. The then head of Epic Records turned to me and asked, "So what do you think of this guy, Puffy? What do you think is going on with him? Do you like his music?"

He directed the question to me because I was the youngest person at the table. I also loved and understood hip-hop, and I was the only artist there. Besides, I'd recently worked with Puff as a producer. The table got quiet as I leaned in and gave my honest assessment: that Puff and Bad Boy were definitely where modern music was headed.

Not too long before, at our kitchen table, Tommy had shared his own opinion with me and my nephew Shawn: "Puffy will be shining my shoes in two years." I was stunned. *Wait. What did he say?* It was one of the very few times I stood up to Tommy, telling him that what he had said was blatantly racist. I was pissed. Shawn had never seen me talk back to him; he was shocked that I showed my anger and became genuinely concerned for my safety. So many people were then.

But that night at the restaurant, what could have been a robust discussion between industry leader and artist about global culture and the future of American pop music became an epic Tommy tantrum instead. As I was finishing my answer, I saw his eyes flash with familiar rage. He jumped up from the table and began pacing, huffing and puffing around the restaurant. He was so livid he couldn't contain himself. The entire table sat in silence as we looked at one another, not knowing what the actual fuck was wrong with him (this time) or what we should do. The whole restaurant witnessed Tommy trying to walk himself back down off a ledge only he could see. Finally, he stormed back. Still vibrating with rage, he slammed his fist on the table and announced, "I just want everybody to know that THANKSGIVING IS CANCELLED!" *Um, okay.*

We were planning to have a festive Thanksgiving dinner party at Sing Sing, but because I had dared to give my honest, autonomous opinion, in public, to someone he admired (who had asked *me* what I thought), he was going to shut down the fun. As if it were my ten-year-old birthday party. Even then, it was laughable, the hubris with which he declared a national holiday *cancelled*. Like, who was going to call Frank Perdue? By God, who was going to recall all the Butterballs?! I'd been asked a direct question. What was I supposed to do, sit there like a dummy and not answer the man? It was all just ridiculous.

What wasn't funny was knowing how I would be punished for my transgression on the hourlong ride home. Something came over me that night, and I decided I wasn't going to take the hit for something that wasn't my fault, *again*. This night, I would not be locked up in Tommy's

Range Rover torture chamber and sent back to prison in Bedford. I decided I was not going to leave with him under any circumstances. I realized I was taking a huge, frightening risk, but because we were in a public place, with a table full of witnesses, I took a gamble, thinking he wouldn't make a bigger scene and I might be safe.

He sat at the table stewing and staring at me. I perched nervously in my chair, my leg literally quivering under the white linen tablecloth, but still full of conviction. Somehow, I stared back. *Not this night.* There was no fucking way I was taking that car ride with him in that state. It was a tense standoff, and everyone at the table was freaked out. They were scared for me; they were scared for themselves. *Everybody* was always scared of Tommy! But I held my position, and finally Tommy walked out alone. Even though he and I both knew there would still be people following me and reporting back to him, this stand was a *monumental* move on my part. Out of respect for our privacy, the chef and proprietor agreed to let me discreetly exit through the kitchen. Josefin and I went out to a little club (which was an *enormous* step for me) to shake it off and have a few cocktails, then we went to a hotel to get a decent night's sleep. It was my first sip of freedom—and how thirsty I was for more.

> *'Cause it's my night*
> *No stress, no fights*
> *I'm leaving it all behind . . .*
> *No tears, no time to cry*
> *Just makin' the most of life*
>
> —It's Like That

The night Tommy "cancelled" Thanksgiving was the first time I stood up for myself and resisted his orders. He never allowed me to have a voice of my own; exhibiting the slightest bit of agency or independent thought seemed to threaten and emasculate him. I had no control over his control. I was the voice of the label, making all kinds of profits and shares for him, and yet I couldn't have a voice at the dinner table. But I wouldn't allow myself to be cancelled.

FANTASY

While Tommy would never relinquish control over my life, at a certain point he did begin to make concessions when it came to the production of the music. He always respected me as a songwriter; he was a music man and knew good lyrics and melody structure. However, not only was I outgrowing some of the producers he had attached to me, so was the music industry. I always resisted their push to make me fit in a neat mainstream "adult contemporary" category. Adult contemporary was what he knew, it was what his guys knew, and I really knew it too. I could write big pop hits like "Hero." I could write Broadway-style tunes. Whatever the occasion required, I could make it happen. But I wanted to make more of my own music with a more modern sound. They kept trying to smooth me out while I just wanted to get a little more rough. I wanted to add dynamics and broaden my reach. And, of course, there was a racial and cultural dimension that came with integrating hip-hop—it was a Black art form. Unlike jazz (which Tommy appreciated) or gospel, hip-hop was radical, raw, and in your face. It was not designed to make middle-aged white men feel cool. Hip-hop didn't really *need* his kind of "hit maker" anymore, and I think it threatened him by endangering his power. And yet he couldn't deny the evidence.

My instincts were making hits. So he stopped fighting me so much on the samples, artists, and producers I wanted to work with.

I knew hip-hop added exciting, young energy to almost any other sound if done correctly. I knew Puff would be the perfect producing partner for the "Fantasy Remix" I was dreaming about. I was so happy with what producer Dave "Jam" Hall and I had done with the single. For the sample, I chose "Genius of Love" by the Tom Tom Club. It was a perfect fun, swinging party song, but I knew it could go to even more interesting places. We kept the Tom Tom Club sample for the remix, even emphasizing and bringing it out further. Puff was pretty enthusiastic about my idea of featuring Ol' Dirty Bastard from the Wu-Tang Clan—that was the *real* genius of love.

The suits at the "corporate morgue" weren't crazy about O.D.B. They actually thought he was certifiably crazy and that I was about to throw my entire fan base into shock. Tommy generally considered rap background noise, and had no idea that O.D.B. was about to bring the noise to "Fantasy." They didn't understand how diverse my fans were, nor did they understand the global impact of the Wu-Tang Clan (I mean "Up from the 36 Chambers!"—come on!). Wu-Tang was a movement, a once-in-a-generation type of group, and O.D.B. was such an extra-special member. I truly believed he would bring something incredible to the remix. Puff got the vision and ran with it. There were also a couple of cool A&R folks who helped me smuggle in one of the greatest rap features of all time.

Of course, the session for O.D.B. was late in the evening, and after I was swooped up by Tommy and brought back to Sing Sing for the night. I had taken a bath, which had become for me a kind of reverse baptismal ritual by which I transitioned from young global recording artist back to caged Westchester wife. I slipped into a white silk nightgown, tiptoed across the white wool carpeting of the master bedroom, and climbed into our opulent bed, outfitted with 1,000 thread count white Egyptian sheets and what seemed like a hundred white down pillows.

Tommy was already in bed in his white cotton pajamas. His side of the bed seemed a million miles away. The sterility had become routine. Suddenly the phone rang. I answered and started to squeal with excitement.

Someone from the studio called to report O.D.B. had completed his session. "Wait, wait," I said, "let me put you on speaker." I pressed speakerphone for Tommy to hear:

Yo, New York in the house
Is Brooklyn in the house?
Uptown in the house
Shaolin, are you in the house?
Boogie Down, are you in the house?
Sacramento in the house
Atlanta, Georgia, are you in the house?
West Coast, are you in the house?
Japan, are you in the house?
Everybody, are you in the house?
Baby, baby come on
Baby come on, baby come on!

Wheeeeeeeeeee! I couldn't contain myself. I may have even started jumping up and down on the bed! Then I heard the next lines: "Me and Mariah go back like babies and pacifiers! Old Dirt Dog no liar. Keeping fantasy hot like fire!"

That was IT! Ol' Dirty Bastard spit crazy brilliance and scorched our pristine white bedroom with the grime and righteous fun I'd been craving! It kept going, and all his crazy ad-libs sent me into euphoric giggles. I reveled in it. I was just screaming and laughing and whooping. But then I looked over at Tommy. His head was cocked to the side with a look of confusion he couldn't contain.

"The fuck is that?" he blurted. "*I* can do that. Get the fuck outta here with that." There it was. That was what he had to say about one of the most unique, amazing things I had ever heard! I think he was in shock, or maybe he *did* think he could do it and that all of us were nuts. It was as if the Starship *Enterprise* had beamed me into another galaxy, far, far away from Tommy. Music was our only true bond, and now we were light-years apart.

Now, *I* was crazy about "Fantasy Remix." It was one of the first of my songs that I played over and over before it was out on the radio. I'd play it on the ride back to Bedford (I'm sure Tommy *loved* that). It felt like all the fun I had missed out on in my childhood. It made me feel happy. O.D.B.'s energy was something everyone could relate to—he was your loving, fun-ass uncle who gets drunk at all the festivities, at Christmas dinner, the cookout, Thanksgiving. O.D.B. and Puff just really helped me create something enduring that all kinds of people connected to. That remix gave us lines and feelings we would use forever. He even brought back Donny and Marie Osmond with "I'm a little bit country, I'm a little bit rock 'n' roll!" Like what made him bust out and sing *that*? Genius. And now when I'm singing it onstage and we have his vocals, it sounds like he's saying "I'm a little bit Roc and Roe"—that always gets me.

Making the "Fantasy" video was really important to me too. I wanted it to feel fun and carefree. In my opinion (which was so rarely considered) almost all of my videos weren't *right*. Tommy never allowed me to work with the directors I wanted, the hot ones at the time, like Herb Ritts, or the cool fashion stylists, who would bring an edge to my look; these were creative people he couldn't completely control. His package for me was so mainstream, but this one, there was no homogenizing this one. Necessity is the mother of invention, right? So, since I couldn't have a director I wanted to work with, I decided to direct the video myself. It was a simple concept: young, fun, and free. It was shot on location at Westchester's Playland Park in Rye, New York. Everyone can relate to the joy and abandon of an amusement park, the feeling of throwing your hands up in the air on the roller coaster. That's the pure fun I wanted to capture. Simple elements, like roller-blading cute kids, bright colors, cutoff shorts, and a clown. There was a night dance sequence with a crew of fresh B-boys and that was pretty much it. That was the pop version. For the remix video, I wanted O.D.B. to do for the video what he had done on the song: bring a zany, grimy element to it.

The day of O.D.B.'s shoot was overcast, and we had one simple setup for him on the boardwalk. I went into his dressing room for our first face-to-face meeting bearing a gift—a silver flask engraved with his initials. We talked over the concept—which, again, was pretty simple, because I didn't want anything to overshadow his performance (as if it were possible for anything to upstage O.D.B.). I told him about the idea of tying the clown up on the pole and really featuring his grills. He was down with all the action, but he had some kind of problem with his wardrobe and wanted a wig.

"I want a wig," he kept saying, "like one of them mothafuckas from the sixties. Like Al Green. I'm like this generation's Al Green."

"Oooooh, I don't know about Al Gweeeeen, but you definitely are something incredible," I respectfully responded. He was already in his full-blown drunk uncle mode. I had to send the stylist out to the mall with him so he could get exactly what he was envisioning. Mind you, we were in Westchester (it was my video, but I was still in Tommy's territory).

When they returned, after an hour or two, the stylist was a wreck. Apparently, O.D.B. was singing and shouting and "woahhhhhhhing" and drankin' all through the mall! But his look was perfect, the elongated and baggy proportions were just right for his dancing and weird, wonderful movements. He used his sleeves and his hood as props. It was spot on. And the scene where he's bare-chested in the straight mushroom wig, with the pointy shades—he was giving a little more Ike Turner than Al Green, but whatever it was, it was unforgettable! His performance was all him, and it was perfect. I know O.D.B. had some real trouble on his soul, but he brought nothing but joy to the remix, to the video, and to my world.

R.I.P. O.D.B.

❧

"Fantasy" was a big record. It was the first single to debut at number one on the Billboard Hot 100 in history by a female artist and the second artist to ever do it (the first was Michael Jackson with "You're Not Alone"). It held the top spot for eight consecutive weeks and remained on the charts for a total of twenty-three weeks. It was my ninth number-one single. Even the critics liked "Fantasy" and the remix (some *really* liked it)—the entire *Daydream* album did amazingly well: certified diamond.

As an album it had some really special enduring singles, like "Always Be My Baby" and, of course, "One Sweet Day," whose lyrics and music I cowrote with Boyz II Men, inspired by the passing of my incredible friend and collaborator David Cole and their tour manager, both of whom died too soon. "One Sweet Day" was the longest running number-one single in American history for twenty-three years.

I was set to perform "Fantasy" and do some other bits at the twenty-third annual American Music Awards, where I was nominated in several categories. It was a big night for me, but winning the best female pop artist and best female R & B artist awards was not the most memorable moment for me.

When I wasn't onstage or waiting in the wings I sat in the front row next to Tommy. We were both outfitted in couture tension (the cover shoot of *Daydream* by photographer Steven Meisel, who was arguably the most prominent in the fashion industry at the time, set the look of the chic black-is-the-new-black style for the tone of the album's promotion). Ironically, my outfit for this performance was giving you pseudo "Militant Mariah" vibes, with black leather pants, a black leather trench coat, and a black turtleneck (I'm sure Tommy liked it because the only skin exposed was my face). Maybe it was a premonition of what was ahead.

Because I had more than just the "Fantasy" performance to do that night, I had a trailer behind the Shrine Auditorium for wardrobe changes and such. I was returning to the trailer to get into another ensemble. Security was everywhere, so I didn't need to be followed for the short walk to where all the artists' trailers were parked behind the theater.

As I stepped out in a complete rush to get back to the stage, I noticed a white Rolls-Royce quietly, slowly approaching. Just as my toes touched the asphalt, the gleaming elegant vehicle came to a gentle stop right in front of my door. It was as if time itself had slowed to a stop. The tinted passenger window glided down.

He was alone, leaning back in the driver's seat, so that the arm that gripped the leather steering wheel was nearly straight. He propped his head back just enough that his luxurious eyelashes didn't cast a shadow and obscure his alert and amazing dark eyes that looked into mine.

"Hey, Mariah," he said softly, my name pouring out of his lips like smoke. Then that spectacular smile burst through everything. In an instant, the window went back up, and Tupac rolled away.

Had it not been for a production assistant or someone calling me back to the stage, back to earth, I may have stayed there stunned for hours. I did my bit onstage and returned to my stiff seat next to Tommy. My heart fluttered nervously, but he didn't know. No one knew. I'd just had Tupac Shakur's eyez all on *me*.

Though I was recording *Daydream*, parts of my life were still quite a nightmare. I was writing and singing upbeat songs like "Always Be My Baby," and sweeping ballads like "One Sweet Day." I was totally inspired by the creative risk we took in collaborating with O.D.B. on the "Fantasy" remix. I was exploring my musical range, but I was also filled with rage. It's always been a challenge for me to acknowledge and express anger. My personal life was suffocating during *Daydream*, and I was in desperate need of a release.

Music and humor have been my two great releases—they have been how I survived all the anguish in my life. So while I had a full band and studio time at the Hit Factory for that album, I created an alter-ego artist and her Ziggy Stardust–like spoof band. My character was a dark-haired brooding Goth girl (a version of her, Bianca, showed up a few years later in the "Heartbreaker" video) who wrote and sang ridiculous tortured songs. At the end of each session I would go off to a corner and, without over-thinking it, quickly scribble down some lyrics. In five minutes I'd have a song:

> *I am!*
> *vinegar and water*
> *I am!*
> *Someone's ugly daughter*
> *I am wading in the water*

And I ammm!
Like an open blister
I am!
Jack The Ripper's Sister
I am!
Just a lonely drifter

I'd bring my little alt-rock song to the band and hum a silly guitar riff. They would pick it up and we would record it immediately. It was irreverent, raw, and urgent, and the band got into it. I actually started to love some of the songs. I would fully commit to my character. I was playing with the style of the breezy-grunge, punk-light white female singers who were popular at the time. You know the ones who seemed to be so carefree with their feelings and their image. They could be angry, angsty, and messy, with old shoes, wrinkled slips, and unruly eyebrows, while every move I made was so calculated and manicured. I wanted to break free, let loose, and express my misery—but I also wanted to laugh.

I totally looked forward to doing my alter-ego band sessions after *Daydream* each night. Tommy was off in Italy a lot at the time, so I had a little space and air to do this bizarre, fun thing that was just for me. The band loved it, and we ended up with an album's worth of songs, which we mixed and everything. My jokey "anger release" project ended up being a weirdly good satirical, underground, alternative rock *thing*. When Tommy and some of the other label folks heard it, they couldn't believe we had done all that while recording *Daydream*. I even got the art department at the label to design a cover I had conceptualized. I wrote the title with pink lipstick over a Polaroid picture Tommy had taken of a giant dead cockroach in Italy. I told them to add a smashed-up eye shadow makeup palette. They laid it out, and it was perfectly grungy and cheeky. I got a lot of personal satisfaction out of making that "alternative" album. I made the sarcastic hardcore head-banging record no one was ever going to allow me to make. My assistant and I used to blast it in the car riding up the back streets of Westchester, singing at the top of our lungs, giving me a brief moment to be outwardly angry, irreverent, and free.

There was a song on the album called "Crave" (that I eventually renamed "Demented"). Tommy knew I had a talent for recognizing talent, so he created a boutique record label for me that I named Crave, inspired by the song.

The first act on the Crave label was a hip-hop group called the Negro League (they have cameos in "The Roof" video). They named themselves after famed Black baseball players like Satchel Paige and Cool Papa Bell, who'd had to form their own league because of segregation. They were young, fun, and *all* of them were fine. I just loved rolling into a party with them—they would chant "NEGROES! NEGROES!" Nothing ambiguous about that, *dahling*.

Later, when it became clear to Tommy that the marriage was not going to make it, Crave quickly became defunct, and the alt album conveniently disappeared. There was one small, sweet residual benefit from Crave and the Negro League. I cast one of my friends from the group as my shirtless, motorcycle-riding, lip-licking love interest in Jermaine's "Sweetheart" video. I called him "Flask" (which was close to his name) because he was so nervous on the flight over to Bilbao, Spain, that he drank and got smashed. But his hangover played well on film, emphasizing his already dreamy eyes. He was my sweetheart for a very short time right after a very tough breakup, which I'll get to soon enough. He was fun, fine, and just the thing to lick my wounds.

ONE SUMMER NIGHT,
WE RAN AWAY
FOR A WHILE . . .

In the wake of the success of the "Fantasy" remix featuring Ol' Dirty Bastard I now had some ammunition that made it slightly easier for me to work with people outside of Tommy's jurisdiction. I was starting to reach out to what I thought were the right collaborators, with whom I could achieve the sound I'd been hearing for a while, which included infusing hip-hop and working with a diversity of rappers. However, the old guard of A&R and music executives at the major labels didn't know how to control or contain hip-hop and looked at me sideways for my suggestions.

Rap was making a lot of money really fast, so the smart execs raced to try to get a piece of it. And Tommy was no exception. He was smart. Though he'd always had a more traditional pop/ adult contemporary style in mind for me, he couldn't deny that the industry and the audience were shifting. It was well established that Tommy didn't particularly like rap or rappers, but he was a shrewd businessman, and despite his initial resistance, he understood that I had my finger on the cultural pulse. I was determined for my next single to sound more like the music I was hearing in my head all day, the music I'd been dreaming of. So began my work on *Butterfly*.

I had gotten to a place where I was trusted to choose people I was inspired by, not the predicable players. One of the most talented was a suave and scrappy producer out of Atlanta with a brilliant ear and instinct, Jermaine Dupri. Like me, Jermaine got in the game early. He was fiercely ambitious and super talented; by the time he was nineteen years old he'd discovered, developed, written, and produced multiplatinum hits for Kris Kross and secured a joint-venture deal for a record label, SoSo Def Recordings, with Sony and Columbia.

I was really inspired by the work he did on "Just Kickin' It" with the fresh girl group also out of Atlanta—Xscape. It was intentionally "under-produced"; his track choices were sonically raw—just what I was looking for. Once I heard that song, I knew we should work together. Jermaine—aka JD, aka Jermash (as I call him)—and I instantly creatively clicked. As producers, we both had a fierce discipline in the studio, but we could also approach the music with abandon, unafraid to try new things. We could focus and flow together. It was a rare relationship, and we knew it.

Our first collaboration was "Always Be My Baby," on *Daydream*. It was the first song we wrote together, but it was as if we'd done it a million times before. We sat in the studio and approached it like a blank canvas—sonically organic. With the gifted Manuel Seal on keyboards, we created this cool, yet endearing, classic song.

In order to make the label happy, I had to deliver several versions of a single, including one that was up-tempo and simple, scrubbed of all ad-libs and "urban inflections." In order to make myself happy and make sure a song I liked could work for the club kids (who have always given me life), I set aside time to make remixes, sometimes several on one song. I often did complete rewrites and all-new vocal tracks rather than recycling from the original—especially when I worked with David Morales. We would completely re-envision a song. We often worked late at night, when I could steal a moment for myself. David would come to the studio, and I'd tell him he could do whatever he wanted with the song. I'd have a couple splashes of wine, and we would just go wherever the spirit took us—which were almost always high-energy dance tracks with big, brand-new vocals. It was one way I found liberation while locked up in Sing Sing.

I had a remix idea for "Always Be My Baby" and asked JD to bring
Xscape and a big, exciting young female rapper out of Chicago named
Da Brat who had a hit record, "Funkdafied," that JD had produced, to my
studio. Knowing how smoothly JD and I worked together, I calculated
that we could bang out a remix and shoot a cool docu-style video all in
the same session. It was an efficient move. It was a very big feat to secure a
hit record; you had to be strategic in your creative choices. We chose "Tell
Me If You Still Care" by the S.O.S. Band as the sample, thinking that it
would be palatable for a crossover audience, and then having Da Brat rap
on it would make it appealing for a hip-hop audience.

JD was down. I knew how I wanted the remix to sound, with
Supremes-style backgrounds. I had to redo all the vocals 'cause it was in
a different key. But because Jermaine was so adept in the studio and so
in tune with all of our styles, I knew he could bring it all together. The
session was set—So So Def was coming to Sing Sing.

As you approach the grounds of Sing Sing, a security station sits to the
right, obscured by trees. Inside were multiple screens connected to all the
cameras throughout the house and on the property. JD made his way up
the long driveway toward the enormous house that rose like a castle from
a thick, fluffy blanket of glistening snow. He wasn't prepared for such
grandeur. I didn't realize the rare air I was orbiting in until I caught that
moment of recognition on JD's face when he stepped out of the car. The
scale and opulence of the mansion suggested not simply "music star" but
the next stratosphere. Sing Sing was supersized. It was the physical rep-
resentation of the combined power and influence of me and Tommy, a
music-industry power couple. And in that moment, we were *the* music-
industry power couple. When he got to the massive front door, Jermaine
looked like Richard Pryor in *The Wiz*. Honestly, the whole lot of us
looked like a group of children playing in a fairy-tale kingdom. But in
actuality it was more like visiting day "upstate." The joy was temporary.

It was refreshing and a much-welcomed reprieve to have a group of
fresh artists at my house to create something we would love and respect.

These were my peers, steeped in hip-hop music and culture—and we were down to make a *hit*. Though we were all very young, collectively we were worth hundreds of millions of dollars in record sales. But once you walked through the gates of Sing Sing, that didn't mean much. We were now all under surveillance. JD, Xscape, and Da Brat took note of the excessive presence of bodyguards and security, but it wasn't immediately clear to them exactly who or what they were guarding.

Jermaine was so focused and serious, he went straight to the studio to get acclimated and organized. He sat at the console, in full command, like the captain of a spaceship. While he worked on the beat, the girls from Xscape and I vibed and talked through the mechanics of the background vocals. It was probably the first time I ever had five women close to my age at my house. Xscape was Kandi Burruss, Tameka "Tiny" Cottle, and Tamika and LaTocha Scott. With their elaborate Atlanta hairstyles, glossy lips, and oversized sportswear, they were super fly and fully captured the glamorous-yet-chill look of women in hip-hop during those years. Their sound and style was exactly the right vibe for the remix and video. I wanted us all to look easy and real, not manipulated by "development executives."

From the studio you could see the massive French windows, which led to the indoor pool area with its museumlike high ceilings. On clear days the reflection of clouds would float on the water's surface from the outdoor pool, which was beyond the walls. From the outdoor pool you could see the pond, and from there, on a clear night, you could catch the twinkling lights of Manhattan way in the distance. We hung out in the marble room with the pool, playing cards, drinking, cracking jokes—almost like actual girlfriends.

And then there was Da Brat. Her energy was irresistible; I adored her, instantly. I was very reserved around new people back then. I had become shy, and it took me a long time to trust (it still does), but Brat broke right through the wall of my fearful past, on day one. We had kindred, childlike spirits, only Brat fearlessly flaunted her little-girl soul, while I was desperately hiding mine. A lot of effort, strategy, and money went into creating my classic-storybook-princess façade, but Brat, with all her irreverent adolescent spirit, armed in a big puffy coat and little braids and barrettes, burst right through my bubble. By this point, my life was so controlled by Tommy and his cronies, I could barely see it anymore. But Brat, with her spontaneity, brashness, and cool-assness, spotted my inner little girl right away and shook her awake.

Brat was from the West Side of Chicago and was clearly mesmerized by the extraness of Sing Sing. There was absolutely no posturing from her; she walked right in the door like, "Dayyyyumm!" I took her on a tour of the house. She never tried to contain her wonder as we ran from room to room. But we were not alone—security was always right there behind us, like a shadow. When we moved, they moved. For the past four years I had been constantly working on such an intense level. I had so many decisions to make, so many people counting on me and looking to me for answers and a payday. If I had any "free" time, I spent it with Tommy or people his age, people on his payroll. I hadn't had any real fun in such a long time, and Da Brat was a one-woman party.

I just wanted to have fun, but I knew we were being watched and listened to. There were cameras and recording devices throughout the house. I wasn't sure where they were all planted—but I knew of at least one place they weren't.

Our next stop on the tour was the master bedroom. Brat was so funny; she squealed when she saw the giant television screen rise, as if by a magic trick, from a case at the foot of our elaborate bed. Brat was no girlie girl— she was wearing oversized jeans, a polo shirt, and Timberland boots—but I made a big deal out of showing her my Coco Chanel–inspired closet and insisted she see my massive fancy shoe collection. I knew if I could get her in the shoe room, security wouldn't see us; I'd designed it and was pretty sure there were no cameras or listening devices among my Manolos. I chatted loudly about stilettoes as I slowly closed the door.

We sat on the floor of my shoe closet and kicked it for a bit. We were both Aries, both super silly, and both believed in an awesome God. I was having so much fun with Brat, but I knew we couldn't stay hidden for too long; surely security would get suspicious and expose my one safe room in the house.

I never knew who was listening, so I whispered to Brat, "Want to go get some french fries?" In any other reality, this would have been a mundane suggestion, but in mine, it was about to be a full-scale caper.

As we emerged from the closet, I put my finger to my mouth and pointed at the wall, giving her the signal to be quiet and follow my lead. I chirped on about showing her around the rest of the property, then announced that I wanted to quickly show her the cars. We skipped along to the garage. Inside there was a fleet of cars. Several of them were mine, most of which I never drove, in part because I was always being driven. I pointed at the black Mercedes convertible and told Brat to get in quickly. I always kept the keys inside the car, so in a matter of seconds I had the engine going. I threw it into gear, and we whipped around the cul-de-sac, then sped down the driveway and out onto the open road. Suddenly, there I was: flying down the street in my sports car, with my new, cool homegirl, laughing deep and loud in the bright wintery afternoon sun. It was exhilarating. Brat and I had broken out da Big House!

While we were out playing Black Thelma and Louise, *Escape from Alcatraz* was not playing so well back at Storybook Manor. I understood that security was necessary, but why was it necessary for them all to be white, with blue eyes and black guns? They were going berserk. Before we got the mile or so down the road to the Burger King, Brat's phone began to ring. I could hear JD yelling on the other end: "Yo, Brat, get the fuck back here; they going crazy!"

Brat laughed into the phone and replied, "I ain't driving; Mariah is!" But JD was clearly upset.

"This ain't fucking funny," he said. "Tommy is bugging out; he got everybody running around looking for y'all; they got guns out and shit!"

Brat shot back, "Damn, we just going to get french fries, JD! If Mariah wants french fries, we getting fucking french fries!" She abruptly slammed her phone shut, and we proceeded to Burger King.

For the twenty or so minutes, while Brat and I sat in the car eating those fries and cracking jokes, I reveled in the simple excitement of being young. I'll never forget it. Jermaine must have called every five minutes, begging us to come back. He went from being angry and annoyed to being nervous to being afraid. Brat was quickly realizing how serious our momentary escape had been. With every ring, she looked at me with increasing concern and sadness. We were really only a mile away, and people were *panicking*.

She said something like, "This ain't right. This is your shit, Mariah. Jermaine, Xscape—we all here because of *you*. You done sold millions of records, girl. You live in a damn palace. You have everything, but if you can't be free to go to fucking Burger King when you want, you ain't got nothing. You need to get out of there." This time she wasn't laughing. If Da Brat, a nineteen-year-old female rapper from the West Side, is afraid for you, you know the situation has got to be dire, *dahling*.

When we pulled up to the property, there were more than ten security personnel standing outside, preparing two large black SUVs to go on a search. They stopped me before I could get up the driveway to the garage, as if I was a fugitive crossing the border. I was promptly whisked back into the house and back into the studio—back into my tower, my jail.

JD was visibly shaken. My spontaneous, mischievous little scheme had had real consequences for him. I hadn't brought my phone, so security had no way of contacting me. There would be hell to pay from Tommy for such sloppy surveillance. While Jermaine was in the studio, concentrating on laying down the beat for the track, security had busted in and interrogated him, with their guns out in broad daylight. I assume they figured that since Jermaine was the producer, Brat was *his* artist, so he was in charge, he was responsible. They yelled at him: "Where is she? *Tell us where she is!*" Of course, he had no idea where we were. He was working. He was at my studio. This was the first time he'd been at my house. He was only twenty-three years old.

After Tommy was assured of my safe return, the situation settled down. Brat rolled a fat blunt, but God knows she couldn't smoke it around me, so she just held on to it throughout the shoot, like a security blanket, and began to work on her rap for the remix. Her nerves were a bit of a wreck now too. In addition to everything else, she probably felt guilty we had caused such drama while recording her first big rap feature with me. But when the mic was hot and the camera was rolling, Da Brat killed it. Her

delivery was happy and hard, playing with clever references and sophisticated rhythms inside the space of the song:

> *Who rocks your Music Box*
> *And breaks down the structure*
> *You fantasize as you visualize me as your Dreamlover*
> *Fuck with your Emotions Unplugged in your Daydream*
>
> —"Always Be My Baby (Remix)"

We got it done: a remix, a video, and a prison break all in one day. You
would never know from the video I directed that we were surrounded by
armed security. I was a master at editing out the pressure.

"Mother" Emma Cutright

Nana Reese in front of her church with her pocket book

Alfred Roy at four years old

[LEFT] Nana Reese with her Bible

Addie looking glamorous

My mother's mother

Pat in her opera days

Alfred Roy in the military

Little One

With Santa Claus for the first time

My cousin Vinny
at age three

With Cuddles the bear on a trip
to Mount Washington with Father

Me with the late bohemian Pat

Hodel with flowers from Alfred Roy

"Far from the Home I Love"

Posing for the guncles

Detangled and swept away

Chess with Alfred Roy

Early on you face . . .

"Lullaby of Birdland" with Clint at the piano

Wayward child

Little Mariah and Pat

Cee Cee, me, and Chris

Ninth grade

Beauty school! 500 hours

Looking In

"The Distance"

With Josefin, making it happen
in the city

Me, Mike, and Shawn. Just for laughs.

With Shawn at Christmas in Aspen

Behind the scenes at a genuine diva moment with the incomparable Ms. Whitney Houston

The two dresses
and Ms. Ross

With Morris, the icon

Theatre producer Kermit
Bloomgarden with Arthur
Miller and Marilyn
Monroe and the piano

Me "with" Marilyn

With The Queen

Backstage "moment" at the World Music Awards in Monaco

Backstage in Taipei on the *Butterfly* tour

Me and Kris surviving *Glitter*

Serving a dip with my dear friend Treymond

[LEFT] Living for my Lagerfeld dress with Rae Rae and Kris

From my pinup board in Franco's garden in Capri

At the Lanesborough hotel in London
with Bailey the puppy

Alternative "Riah"

With Luis Miguel,
the Latin Elvis

Opulence and decadence on Roberto Cavalli's yacht

[LEFT] Bianca after dark

A puppy love moment . . .

President Obama making Roe laugh

With Nelson Mandela

Prince helped me on a soul level
when I needed it the most, and
through his music he continues
to save the day, every day.

With my all-time favorite,
Stevie Wonder

Liron and I having a laugh

Shawn and me with sunflowers for Alfred Roy on our last Father's Day together

Roc and Roe in Italy learning to swim

Alfred Roy in the Porsche

My son, Rocky, in his grandfather Alfred Roy's car

SIDE EFFECTS

I was a girl, you were "the man"
I was too young to understand
I was naïve
I just believed
Everything that you told me
Said you were strong, protecting me
Then I found out that you were weak
Keeping me there under your thumb
'Cause you were scared that I'd become much
More than you could handle
Shining like a chandelier
That decorated every room
Inside the private hell we built
And I dealt with it
Like a kid I wished I could fly away
But instead I kept my tears inside
Because I knew if I started I'd keep crying for the rest of my life with you
I finally built up the strength to walk don't regret it but I still live with the side effects

—"Side Effects"

When Tommy suggested we go to couples therapy, I was sur-prised. Unsurprisingly, he told me it would have to be with *his* therapist, who he had been seeing for years. Neverthe-less, this was a monumental step for both of us. Our careers, and con-sequently our marriage, were constantly in the public spotlight. But no one had ever been allowed into the dark interior of our relationship. I'd never had anyone to confide in about how I was living—or not living. I had carried the burden of believing that because I was able to write, sing, and produce my songs, become famous, and gain access to unimaginable wealth, I didn't deserve personal happiness too. I truly believed everything good in my life would cost me, and that Tommy's control was the price for my success.

Honestly I was really only trying to gain five minutes of peace—the opportunity to be able to walk down the stairs into my own kitchen to grab a bite to eat without the hiss of the intercom and his menacing "What ya doin'?" buzzing out of it. Also, I didn't trust anyone—by then I was estranged from my immediate family, and everyone around me was connected to Tommy and scared of him. I knew that anything I said would get back to him, and I would suffer his constant rage.

I had started to develop hives-like breakouts. I went to see the dermatologist, who assured me that my otherwise unblemished skin was having a reaction to severe stress. It was suggested I make some dietary changes and add a few new cleansing routines to help soothe the symptoms. When I told Tommy the doctor's diagnosis (it was not good business for your top-selling artist to be hived out), he barked back, "*Stress*?! Fuck you got to be stressed about?" Lawd, let me count the ways.

Therapy was a lifesaver. Our therapist was a kind, older Jewish woman with short amber hair and alert eyes. She had a cozy office in her classic Westchester home. I liked her more than I thought I would, as I assumed she would be on "Tommy's team," but she was refreshingly impartial and a real pro. And he respected her. (Which was a *major* thing.) At that point in my life, I didn't have many relationships with stable, professional adults whose livelihoods weren't connected to my record sales. There were very few places where I wasn't overcome with anxiety: first, there had been the recording studio, and now there was the therapist's office.

Though even in my "safe" spaces, Tommy's presence would infect the atmosphere. I would be in the recording studio writing and vibing with producers or other artists, and he would often crash in at 6:00 or 7:00 p.m. to pick me up, as if I was his nine-to-five "office girl" and not a recording artist who had her own creative process, which you couldn't place on a timer. (Not to mention, who collaborated with various rappers and hip-hop producers, many of whom—like me—don't recognize time, especially *day*time.) As soon as he walked in, tension would eclipse the lightness of creating; all laughing would cease, and we'd all shrink a little to make room for the pressure that accompanied him. And while I can't say I felt completely safe or equal in the therapist's office (or anywhere), it was the closest thing we had to a neutral space where Tommy and I could attempt to communicate.

It was a profound breakthrough for me that she listened to both of us objectively. And she *believed* me. She had been treating him for years, like Tony Soprano and Jennifer Melfi, except she was more mother figure than sexy scholar. She might have been the only person who had some kind of insight into his psyche and could completely conceive of the repressive and paranoid conditions he imposed on me in our marriage and home life. She was the first to recognize and name the abuse I was living under. I already knew the havoc it was wreaking on my spirit, but she identified the damage it was doing to me emotionally.

After some of our sessions she would ask Tommy to go sit and wait for me in the car, so that she and I could decompress and speak honestly. Once, during our alone time, I asked her, pleading really, "Why can't he just let me go to the spa or to the movies, or do *anything*? I did nothing wrong!"

She took a pause and said, in her dry, matter-of-fact New York accent, "Sweetie, it's not *normal*. Why are you acting as if you're dealing with a normal situation? It's not normal!"

But I had no frame of reference for normal. Our marriage had been a demolition site long before we made it to therapy.

🦋

After our eight-year relationship my life had become like a psychological thriller. It had gotten to the point where Tommy's very presence to me was a hostile occupation. Tiptoeing around and protecting myself was my daily existence. I never thought I would be strong enough to leave Tommy. I thought I would just continue to deal with it. I prayed that he would realize how he was stifling me, and that he would do the work and things would change. Some days I really did just want to be like Peter Pan and fly the fuck away. Mostly I tried to just take whatever shit he was giving, no matter how outrageous, and just hope he would become more lenient. Being married to him really was the equivalent of having a strict father who ruled with fear and controlled everything you did. I kept hoping he would just ease up and give me space to just be, so that we would have a chance. It was our only chance.

I wrote in *Butterfly* what I had so hoped Tommy would be able to see, and say, to me:

> *Blindly I imagined*
> *I could keep you under glass*
> *Now I understand to hold you*
> *I must open up my hands*
> *And watch you rise*
> *Spread your wings and prepare to fly*
> *For you have become a butterfly*
> *Oh fly abandonedly into the sun*
> *If you should return to me*
> *We truly were meant to be*
> *So spread your wings and fly*
> *Butterfly*

Right away Tommy's therapist advocated for me to have more independence. She supported the idea that I had to create some boundaries for myself and encouraged me to go places on my own. It seemed like a miracle—I'd never had an ally before. She recommended we do things in stages, something like probation. But unlike probation, the purpose was not for me to get reacclimated to society, but to moderate Tommy's behavior, since he was so extreme. He had control over me as an artist. He had control over my personal life. He had control over everyone in my professional life. And even though I was the biggest artist on the label, he was still the most powerful person in my life, and seemingly everyone's life. Everyone was scared to death of Tommy—the executives, the management, legal, other artists—*everyone*.

After ferocious negotiation with the therapist, we agreed the first step toward independence was that I would finally attend acting classes. For years I had wanted acting training. Songs are like monologues, so I knew I had good raw material and certainly a range of emotions and life experiences to draw from. But I hungered to learn some craft, to explore, develop, and discipline another passion brewing inside me. As with singing, from an early age I was obsessed with films and often memorized lines as an escape. Acting was both a dream and something I felt I needed to do. Tommy "agreed" I would have private acting lessons—unsurprisingly, again, with a coach he knew and approved. Like the therapist, this acting coach was very qualified and worked with incredible, world-class actors.

The acting coach was an ample woman who seemed to thoroughly enjoy her voluminous breasts and the fleshiness of her body. She moved with abandon. She swished around in layers of Stevie Nicks–esque flowy garments and made grand gestures with her arms, even during casual conversation. She was part earth-mother hippie, part privileged princess, part aspiring guru, and I liked her.

She taught out of her bohemian-luxe Upper West Side apartment. Like her, the space was eclectic and welcoming. It was filled with the scent of Nag Champa, which impressed me the most because it was immediately soothing, and back then, I was not easily soothed.

In our first session, she had me lie on a mat on the floor and close my eyes to do some basic deep breathing and relaxation exercises. Sitting in her chair on high, she instructed me to breathe deeply and try to relax. "Relaaaaaaaax." (Easier said than done, lady.)

"Close your eyes. Breathe. Breathe." I was struggling but listening and trying to follow her instruction. "Relax, Mariah. Relax your muscles; breathe and relax your body." It was then I realized my shoulders were shoved up to my earlobes. Even lying on the floor I was in a tense fight-or-flight stance—mostly fight; I'd been protecting myself for so very long.

"Breathe. Breathe. Check in with yourself," she said calmly. Check in with myself? I didn't know what that meant.

Sensing my resistance, she said, "Go to a place where you feel safe."

Nothing.

"Do you have a place where you feel safe, Mariah? Go there. It can be from your childhood."

Nothing.

"Imagine you're little, you're six. Go there."

I was in the deli house. Not safe.

"Maybe you're a little older. Go there."

I was back in the shack. Not safe.

She kept pushing, thinking certainly there had to be a place. "It could be sometime more recent. Just go to a safe place."

I was feeling nothing in nowhere. I could only feel the hard floor flat against my back as I searched around in my own emptiness. I was looking for a space in my mind and waiting for a comforting vision to arrive. There was nothing. I was blank. I opened my eyes and stared at the ceiling. Suddenly I felt cold and alone. It dawned on me that there was nowhere, inside or out, where I felt safe.

Then the coach asked, "How are you doing, Mariah?" A wave of sadness rushed through me and poured out in a deluge of tears. My entire being was heaving, sobbing; I was unsure if I would ever be able to stop.

Eventually the storm of tears subsided. I don't think I had cried openly the entire time I had been in the relationship with Tommy. Crying with him would've taken too much cleanup, and the emotional cost was too expensive. He'd surely punish me if I cried. *He* was the one who cried during some of our more explosive fights. And I would end up consoling *him*, completely abandoning my needs, my pain. It was ruthlessly manipulative.

Don't tell me you're sorry you hurt me
How many times can I give in?
How many battles can you win?
Oh, don't beg for mercy tonight.
Tonight, 'cause I can't take anymore

—"Everything Fades Away"

However, the crying exercise was a release, albeit a tiny one. I'd been holding so much for so long. I began to breathe, a little.

My acting coach hovered over me, and I could smell essential oils, patchouli perhaps, seeping from her pores. She placed her hands on my shoulders and began to gently push them down toward my ribcage.

"Let go of the fighting stance and just breathe," she whispered. I hadn't realized how high and tight I was gripping my body. My breakdown was encouraging to her; I had freed some of my suppressed feelings. Now she told me she wanted me to "feel free in the body." I was a bit wobbly when I stood to watch her demonstrate the exercise. She closed her eyes and began rolling her shoulders from side to side, letting her head fall back and around with them. Then her hips joined in an aimless sway. She lifted her arms up and began flailing them like those weird inflatable tube men at the car wash. "Free in the body!" she chanted. "Come on, get free in the body, Mariah." I was watching her do her erratic, ecstatic dancing and just couldn't make the leap. Just as I couldn't dance for Addie, to prove I was Black, I knew I was *too* Black to do interpretive dance with her, even if it was a private session.

What I remember most clearly was the acting coach telling me I had difficulty accessing my anger. I thought back to something the therapist had once told me: often sadness is anger turned inward. Of course I kept it all inside—how else would I have survived? I realized I couldn't express anger because I was never allowed to. Who was I ever safe to be angry with? Not my brother, certainly not my sister, not Tommy, not my mother, not anyone. There was no safe person and no safe place in my life. There never had been.

That woman-child failing inside
Was on the verge of fading
Thankfully I woke up in time
—"Close My Eyes"

The crush of Tommy was relentless. After countless painful and dramatic fights, and after I began some genuine soul searching, Tommy and I began to broach the notion of temporary separation in therapy. It took a lot of personal work and getting in touch with myself to even touch the concept. I was so scarred on so many levels. The emotional struggles with Tommy had been nonstop, and I couldn't yet even begin to know the effects of the trauma, but getting to where we could discuss a reprieve from the pain was major. He had pulled a lot of strings to tie me up. I really didn't know how I would be able to escape him while he was still alive. He could be incredibly vindictive. And his network was so far-reaching. I had a very real feeling my entire safety was at risk. With a little support and a few new tools, I was able to clearly see that living with him was killing me. I needed to create a place for me to breathe.

I was certain I needed to escape Tommy's fury and access my own, and this would take some help and strategy. Because we were in therapy, I didn't have to be the one to "bring it up." It was the therapist who told Tommy he would lose me forever if he didn't try to give me a little space. So it was discussed as a temporary Band-Aid to "treat it like a separation." She was trying to convince him to let me go hang out with other people, for God's sake—for *my* sake.

After so much prodding and much ado, Tommy agreed to try the therapist's advice and made a deal to take certain steps to see if we could find a way to continue to live together. I remember the therapist saying, in her motherly way, "Mariah has to start going places by herself, Tommy. It's not fair. You're stifling her." I was at a breaking point, and something had to give. I wasn't even asking for much, just a little time with friends. I was drained of my spirit, and at this rate, the relationship was threatening to take the remaining bits of my very soul.

My acting teacher's building was connected by a private passageway to the building next door. It was possible to access the neighboring building by going through the front entrance of her building. It was like something out of the opening of the 1960s comedy show *Get Smart*: you had to go through a nondescript side door and walk down a concrete corridor and through an enclosed back alley, but it was possible to go from building to building without ever going outside.

So I secretly rented a small apartment in the building next to hers. I was able to work with the building's management to arrange to have things brought in for me under a fake name. I had it set up very simply, with a convertible couch so I could sleep—by myself. I would tell Tommy that I was tired from acting class and staying overnight with my teacher, then slip over to my own little place and exit in the morning from my teacher's building. It was sneaky, but I was at the end of my fucking rope! There was always someone watching my every move. This was basic survival.

Later on, my survival cave became my personal office and private studio. I had a simple wall of mirrors installed, and it was there I did the best bodywork in my career with the incomparable Debbie Allen. Ms. Allen had gotten in touch with me and said she wanted to work with me because she really connected with my music. What a Godsend! She was masterful. She analyzed how I moved or didn't move. She taught me stretches and other tools to help liberate and ground me. She worked with me on choreography for performances. She created moves that worked for *me*. She had dancers surround me, literally giving me support. And that was what I had needed for so long—someone to be patient with me as I discovered my own body.

I had been totally disconnected from my body for so long. I only knew how to let myself be completely taken over by a song. I had no clue I fluttered my hands the way I did until I saw one of my early performances on TV! It took the fabulous Kiki Shepard to discover I didn't *really* know how to walk in heels. She pulled me aside and had me walk up and down the stairs on the side of the stage at the Apollo until I got it right. Pow.

Guardian angels do exist—Debbie Allen was surely one of mine.

The therapist put together a plan for me to go out socially without Tommy for the first time. This was major. It was going to be new to me too: I had gone straight from a complicated and careless childhood into the treacherous music industry and a toxic, tumultuous marriage. And I was barely in my midtwenties. But I was finally starting to access a different kind of courage—one that was there to protect my life, not just my songs.

Tommy had been adamant about me not acting because he feared I would be on glamorous sets with attractive actors or directors or whatever. The fact that he conceded to me having an acting coach (who he thought was loyal to *him*) was mildly promising. He didn't have the same pull in Hollywood as he did in the music business. Me taking acting classes in the city perhaps wasn't so threatening to him, because New York was his town and he had eyes everywhere. But me being out with my peers, people my age, for *fun*? That was deeply threatening to him. What was scariest of all was the notion of me being seen without him and, God forbid, photographed without him. He couldn't bear to think people would see Cinderella out at the ball without her prince and savior.

Controlling public perception was vital to Tommy, and before social media and smartphones, it was fairly achievable. So the deal was, we would go to a big event together, be seen, have it documented, and then afterward we'd split up, and I would be able to hang out with my friends. Tommy was likely less afraid of losing me to cheating (which never crossed my mind) and more afraid that he would lose his influence over me, which was far more valuable to him than my fidelity. Though he was opposed, he knew he had made a deal, and in his world, a deal is a *deal*. So we negotiated my first solo flight as a social butterfly.

Our relationship was very much like a teen-and-parent arrangement where independence is earned in increments. I was close in age to a teen, but it was Tommy, clearly my senior, who needed to be taught to be an adult about the matter. It was all so twisted, but we were trying to give *normal* our best attempt, sweetie.

THE MAN FROM
KALAMAZOO

Operation Mariah's Solo Test Flight Night had a strict itinerary: First, Tommy and I would attend the Fresh Air Fund gala together, which we'd done in previous years (*acting* normal). Afterward, I would have dinner with a group of friends (*actually* normal). Being out with Tommy had become such a strained performance, I was riddled with a horrible cocktail of anxiety and boredom.

Fortunately, that night, I knew that some of my peers, like Wanya Morris from Boyz II Men, were also going to be at the gala, so I wouldn't have to wear such a heavy mask all night. I held on to the fact that on the other side of the photo ops, thousand-dollar plates, and platitudes was not the usual silent, suffocating ride back to Westchester together but the possibility of *fun*. I could get through this one. I slid into a chic red floor-length Ralph Lauren matte jersey slip dress and hit the red carpet, propped on Tommy's arm.

All the photos from that night showed us looking in different directions, my body stiff and an awkward smile plastered on my face. There was nothing to smile about. Quite honestly, I was afraid to smile in most photographs, as I'd been told as a little girl that my nose was too wide and smiling made it spread more. That shot of insecurity was followed by a chaser from Sony's artist development executive, a rotund and imposing lady who told me when we first met, before my first record: "This is your flattering side. You should *only* ever be photographed on this side of your face." (It was the side *without* the beauty mark. Who *are* these people? Who. Are. They?)

I was too young and didn't have the confidence to challenge her opinion, so I obeyed. I internalized so many of the damaging and cruel critiques older people had given me as a child and young woman; some have burrowed so deep down in my psyche that I will never be able to root them out entirely. To this day I unconsciously turn to the "flattering side" if there is a camera around; it's a *thing*.

The gala was your typical celebrity-studded chicken-dinner charity event. I sat up straight, sucked in my stomach, and held my breath until it was over. Tommy and I faked it all night without incident. We both had quite a bit of practice in faking it. Then it was over: I had given Tommy his public moment, and now I was free to go! This was a big friggin' deal! I was never allowed to go *anywhere* social without him. I couldn't believe it! I was free to laugh and have fun, like a human being, without being shushed and silenced and sequestered. I felt kind of like Cinderella in reverse; it was the fancy ball that was the chore.

In the 1990s, Giorgio Armani was the pinnacle of a luxury fashion house. Armani was the go-to designer of all the A-listers. Tommy, of course, wore Armani and he was always trying to class it up. And I occasionally wore Armani too. There were several cool and connected people who worked for the designer and hung out with their cool clients. After the gala, our plan was to go to a dinner party at a restaurant that some of the Armani insiders had arranged. My assistant and I went, and Wanya met us there. It was a fab downtown scene.

The lighting in the place was low, and twenty of us were seated in the back against a gigantic wall of windows, around a large dining table crowded with beautiful bottles of wine and candles. The air was electric with playful chatter and laughter. And there was great music playing in the background, with Wanya occasionally breaking out into riffs. It was an ordinary night to everyone else there, but it was a revelation to me, being out socially with my peers and listening to the music of my time.

Though I was still being watched, I felt lighter than I had in a long time. I felt young and unchained. It was not uncommon for a dinner party of this kind to have guests come and go in waves, so when Derek Jeter and his friend came in and sat down across from me at the table, they didn't command any of my attention. I found them both ambiguous. After I briefly glanced up at them I thought, *Who are these guys?* my attention went right back to the more interesting dinner guests.

I was never drawn to the jock type, not even in high school, where athletes were at the top of the food chain. Derek and his friend were no exception to my rule. His Armani suit didn't cover up the Kalamazoo in him. He didn't have the New York slick vibe that I had become so accustomed to. I'm not being shady, but he had on *pointy* shoes. Artists can be very tribal, and compared to the hip-hop and R & B stars, models, fashionistas, and cool kids in every hue at the table, the two of them presented as rather pedestrian.

The restaurant was moody, but our table was buzzing, and at some point the conversation moved to "inconspicuous Blackness"—passing, but with more nuance. I was riveted. We discussed who we thought was secretly Black or else could have some Black running through them, how they might or might not identify and how they were often misidentified. I had never had an open conversation about biracial or multiracial aesthetics, *ever*. My parents didn't have the language for it, and Tommy never wanted to talk about my biracial identity; if he wasn't ashamed of it, he certainly didn't want to promote it. I couldn't believe it: it was my first night out without him, and suddenly I was in a dialogue about race and identity with young, smart, and creative people!

Eventually the debate turned to *me*. One of the guys from Armani said he couldn't tell if I was part Black (*no* parts of him were Black, by the way). Wanya wasn't having it. His voice got up in his high register: "Naw, man, come on! *We* all know; how could you not know?" I was laughing, but I was also deeply interested.

As if on cue, another person from the Armani team chimed in, "Derek, your mother's Irish and your dad's Black, right? Like, so what do you think about all this?"

All of a sudden, it was like the moment in *The Wizard of Oz* when the screen went from black-and-white to Technicolor. I was in a new moment, a new room; it was a new night and perhaps a new world. When I heard "Irish mother and Black father," my head snapped up involuntarily and turned toward Derek. Our eyes locked. A deeply suppressed sadness I had buried inside since the first painful blow from someone saying I was not white enough or Black enough, which translated into "not good enough," both rose and began to dissolve, and a longing to connect took its place.

It was as if suddenly I could *see* him. Derek was definitely no longer pedestrian; he was closer to a Prince Charming. This first moment of connection was so profound. I had created an endless number of romantic moments in my songs, and I had been incredibly sad for so long. Finally, it was if I was actually *living* a dream. I saw his eyes—enormous twinkling jade pearls floating in a golden-brown pool. It was as if there was no one else in the restaurant or the universe. We began talking across the table; the banter was lightweight, sparkly, and deeply flirtatious. I couldn't recall the last time, if there had ever been one, that I'd felt butterflies talking to a man.

The rest of the evening we talked, soft and easy. Eventually I realized how aware everyone was of our attraction, but I didn't care. This was my night out, and I was feeling the sweetness of freedom, the rush and allure of it all. I knew I was being watched, but to hell with that. Derek was young, mixed, ambitious, and doing his dream job, just like me! In the midst of all the people, lights, and music, it felt like we were the only ones in the world. Even though it was just a flicker, it was still *fire*.

Brazen as it was, I allowed Derek to walk me to the car, where a driver—aka Tommy's agent, of course—was waiting. Being with him in that moment felt like *living*. I'll never forget walking next to him that night, looking *up* at him, with his height and the way his athletic body moved. I felt diminutive next to him. It was such a different experience. This two-minute stroll on the pavement was more exhilarating to me than walking a thousand staged red carpets. It was a real moment. I was loose on the streets of New York, the sultry late-night breeze blowing my hair and pressing the delicate jersey of my dress against my body. I actually felt good. Unencumbered.

SHOOK ONES

Standing alone
Eager to just
Believe it's good enough to be what
You really are
But in your heart
Uncertainty forever lies
And you'll always be
Somewhere on the
Outside

—"Outside"

Knowing there were eyes on us, my assistant discreetly exchanged information with Derek's friend. I'd been in such a dark and lonely place for so long in my relationship. I finally had some hope, because I had found someone like me who existed in this world. As a child I used to pray I would meet someone who would understand me for what I was and not feel superior to me.

Our encounter also had a genuine air of innocence. It reinforced the many pure ways I wrote about romance in my songs. It was like the movies I idolized. But though it felt that way to me, it turns out Derek hadn't just walked into a room and into my life. My manager knew Derek really wanted to meet me; he had begged me once to sign a photo for "this kid who's crazy about you" so he could get World Series tickets—an incident I totally forgot about. That night he and I met, he told me "Anytime You Need a Friend" was his favorite song and that he listened to it before every game.

Anytime you need a friend
I will be here
You'll never be alone again
So don't you fear
Even if you're miles away
I'm by your side
So don't you ever be lonely
Love will make it alright

If you just believe in me
I will love you endlessly
Take my hand
Take me into your heart
I'll be there forever baby
I won't let go
I'll never let go

Among all of my songs that one was especially significant, because I was desperately alone, removed from friends and full of fear. My belief in God kept me alive—I wrote that song thinking about what I thought God would say to us in times of fear.

When the shadows are closing in
And your spirit diminishing
Just remember
You're not alone
And love will be there
To guide you home

—"Anytime You Need a Friend"

It was uplifting, rooted in spirituality and a message of faith, and that, too, made me feel safer and connected to Derek. It also let me know he was actually a fan—and the fans were the only people I really trusted.

We started a clandestine communication, texting each other cute, short messages whenever we could and planning times to talk. Needless to say, I was terrified to talk to him if Tommy was anywhere near. But I would steal moments. If we were at the studio or at dinner, I would pretend to need to use the bathroom. I enrolled my assistant. We'd stage an errand and leave in her car, and I would talk to him. Sometimes we would go to her house, and I'd sit in her modest little living room and talk to him in a whisper—I was *that* afraid of Tommy. Every call was brief. I was riddled with fear, but it was thrilling. While the energy was definitely exciting and romantic, our actual conversations were on the light and banal side. I didn't care; it was *something*. Planning and communicating with Derek felt like someone had smuggled a file into my jail cell. Each time we connected, it was as if I had worn down a bit more of the bars that held me captive.

Every little move we made built toward a bigger idea: freedom. I had become completely accustomed to nonstop work, looking over my shoulder, and warding off despair; it was life affirming, as a young woman, to feel giddy and girlie. Through all the darkness, I discovered I still had some whimsy reserved for me and my own heart. I even began watching baseball in the studio when he was playing. To add to the perfect fantasy of it all, Derek played the same position the great Joe DiMaggio (Marilyn Monroe's iconic second husband) played on the Yankees, connecting him to my Marilyn fascination. I literally met the person I had imagined. I was living in my own love song.

The weeks of covert communication built up to arranging an encounter. I was still painfully aware that I was married, and I didn't plan to break any of my vows. The plan was, I would meet him at a low-key pizza spot near his apartment, and we'd sneak out and go to his place. I was freaked out about taking the risk, but I had to see him; I had to know I was alive. I recall the care with which I chose my ensemble. I wanted something sexy of course, but certainly classy, youthful yet chic. I put together a warm chocolate moment: a soft and creamy chestnut-colored quilted Chanel leather miniskirt paired with a russet fine-knit bandeau top and layered with a matching cardigan. There were brown ribbed Wolford tights underneath, leading into a sleek round-toed mocha Prada boot. I *loved* those boots. I was serving textures in cocoa flavors. It was November, so I was giving an "autumn in New York" moment. To top it off, I wore a brown baseball cap over the volume of my curls, the brim pulled down low to hide my face.

I was scared (ooh, was I *scared*). The stakes were incredibly high. I'd never tried anything this dangerous before, and I had seen firsthand how Tommy could destroy people. He certainly tried to destroy me. As I remember it, the procedure for the covert operation was: My assistant and I would tell my driver (aka Tommy's spy, on *my* payroll) we wanted to grab dinner at the pizza parlor. We'd walk in together, and when Derek came in, we'd give my driver the slip. Derek lived nearby, somewhere we could be private and just chill. My assistant would act as a decoy, and Derek and I would duck out together.

I was nervous on several levels. In addition to being terrified of Tommy's wrath, I was also feeling naïve. Even though I'd been all over the world, I had nearly nonexistent experience in dating. The thought of the simple pleasure of just being close to Derek was liberating.

My assistant and I sat on stools at the counter, staring at the large storefront window, adrenaline pulsing through us both. In walked Derek—in a basic sweat suit and baseball cap, of course. My heart was pounding. We were finally in the same room together, but the most treacherous move was ahead: we had to escape the pizza parlor without the spy seeing us. I believe my assistant went out to the car pretending to retrieve something. When she went up to the driver's window, Derek and I pulled down our hat brims and ducked out the door and around the corner into a small backstreet. Tucked under his arm, I was consumed with relief and excitement. We slipped through a couple more winding backstreets to his apartment building.

I was anxious beyond belief, and a shyness I desperately tried to hide washed over me as soon as the door to his place closed behind us. Had I ever been alone with a single man in his apartment—or anyplace—before? I wasn't sure. This was all new. Would the spy discover me missing and foil our covert op? The butterflies in my stomach were in a complete frenzy.

I took off my cap, shook out my curls, took a breath, and tried to calm and orient myself by focusing on my surroundings. I don't recall many details. It wasn't a particularly impressive place, just practical and neat. I stood in the living room a bit awkwardly, very smitten and still scared. Derek said there was a roof deck on the building and asked if I wanted to go up there. I agreed.

He disappeared from the living room and returned with a frosty bottle of Moët. "I've been saving this, because I thought one day you might come over here." I smiled and said, "Yeah, we're gonna need that." (And so it really was a bottle of "Moe-ay" that got me feeling liberated.) We went up to his roof, laughed, talked softly, took sips of cold champagne straight to the head, and reveled in our bodies embracing.

The fall moon was bright, and a warm, heavy mist covered the night. For this brief moment, I was in rapture, alone on top of the city with a man who seemed to have stepped out of my dreams. We whispered a few things, giggled some more, and then drifted into the romance of the moment. We leaned in, an inch at a time, and melted into a warm, slow, intoxicating kiss. I felt an invisible veil of sadness begin to slip off of me and melt into a puddle at our feet.

And in that instant, the sky gave way, and it began to pour. We held on to our kiss; our arms didn't relax their embrace, and our bodies remained fixed. The rain came so suddenly, but we had already disappeared into the dreamy encounter we had anticipated, planned, and risked so much for. I was so caught up, not once did I think about my leather Chanel skirt or Prada boots in the elements. And thank goodness my hair was naturally curly, because had it been straightened, I might've broken and run to save the blowout!

What broke the trance was not the rain but fear again. How long had we been gone? Did Tommy already know? I had to go! I two-wayed my assistant that we were on the way back. Derek dashed me back through the wet streets and left me right before the pizza parlor, where my assistant was waiting with wild eyes. She ran out when she saw me, and we jumped into the limo. We plopped into the backseat breathless, covering our mouths to muffle the laughter. Surely the driver noticed I was soaking wet, but I didn't care! I didn't care that he was without a doubt going to report my disobedience. I had stolen away to claim a moment that was all mine and that was *real*. I left just a little bit of sadness on that rooftop, and I was not turning back to reclaim it.

Once the driver dropped my assistant off, I was alone in the long leather backseat of the limo for the tedious ride back up to Sing Sing. My mind was racing and my heart was pounding. *Did that really happen? Did I really do that? Tommy is going to go insane!* I turned on the radio to help calm me down. Out came blasting a grimy, dangerous, sexy-ass beat, then the hook:

> *Scared to death, scared to look, they shook*
> *'Cause ain't no such things as halfway crooks*

I was certainly shook when we pulled up to the tall, imposing black wrought-iron gates that led to my mansion. It appeared menacing in the dark rain—and in light of what I had just done. Tommy was supposed to be out of town, but once I got on those grounds I never knew what to expect.

I slowly entered my gorgeous penitentiary; all was quiet, and not quite as scary. A mercy. He wasn't there, so at least I didn't have to concoct a story about why I was dripping wet. Exhausted, I sat on the grand staircase, removed my boots, and tiptoed up to my bathroom. I didn't bother to turn on the lights. I wanted to stay in the quiet of the expanse of the cool, soft-pink marble that surrounded me. I wanted to luxuriate in the poetry of the dull reflections of the opulent crystal chandelier bouncing against the dark. I pulled off my drenched knit top, which had become like liquid skin, and stepped out of my damp leather skirt. I sat on the edge of the massive tub to peel off my resistant, thin wool tights. I took a quick warm shower, letting the water wash off some of my anxiety. Wrapped up in a plush white terry robe, I walked up to the mirror and looked at myself. I stared into my own eyes. They were a little brighter. I caught a glimpse of the Mariah I remembered from before all the terror peeking through. I saw a bit of exuberance, a bit of hope, a bit of courage. I saw the glow of the promise of freedom.

After such a dangerous, sexy, and grimy night the big all-white bedroom with the big all-white bed was more foreign than ever. I pulled the fluffy white goose-down comforter up to my neck and closed my eyes. Immediately I wanted to go back to the roof and relive the splendor I had just escaped. Involuntarily, my head started a gentle bob on the pillow and a beat began to faintly roll in. The song I had heard in the car, "Shook Ones, Part II," by Mobb Deep, started to play loudly in my head, and I began to whisper:

> *Every time I feel the need*
> *I envision you caressing me*
> *And go back in time*
> *To relive the splendor of you and I*
> *On the rooftop that rainy night*

I drifted off to sleep.

The next day I called Poke and Tone from Trackmasters. We got the sample and got busy. "The Roof (Back in Time)" was my first complete docu-song.

> *It wasn't raining yet*
> *But it was definitely a little misty*
> *On that warm November night*
> *And my heart was pounding*
> *My inner voice resounding*
> *Begging me to turn away*
> *But I just had to see your face to feel alive*
> *And then you casually walked in the room*
> *And I was twisted in the web of my desire for you*
> *My apprehension blew away*
> *I only wanted you to taste my sadness*

As you kissed me in the dark. Every time . . .
And so we finished the Moët and
I started feeling liberated
And I surrendered as you took me in your arms
I was so caught up in the moment
I couldn't bear to let you go yet
So I threw caution to the wind
And started listening to my longing heart
And then you softly pressed your lips to mine
And feelings surfaced I'd suppressed
For such a long long time
And for a while I forgot the sorrow and the pain
And melted with you as we stood there in the rain

—"The Roof"

It's exactly what happened.

THE LAST SHOW
AT SING SING

With the downpour on the roof, a dormant seed of self had been watered, and a bit of the humidity of Tommy lifted. I gained just enough confidence to appear defiant. Look, I—both of us—knew we were at the end of the road long before I left. I began leaving in increments, and in response, Tommy started making desperate last-minute attempts to get me to stay. He bought me a gorgeous but pointless Carnival red convertible Jaguar with a crème leather interior and matching drop top. It sat in the driveway of our thirty-million-dollar mansion—one more expensive thing to add to the lavish scrap heap that was our marriage.

One evening I was working with two men I had a significant creative and professional relationship with, whose duty it was to have moblike loyalty to Tommy. These three men, to whose wealth and prominence I had contributed considerably, and I were sitting in the kitchen, about to have a meal break. Even though we were all "friends" sitting around the table, facing a large, rustic fireplace with the now sadly ironic phrase "Storybook Manor" etched in the limestone mantel (I named it that, desperately believing I could wish and will my nightmare into a fairy tale), the atmosphere was anything but warm. It was cold, quiet, and pungent with pain and conflict, evidence to all that a dynamic in me had shifted. I think it embarrassed Tommy that he had lost control and lost his "woman" in front of his "boys." Embarrassment enraged him.

He began an awkward and creepy little rant about the beautiful car he had just given me, and our fabulous estate (which I designed and half financed), and how in spite of all of it, I wanted to *leave* him. I was sitting still, looking down at the table, when Tommy walked over and picked up the butter knife from the place setting in front of me. He pressed the flat side of it against my right cheek.

Every muscle in my face clenched. My entire body locked in place; my lungs stiffened. Tommy held the knife there. His *boys* watched and didn't say a word. After what seemed like forever, he slowly dragged the thin, cool strip of metal down my burning face. I was searing with rage from the excruciating humiliation of his terrifying, cowardly performance in my kitchen, in front of my "colleagues."

That was his last show with me as the captive audience at Sing Sing.

So many I considered closest to me
Turned on a dime and sold me out dutifully
Although that knife was chipping away at me
They turned their eyes away and went home to sleep

—"Petals"

I was locked way in the bathroom, which now felt like a mausoleum, sitting on the edge of the cold tub trying to muster up the courage to leave, completely. Then the words softly came fluttering into my head: "Don't be afraid to fly. Spread your wings. Open up the door." I hummed the melody, which would become "Fly Away (Butterfly Reprise)." And I descended the grand stairway for the last time. I truly believed I was going to die in that house I built in Bedford and haunt it forever. I could just see what they'd make of it: a morbid yet festive tourist attraction, "The Famous Ghost of Mariah Mansion," like a tasteful Graceland, where you could hear me hitting high notes in the halls at night.

When I finally walked away from Sing Sing, with little more than my wardrobe and personal photos, the only thing I really wanted from the house was the beautiful hand-carved mantelpiece. A masterful Eastern European craftsman had carved it exquisitely to my very specific design directions. As I was leaving the house, I ran my fingers along its smooth and intricate curves for a final farewell. Only then did I notice there was a butterfly in the center of the heart that was in the center of the structure. I did not request it but its open wings were the sign I so desperately needed when I let that door close behind me.

Natural disasters eventually tore down all the walls that held so much of my misery. A few years after I left Sing Sing, it burned down to the ground. And Hillsjail was completely destroyed by a tornado. I was in my Manhattan penthouse when I received a call from a woman who was the former owner of my former house. She had removed the mantel but put it into storage, because she found it so personal and thought I might want it. I retrieved it and had it painted a fresh white lacquer, just as Marilyn did with her mother's piano. That mantel is now in my most personal room in my house, along with my family photographs and other precious things of mine. And I didn't let my spirit die.

JUST LIKE HONEY

The rendezvous with Derek was just the push I needed to cross over into the Promised Land. I had proof that I could have something beautiful on the other side of the hell that was my marriage. Tommy's dark reign over me was now crumbling. Derek was outside of Tommy's world; Tommy couldn't destroy him, and I felt the possibility of my own destruction coming to an end.

"The Roof," as a song and a video, painted a deeply passionate and very accurate picture of my experiences. It was *major* for me, not for any salacious reason but because any intimacy with another human being was not something I had experienced before, ever. It was an amazing feeling, and I was obsessed with replaying the encounter and fantasizing what it could lead to.

I romanticized so much about that night that I believed it was part of my destiny. I thought I had met my soul mate. I was driven. My whole being ached to see Derek—or, more accurately, to experience how I felt when I was near him.

In creating the video concept for "The Roof (Back in Time)," I wanted to capture the feeling of the night—the crazy anticipation and the strong sensual undertones. I wanted it to be a little raw and sexy. We played on the "back in time" theme with a stylish old-school eighties hip-hop vibe, which was not a common era to reprise in 1998. The wardrobe stylist had to scour thrift stores and costume shops to get Adidas tracksuits, Kangol hats, and Sergio Valente jeans; and Serg Normant the hairstylist worked overtime to achieve my Farrah Fawcett layered, feathered moment. We featured Mobb Deep, members of the rap group the Negro League, and legit break-dancers. I knew it was a very cool video, good for both the "urban" and "mainstream" markets.

But anytime I made a move forward for myself, there would always be backlash. The "show" that was my marriage might have been over, but the aftershow—the "meet and greet," the dismantling of the stage—took a lot of delicate planning. There was quite a bit of upheaval. My life was thoroughly intertwined with Tommy's; I needed time, and counsel on a clean (as possible) exit strategy. I moved into a hotel on the Upper East Side and continued therapy.

I was still absorbed in the memory of the roof and wasn't willing to fall back into the mud of despair. A new part of me was alive, and I was intent on feeding it. I heard from one of the Armani people that Derek was going to be in Puerto Rico. At our next therapy session, I announced to Tommy that I needed to go on a trip. I made the case that it was time for him to honor the scope of our new agreement: he was supposed to let me go, and we could see other people. I'd been out alone socially, I'd been in recording sessions without him picking me up, I'd been taking acting classes and spending the night at my teacher's house (*right*), and now it was time to go somewhere, just for me. (Okay, maybe I felt a teeny bit bad about that last part—but ya gotta do what ya gotta do to survive.) I made it sound super reasonable: perhaps me and my assistant, or maybe another girlfriend, would go away for the weekend, to somewhere where I could swim in the ocean and chill in the sun and write (keeping in mind I'd *never* done anything like that while at Sing Sing, *never*)—somewhere beautiful and close, like Puerto Rico. My assistant was totally into it. She was still young herself, and this was a legitimate secret romance. We were all caught up.

We stayed at the El Conquistador Resort, a lovely collection of villas in a gorgeous, classic, old-style Spanish-Caribbean hotel on a lush private island. It was tucked into green hills and right on an exclusive beach. We decided to go to the popular dance club Egipto, which was in Old San Juan, nearly an hour away. It was designed like an Egyptian temple, and as if in a scene in *Antony and Cleopatra*, in walked Derek. We had not orchestrated this meeting, but I just *knew*. I so believed in my heart he would be there at the club that I had had my assistant book a villa at another resort, El San Juan Hotel, that was nearby. We stayed at the club briefly, and I informed him I had secured a little hideaway.

So there we were again, sneaking around to avoid my security. We went out the back door of the club and walked through a maze of small pathways through the palm trees and blooming bushes to the resort and my villa, accompanied by sultry night air. We got back to my room, and that familiar dance of the butterflies began. Being alone with someone I had a genuine attraction to was all so new to me. And again, I threw caution to the Caribbean breeze and surrendered into his arms and the moment. We lay for the night in one embrace, engaging in one, single, long kiss. It was the sexiest moment—without sex.

I knew my security saw me and saw Derek leave my room in the morning, but I finally felt something stronger than fear of Tommy's revenge. Now that I had it, I couldn't imagine life without this feeling. Desire became my reason for living, my all. Sleep didn't come on the plane ride back to New York, but a song did. I started writing.

> *I am thinking of you*
> *In my sleepless solitude tonight*
> *If it's wrong to love you*
> *Then my heart just won't let me be right*
> *'Cause I've drowned in you*
> *And I won't pull through*
> *Without you by my side*
>
> —"My All"

Going to Puerto Rico was a paradigm shift. After that trip, I strategized and carried out another coup on behalf of my heart: I put everything I was feeling at that time into a song. It was a gigantic risk, because I knew Tommy assumed I was having a sexual affair (even though, technically, I wasn't yet). It was also a revelation. There was an excitement and purpose awake in me that fueled me to a new level in my creativity. I was hearing different melodies, and I had new, real experiences to draw from. So I did something dangerous and beautiful for *me*—and everyone was scared *for* me.

I'd give my all to have
Just one more night with you
I'd risk my life to feel
Your body next to mine
'Cause I can't go on
Living in the memory of our song
I'd give my all for your love tonight

There would be hell to pay, I knew. I truly believed I was actually risking my life, but I felt life wasn't worth living if I couldn't have what I'd had that night. "My All" was the realest, boldest, most passionate love song I'd ever written. I brought to it the Spanish undertones, the warm breeze, the ecstasy of desire, and the agony of separation that I remembered so clearly.

Baby can you feel me?
Imagining I'm looking in your eyes
I can see you clearly
Vividly emblazoned in my mind
And yet you're so far, like a distant star
I'm wishing on tonight

I'd give my all to have
Just one more night with you

—"My All"

This song was about life and death, and I didn't want it to get lost in any over-the-top schmaltz. I needed it to be strong and simple. I wanted the vocals to be the centerpiece, the focal point in the mix, with a stripped-down track behind them. It was all about the emotion, the soul, and I sang it as if my life depended on it.

I first played the song for Tommy and Don Ienner, the then chairman of the Columbia Records Group, in the Range Rover, on our way to a restaurant in upstate New York. Don knew it was a hit. Tommy knew it could never be about him. A new place inside of me as an artist that had previously been sealed off was now fully exposed. And "My All" *was* a hit, a platinum hit. Later, Jermaine (Dupri), The-Dream, and Floyd "Money" Mayweather, three solid dudes, told me "My All" is their favorite song of mine. As creators, they know love is life, and there's nothing more real than that.

I had already begun working on *Butterfly* before my encounters with Derek, but they inspired some of the growing maturity and complexity in my songwriting and structures. The narratives and the melodies were coming from a fresher place. I was hearing things in a more layered, raw, and sophisticated way. I was feeling freer and less apprehensive to spread my creative wings. I advocated for the sound I wanted. I reached out to new producers who could bring that smooth, sexy edge to it. I started working on "Breakdown" with Stevie J, one of Bad Boy Records' "Hitmen," and Puffy. I brought Stevie, Puffy, and Q-Tip—one of the coolest and most creative guys out there—together for what would become the album's lead single, "Honey." I'd begun the lyrics and basic melody in Puerto Rico. Q-Tip made this amazing sample of "Body Rock," by the Treacherous Three. I told them I also wanted to include the 1984 hit "Hey! D.J.," by the World's Famous Supreme Team: "*Hey! D.J. just play that song / Keep me dancing (Dancing) all night long.*" Little did they know it was a secret shout-out to Derek Jeter. "Honey" was a song about jonesin' for that DJ feeling.

> *Oh, I can't be elusive with you honey*
> *'Cause it's blatant that I'm feeling you*

And it's too hard for me to leave abruptly
'Cause you're the only thing I wanna do
And it's just like honey

—"Honey"

When I played "Honey" for Tommy, he quipped, "Well, I'm glad you were so inspired." The bitterness! I was like, "What? *Now* you're mad? Why didn't you get mad about 'Fantasy' or 'Dreamlover'?" It's blatantly obvious I wasn't talking about Tommy in that song! I wasn't talking about him, or any actual person, in practically *any* romantic song. Before I met Derek, they were mostly imaginary characters. I'm sure Tommy could sense that the songs written for *Butterfly* were no longer about far-off, fictional lovers—these songs, though certainly poetically embellished, were full of specific details and sensual realness.

Tommy and the label were also resistant to what my new sound represented. Again I heard the refrain "too urban," which of course was code for "too Black"—and yeah, I wasn't ever going back.

"Honey" was the first time I felt I had full creative license in making a video. We were making a mini-comedy–action thriller, and it was possible thanks to an insane two-million-dollar budget. The video allowed me to really explore my kitschy humor, with Frank Sivero as the gangster character with the crazy hair. I also included Johnny Brennan from the Jerky Boys—"Honey pie, sweetie pie, cutie pants." I *lived* for the Jerky Boys; they were so silly. Come on, I wasn't trying to ridicule Tommy—I was just playing with cinematic stereotypes, juxtaposing Johnny's character with Eddie Griffin's. My Spanish line—"*Lo siento, pero no te entiendo*"—was delivered with a wink.

What I did in the "Honey" video is what I had always wanted to do. I got to explore creative and fashion influences without label restrictions. My look was inspired by Ursula Andress in the 1970s 007 movies. I wanted to look glamorous, dangerous, and badass, like a Bond girl. And I finally had the freedom to access the right creative team to achieve the looks. Emerging out of the swimming pool in the beige bombshell bikini? *That* was me. I was also finally able to work with a young, hot

Black director, Paul Hunter, who got all my jokes and James Bond references, but who also made sure the video had a contemporary and stylish look. The whole crew and vibe was just young, fiery, and fun. The experience was such a contrast to all the videos I made while sequestered in upstate New York, where everything had to be done within a twenty-mile radius of Sing Sing. The whole message in the "Honey" video was that I was breaking free—although no one understood the insanity, toxicity, and abuse I was living inside. They had no clue.

While we filmed the video, in Puerto Rico, I could often see my manager in the distance on the shore, hard shoes off, khaki pants rolled up at the ankle, pacing along the beach with his phone glued to his ear—talking to Tommy incessantly. Even though we were technically separated at that point, I was still the top Sony artist. Plus, knowing my every move was a hard habit for Tommy to break. My manager was reporting but not giving him the blow-by-blow. It would've made Tommy nuts to know I was having such a good time.

As much as I loved "Honey," my only major disappointment was that Biggie (the Notorious B.I.G.) never made it onto the remix. Puffy and I had talked about bringing to "Honey" a similar blend of my raspy, silky vocal texture with the kind of grit and flow ODB brought to the remix of "Fantasy." I had never met Biggie, but there was a running story that I had beef with him because of his song "Dreams of Fucking an RnB Bitch":

> *Jasmine Guy was fly*
> *Mariah Carey's kinda scary*
> *Wait a minute, what about my honey Mary?*

I was kinda scary? What does *that* mean? Fuck him. If he only knew some of the scary shit I'd *actually* been through. Puffy called him one day while we were working in the studio and put me on the phone. In true Biggie form—half pimp, half preacher—he said, "Naw, ma, you know, no disrespect," assuring me the song was all in fun. So things were cool between us. On the call, we talked about the music and flow, and even clowned a little bit. It was a chill and creative conversation. He was confident about what he wanted to bring to "Honey," and I had no doubt he would come in the studio and crush it; that's what Biggie did. Tragically, he didn't live long enough to make our studio date. The "Honey (Bad Boy Remix)" featuring Mase and the Lox was a smash, but there's a part of me that still misses Biggie on that song, and certainly in this world.

Producing the songs for *Butterfly* was what got me through that period in my life. I was writing about everything that was actually going on. It was the beginning of another level in my healing process. After the failure of the fake separation, after Puerto Rico, after the sexy-ass songs started pouring out, after all the pain we triggered in each other, after all the crazy normalcy we pretended to have and the stifling grip of his control had finally loosened, Tommy knew there was nothing left of the marriage.

I got a new lawyer, someone outside of Tommy's circle of power. I had her draw up the papers. Tommy signed, and I boarded a jet to the Dominican Republic, where mutual-consent divorces for foreigners are processed with the quickness. I flew into Santo Domingo, saw a judge, got my freedom papers, hopped back on the jet, and went straight to Tampa, where Derek was at spring training! I finally felt like a butterfly.

> *Don't be afraid to fly spread your wings*
> *Open up the door so much more inside*

On that flight, I wasn't afraid. I was incredibly vulnerable and raw. I'd closed *and* opened a door. I knew I had so much life, and work, ahead— and at the time I thought that life would include being happily-ever-after with Derek J. My romantic life up until then had been so grim, why not believe in a fairy tale? I couldn't wait to fall into his arms with divorce papers in hand. Finally!

Neither of us had wanted to cheapen our romance by cheating on my marriage. I know plenty of women would've had sex on that roof in the rain, or in the villa on the beach. It would've been justified—they were such seductive situations, and my miserable marriage was in ruins at best—but it wouldn't have been right. I wanted to wait until it was *right*. I'd waited all my life to really desire a man. It was worth waiting for it to be how *I* wanted it to be.

I'd had so many threatening experiences with men, and I had no real concept of choosing and being chosen on my own terms. I'd never been hungry for sex—not on my wedding night, not ever. I saved all my passion for my music. This time, Tommy was right; I was *inspired*. It was so sensual—everything was so new and sweet, down to the smooth texture of his honey-dipped skin. It was how it was *supposed* to feel. The months of anticipation had built an intensity I could not have manufactured. It was so heady, so intoxicating, and I was so vulnerable. I was in touch with a fire I didn't know I had inside.

Derek confessed to me then that he was "in on" our divine dinner meeting. He had apparently told several folks he wanted to meet me, including his contacts at Armani. He revealed that he and a friend had had posters up on the wall in their bedrooms: his friend's was of Alyssa Milano, and his was, you guessed it, of me. Apparently, plenty of people were aware he was a fan, long before we ever met.

"I had this plan," he told me. "I was going to come to New York. I was going to get on the Yankees. I was going to meet you, and I was going to steal you away from Tony Sony"—his name for Tommy—"and then we were going to get married." My grin was a mile wide. "Okay. I like that plan." Only, he didn't steal me from Tommy—I liberated myself.

There was nothing salacious about my relationship with Derek. Even on the night of our consummation, when I slept over at his house in Tampa, his sister was there, so basically it was an eighth-grade event. I remember waking up the next day, enthusiastically thinking, *I'm going to make breakfast for him!* just like in the movies. I tiptoed down to the kitchen with passion-tousled hair, wearing his oversized Yankees jersey.

I looked in the refrigerator to find three lonely eggs and not much else. His sister found me searching, and we laughed at my foiled rom-com plans. She was kind, and I related to her instantly. I didn't know many mixed-race young women. She was beautiful, with an open heart and an honest laugh.

His entire family moved me. All my life I had blamed the dysfunction in my family on race, but meeting the Jeters dispelled this myth. My family's brokenness was deeper than Black and white. This family was close in composition to mine but so different in actuality—they were close and loving. They interacted with each other as if they really knew, and cared for, one other. They were solid people, with a clear moral code. They held each other up. And they were lovely to *me*, all of them. This was a powerful example: a Black father and a white mother existing as partners and parents. A sister and a brother who were proud of each other, not enemies. Here was proof that a family that looked like mine could be unbroken. Perhaps that notion, that there could be a mixed family that was perfectly matched, was the most lasting thing Derek gave me in our brief relationship. The image of the Jeter family gave me hope.

But Tampa was only a weekend wonderland, and I had to return to New York and *Butterfly*. I had to prepare for the tour, which would be my most extensive to date. A couple of my girlfriends who were excited to celebrate my emancipation from my marriage to Tommy came to meet me, and we all flew back to NYC on a jet. It was difficult to leave what seemed like a dream, but I was also anxious to get back to work. Derek gave me a little gold ankle bracelet and a giant stuffed puppy dog as going-away presents. Cute. I only had whatever short-skirt outfit I had worn to the Dominican Republic, so he gave me one of his sweat suits to wear on the plane.

We arrived at the private airport where the jet and my girls were waiting. Derek opened the car door for me, and I stepped out into the Florida sun, cheeks flushed, lips plump, hair still holding on to the morning's frolicking. My large, dark Chanel sunglasses rested low on my nose, and my frame was drowned in his oversized sweatpants, which were rolled up at the cuff and down at the waistband, revealing my ankles and my navel. I had the sleeves of the jacket pushed up too, its wide bottom swinging in the wind, flapping around the cropped top I wore underneath. Balancing precariously in my six-inch mules, I struggled to manage the huge stuffed animal on one arm and my Louis Vuitton hobo bag on the other.

As I approached my girls, I could hear them shouting "Oooooooh, *hel*-lo!" They claimed I was strutting down the tarmac like a cowboy in pointe shoes. We sipped champagne and toasted to acquiring freedom papers and finally getting a shot of good vitamin D. We giggled the entire flight back.

Derek was only the second person I had slept with ever (coincidentally, his number was 2 on the Yankees). Just like his position on the team, our relationship was a short stop in my life. It was a very critical transition for me, and maybe a dream come true, or maybe an accomplishment, for him. I don't know. Very soon it became clear we weren't meant for the long run. For one, there's a great gulf between athletes and artists, and honestly it's hard for two stars from any industry to make it work.

My time with Derek was a sweet and short dream, yet its impact lingered. I thought about it from time to time for years after. Once, I was feeling intensely melancholy while recalling our short love affair to a friend. In my best Joan Crawford voice, I lamented, "The mother loved me! The sister loved me! The father loved me! It could have been *perfect*!" There was so much energy surging through my body that the champagne glass I was holding completely shattered. I took that intensity and put it in "Crybaby."

> *Late at night like a little child*
> *Wanderin' round in my new friend's home*
> *On my tippy toes, so that he won't know*
> *I still cry baby over you and me*
> *I don't get no sleep*
> *I'm up all week*
> *Can't stop thinking of you and me*
> *And everything we used to be*
> *It could have been so perfect*
> *See, I cry. I cry. I cry.*
> *Oh I gotta get me some sleep*
>
> —"Crybaby"

Let's be honest, as an artist, I am the Queen of taking one morsel and making many meals from it. I milked and mined my limited time with DJ for much more than it was worth. My sixth studio album, *Butterfly*, was released into the world and has since sold more than ten million copies.

Though our relationship was just a moment in my time line, Derek served a very high purpose in my life. He was the catalyst I needed to get out from under Tommy's crippling control and get in touch with my sensuality. And the intimacy of our shared racial experience was *major*—to connect with a healthy family who looked like mine was very inspiring. He was in the right place at the right time, and he was there for the right purpose.

DJ was a love *in* my life, not *of* my life. It was the idea of him, rather than the reality of him, that was so magnetic. In the end, I'll chalk up our ending to the fact that we couldn't live up to each other's fantasies. One can never compete with the fantasy. You just can't. It's like Marilyn used to say: "They go to bed with Marilyn Monroe, and they wake up with Norma Jeane."

The hard way is the way I have learned the most. There is no "Dreamlover" coming to rescue me and no Prince Charming or Joe DiMaggio to sweep me off my feet. I got swept away by a shortstop, but only God Almighty is my All.

A VISIT TO
THE PRESIDENT

I had to go get what I wanted, and I wanted freedom. I needed not just freedom from my marriage to Tommy, but freedom from Sony, as they were inextricably linked.

The executives at Sony used to call me "the Franchise" (crazy, right?), so when I was ready to get off the label, they made it difficult for me. We went back and forth with the lawyers about what obligations I would be expected to fulfill. We agreed to an unnamed studio album (which would eventually become *Rainbow*).

They wanted a greatest-hits album too. I was resistant to this because it felt so premature, as if they were trying to sew me up with the nineties.

No matter who I was talking to at the label, Tommy was still in control. There was no one above him at Sony Music—everything had to go through him. When I began to have conversations about getting off the label, I was blocked at every turn. Tommy had a vendetta against me, and he used his power to hold me hostage. When things still weren't moving along, I felt I had no more options, so I decided it was time to pay a visit to Norio Ohga, the president and chairman of Sony Corporation. I had never done anything like this. Tommy was the biggest boss I'd ever faced until then. Going above his head seemed like a wild, dangerous idea and was certainly a last resort. But I had no choice: this was my freedom, my career, my life.

I knew I was the most successful artist in Japan that Sony had at the time, so I figured I could at least get a sit-down. My executive assistant made the travel arrangements for the two of us—nobody else, not even my lawyer.

I called ahead and said, "I'm going to be in Japan. I'd like to come see Mr. Ohga." Meanwhile, the people at Sony were probably busy working on the next big global technology or whatever. At the time, I wasn't thinking that what they made from the music business was small potatoes compared to everything else. All I was thinking was that there had to be someone above Tommy. There had to be some way out, and I was willing to do anything. So, I decided to pack my bags, fly to the other side of the world, and talk face-to-face with the man who was really running things.

Mr. Ohga's assistant was a woman who was very kind to me and helped me throughout the trip. We remained friendly for years after. Mr. Ohga spoke English, but there was always an interpreter present. I had been to Japan several times and was somewhat familiar with their cultural norms, particularly with regard to showing respect and never losing face. What was more difficult to navigate were the cultural expectations around gender. Mr. Ohga was very old school, and I'm sure being confronted by a young woman was startling to him, even if that young woman was the best-selling artist on his label. And honestly, I don't even think he knew that I was mixed race, so he didn't know a young Black woman was coming to his headquarters, petitioning for her freedom. It was a ballsy move, but I had the numbers to back me up. Back then it wasn't about streaming numbers. Sales were physical objects, things that people had to go out and buy—a hundred million albums, DVDs, CDs, VHS tapes! They bought products and posters. After all, I was "the Franchise." To this day I still don't know how much money I made for Sony. I've been told it's billions.

Like the man himself, Mr. Ohga's office was serious and elegant, dimly lit with a large, traditional black lacquered table as its centerpiece. Mr. Ohga was formal and laser focused. I wasn't quite prepared for the extent of his formality, honestly. I hadn't consulted with a prep team or advisers. So there was no *preparation*, but I did have a clear purpose. My intention for the meeting was for us to decide on an exit strategy. We would need to figure out the terms of a deal, and I wanted to make sure there would be marketing support from Sony for the work I would deliver. Despite how badly I wanted to get off of Sony, I knew my fans deserved the highest-quality music I could make, and I would give them nothing less. I wanted Sony to know that I would work hard and promote tirelessly. I wanted to be seen and heard; I wanted them to know that I was here, I was paying attention, I was serious, and I was willing to speak up for myself.

I had to be sure that if I fulfilled my end of the bargain with these new albums, they wouldn't cheat me by failing to support them. If I was going to put my heart and soul into this work, I needed to have their word that they would throw everything they had behind it as they used to do. It was a brief meeting that would have long-lasting impact.

Tommy himself had once gone straight to the Japanese executives to oust Walter Yetnikoff, a former mentor turned rival. These powerful men were not only well versed in these kinds of cutthroat business dealings, they were encouraged to stand up for themselves. Though I wasn't a male artist and I had no parental support or lawyer in the room, I was stronger now, and I wasn't going to let myself be played ever again.

I may have had big boss energy, but I was also deeply saddened by the whole process. I wanted to stay on at Sony, but I didn't know how to move forward in the midst of my marriage to its CEO coming to an end. Deep down I was hoping they'd just fire him so I could stay. It wasn't the first time he had caused problems—there was a lawsuit with George Michael, and Michael Jackson eventually launched a campaign against exploitation of Black artists, explicitly aimed at Tommy, with Reverend Al Sharpton at the National Action Network's Harlem headquarters.

Mr. Ohga may not have agreed to fire Tommy the very next day, but when I went to Japan, people took notice. They were now listening. My music had made an impact in that culture, in that country, and in that company. Going to Japan was a stretch for me, but it changed my life. I took a stand, *by* myself and *for* myself. I had made it happen, and soon I would be free.

Though I expected to have more time and a more in-depth meeting, ultimately I was grateful Mr. Ohga respected me enough to take that meeting and make a deal with me; it's why years later I was able to return to the company with *Caution*, which interestingly enough is my most critically acclaimed album. When I got back home to deal with the powers that be in America, we arrived at a final deal that included four albums to be delivered over the next five years: *#1's*, *Rainbow*, *Greatest Hits*, and *The Remixes*. *#1's*, which I had conceptualized and proposed to Columbia, would be the first to come out, in 1998.

I was reluctant to rerelease old music, so in addition to the thirteen number-one hits I'd had by then, I added four brand-new tracks to the album. Brian McKnight and I recorded a totally new duet version of "Whenever You Call," from *Butterfly*. I also did a duet with Jermaine, a cover of Rainy Davis's "Sweetheart." I did a cover of "I Still Believe." Last, but certainly not least, *#1's* included my duet with Whitney Houston from *The Prince of Egypt*, "When You Believe."

The recording of that song was interesting. Jeffrey Katzenberg, from DreamWorks, brought me the song and asked if I would consider recording it for the soundtrack for an animated film. The soundtrack was heavily laden with R & B and gospel influences and featured K-Ci & JoJo and Boyz II Men. After I saw the movie, I knew it was something special that I wanted to be a part of (it went on to gross $218 million worldwide, making it the most successful non-Disney animated feature of the time). But most of all I was excited by the prospect of working with Whitney!

It was a major pop-culture moment that Whitney and I were collaborating, but I was personally so happy we did because we ended up having a wonderful time together. Everybody wanted to pit us against each other in some "battle of the divas"—a tired but pervasive pathology in music and Hollywood that makes women compete for sales like emotional UFC fighters. This narrative just supports the stereotype of all women being petty and not in control of our feelings, yet totally controllable by the boys in the industry.

Obviously, Whitney was formidable. Who wasn't inspired by her career, who she was as an artist and as an anointed vocalist?! But we were very different. I loved (and still love) layering the background vocals, writing, producing, and doing behind-the-scenes stuff like that. She was kind of born into it, like a royal singing princess. To us, it never felt like a competition. We *complemented* each other. We both had our hearts anchored in the Lord, and *that* was real, even though so much of what was happening around us was surreal. After the initial iciness (built up by outside forces) wore off, we developed a real fondness for each other. She had a marvelous sense of humor. She started using my words and calling me "lamb"—it was just pure fun.

Bobby Brown was around, and I don't know what else was going on, but that wasn't my business. I just know we had fun and laughed a lot. Doing the video was great fun too; we had many incredible moments together. Every day we spent together was special, and I'll always cherish the memory of that time and of all that she left behind. "When You Believe" stands as a testimony to the power of faith and, to me, sisterhood here on earth as it is in heaven.

Rainbow was released the following year and was a very different endeavor than *#1's*, which was a compilation album. It was much more involved. For obvious reasons, there was a huge push to get it done, so I wrote and recorded *Rainbow* in three months. I was desperate to work without distraction. My longtime friend Randy Jackson suggested I check out a very cool and secluded recording studio in Capri (which I love more than any place on Earth). In this paradise tucked in ancient limestone mountains towering out of the Gulf of Naples, I had a lovely little studio apartment that was flooded with sunlight and privacy every morning. I'd sit in a room in the studio filled with candles and creativity and hunker down for hours, just writing and laying down tracks. I wrote by myself and occasionally with the incomparable Terry Lewis, whom I love as a writer, while *the* Jimmy Jam added his brilliant musicianship. (Together they are responsible for forty-one US top-ten hits.) Without them, the album would not have come together so smoothly. The three of us worked together all the way through "Can't Take That Away (Mariah's Theme)," which I brought to Diane Warren, who plucked it out on the piano as I sang the lyrics and melody to the first verse. We wrote the second verse together. That song was actually about the professional and personal situation I was going through:

> *They can say anything they want to say*
> *Try to bring me down, but I will not allow*
> *Anyone to succeed hanging clouds over me*
> *And they can try hard to make me feel*
> *That I don't matter at all*
> *But I refuse to falter in what I believe*
> *Or lose faith in my dreams*
>
> *'Cause there's*
> *There's a light in me*
> *That shines brightly*
> *They can try*
> *But they can't take that away from me*
>
> —"Can't Take That Away (Mariah's Theme)"

Since I was a child, I had often had to turn to the "light in me / That shines brightly" just to get through, just to survive. So that was a song about many things, but when I wrote it, I was thinking about all that was going on at the time, about Tommy and the many years I had spent under his control. That was my theme—"They can try / But they can't take that away from me / From me, no, no, no."

The video (which I produced and paid for), while not the slickest in terms of tricks and production values, was a real change. We shot it in Japan. At the time, it was uncommon to incorporate real fans and user-generated content into videos. It was important for me to center my fans and express how they felt about the songs I was writing about my life for *them*. We collected a bunch of materials: footage of everyday people, real people who had overcome the odds to accomplish extraordinary things. The video also included superstar champions like Venus and Serena

Williams, but mainly people in my life who I cared deeply about, like my nephew Shawn, who, despite being the child of a troubled teenage mother, went on to graduate from Harvard Law, and Da Brat's grandmother. It showed triumphant moments, emotional moments—and it was real and raw. I wanted to utilize the theme of my core belief that all things are possible. I wanted the video to be a tribute to all the fans who helped me get through everything.

The song didn't do anything on the charts because the label barely promoted it—and this marked the beginning of their sabotage campaign. But it mattered for the *fans*. It mattered for the people who needed to hear it. And it matters for me. To this day, I still listen to it every once in a while. I still need it.

❦

Another important song on *Rainbow* was "Petals." It was, and still is, a painful piece for me. It's about my life, my family, my growth. It was both a thank-you and a farewell to the toxic influences in my life.

> *I've often wondered if there's ever been a perfect family*
> *I've always longed for undividedness and sought stability*
>
> —"Petals"

In a way, "Petals" told part of my life story through snapshots of the formative relationships that touched and changed me. With that song, I wanted to offer forgiveness and to imagine another possible life in the future—one with less hurt and more healing. So I wrote the song to release some of the pain. But there are still times when the hurt chokes me and I cannot sing the song.

Rainbow had two number ones—"Heartbreaker" (my fourteenth, featuring Jay-Z) and "Thank God I Found You" (my fifteenth, collaborating with Joe and 98 Degrees, and with Nas on the remix). It was important to me to pull together the artists I felt were defining the time, and Usher, Snoop Dogg, Jay-Z, Da Brat, Missy Elliott, Mystikal, and Master P were also part of the album.

After working at Jimmy and Terry's Minneapolis studio, I returned to New York to do "Heartbreaker" with DJ Clue. Jay-Z jumped on that track, and it became the hit we all know and love. We did the "Heartbreaker" remix between New York and Los Angeles. DJ Clue brought in all kinds of cool artists, like Joe and Nas on "Thank God I Found You (Make It Last Remix)." *Rainbow* closed out the twentieth century and, for me, was the bridge to freedom. But as they say, freedom ain't free.

Recording the album was a whirlwind, but it was fulfilling as well. By then I had a real sense of my rhythm and specific preferences for how I would craft a song. I would often create different parts of a song in different places. I really love the process of writing in a collaborative way, but doing my vocals is a more intimate process for me. While writing I like to do a scratch (first draft) vocal, sometimes without lyrics or with partial lyrics, and then take that basic track, complete the lyrics, finish the vocals, perfect it, and layer in background vocals. I like to do the lead when no one else is there, just me and my engineer. If I could do my own engineering, I would record like Prince and be completely alone. I prefer not having to consider other people's opinions in the development of vocals. I like a calm space where I can get to work and focus; I need to be able to hear my thoughts and see the vision in my head. I need to be able to play with the song, tweak it, and I definitely need a chance to sing it through a couple of times. Where does it feel natural to go up? Where doesn't it? Making records is kind of a spiritual science compared to a live vocal performance. I'm at my best when I can take my time and really live with a record.

We put out the *Greatest Hits* album for Columbia in 2001. It was a double album, which included the commercially successful hits and some personal and fan favorites like "Underneath the Stars" and my duet with the truly legendary Luther Vandross, a remake of "Endless Love." My last album for Columbia, which would mark the end of my obligation to Sony, was *The Remixes*. By the time it came out, in 2003, Tommy had stepped down from Columbia/Sony, so I had more creative input into the album and was more invested.

The concept of the compilation was unique: It was a double album like

Greatest Hits, only the first disc was all the club mixes, and the second was all the hip-hop collaborations and remixes, from "Honey" to "Loverboy (Remix)" to "Breakdown," featuring Bones, Thugs, and Harmony. It even included the So So Def remix of "All I Want for Christmas" with Lil' Bow Wow (he was still lil' then) and my hit song with Busta Rhymes and Flipmode Squad, "I Know What You Want."

But before these final two albums, I sealed the new deal on my freedom. After meeting with all the major record labels, I settled on the more eclectic Virgin Records, which was very artist friendly (they had Lenny Kravitz and Janet Jackson). I believed if I had enough money and marketing support, we would have success. With a fresh, historic record deal, I was about to embark on the project that changed my life—*Glitter*.

PART III

ALL THAT
GLITTERS

FIRECRACKER

"He knows we just did this shit with
Mariah . . . and he's trying
to fuck with Mariah."
—Irv Gotti

The saga of making *Glitter* was a collision of bad luck, bad timing, and sabotage.

The soundtrack and film began as *All That Glitters*, and though I first began to work on the project in 1997, we had to put it on hold for several years so I could fulfill more pressing obligations to Columbia. While I had significant creative control over the soundtrack, I had virtually none when it came to the film. The initial concepts I developed for the story were almost entirely rewritten. I started working on the script with my acting coach and Kate Lanier, who had written *What's Love Got to Do with It*. She's such a talented and gifted writer, and I really trusted her. But every day we kept getting more and more studio notes.

Tommy could not give up control, especially now that I was doing what I had always dreamed of and he had always feared: acting. *Glitter* was being produced by Columbia Pictures, which was owned by Sony, which connected it to Tommy. The chair of Columbia Pictures at the time referred to him while we worked as "the white elephant in the room"— that silent, invisible force we could not discuss. Anything that might have pushed the envelope, that would have made it an R-rated or even PG-13–rated movie, was swiftly vetoed. Nothing could be too real, too edgy, too sexy, or *too* down-to-earth. There was a much grittier script to be had (come on, it took place in the eighties!), but we ended up with something very bubblegum.

As a result of continual back-and-forth and Tommy's stifling control, we had script changes every day. No one knew what was happening from moment to moment. In addition to a vastly different script, I had also wanted Terrence Howard in the lead (I envisioned him in this kind of role before *Hustle and Flow*, mind you). But the powers that be were dismissive of the idea of a romance between Terrence and me. I suspected it was because he looks Blacker than me (though he is also mixed!) and they didn't understand how that was going to *work*, if you catch my drift. So *that* was disappointing. No shade to Max Beesley, who was great.

In addition to a lack of creative control, I felt my acting was really inhibited for many reasons by the acting coach, who by this time I believe had become too invested in my career. I don't want to slay her, but she prevented me from doing my best by projecting her own personal shit onto the movie. I've heard this often happens in collaborations; it got very Marilyn and Paula Strasberg–ish. With all due respect, it became an ego fest (I'm sure she would agree with me now). What was important to me was that the extras and other people on set—from actors to crew— knew that I was serious, ready to learn, and ready to work just as hard as them. Though the whole process wasn't great, I did feel I gave some good performances (which would have been more evident with different edits). I wasn't upset because it was such a new medium for me, but I think at every turn there were missteps.

But there was light at the end of this glittered tunnel. Frank Sinatra once said Dani Janssen was one of Hollywood's "original broads," and I love a good broad, especially one who knows how to throw a good party. Dani Diamonds's (as she was famously called) Oscar parties are *legendary*— and I do not throw the L word around haphazardly. Most guests either have to have an Oscar or have been nominated for one in order to be invited.

Her regulars are all legends—Sidney Poitier, John Travolta, Quincy Jones, Oprah, Babs (Barbra Streisand), and on and on. And each year a hot new crop of fresh Oscar winners mingle with icons amid her massive collection of white orchids. One year, I was fortunate enough to receive a surprising and very special invitation (naturally, Dani and I hit it off famously). One of the hottest leading men at the time, a two-time Academy Award winner (Dani's code of no "networking" or name-dropping is taken very seriously, so he shall remain anonymous), came up to me and said about my work in *Glitter*, "I know people give you shit about it. I've been there. You were really hitting some things that were very genuine, and I think you should stick with that. Don't let them make you feel like you can't go there anymore." He made me feel so much better because of the immense respect I have for him as an actor. And it was a good thing I didn't give up—because a few years later something truly "precious" would come my way.

Much of what went wrong with *Glitter* led back to Tommy. He was angry about the divorce and my departure from Sony, and he used all his power and connections to punish me. And everybody else around me knew it was happening, including my new label. Tommy and his cronies went as far as taking promotional items, like my stand-up advertisements, out of the record stores. It was a real fight. He didn't want it to look like I could succeed on my own, without him, so he even interfered with the *Glitter* soundtrack. I worked on it for a long time with people like Eric Benét and Brat, who were both in the movie. Terry Lewis was able to get us the original music for "I Didn't Mean to Turn You On," since he and Jimmy Jam produced it, of course! And having Rick James (who required a white suit, a white limo, and perhaps some other white accouterments for his session) on "All My Life" was priceless.

The whole experience felt like a dream. And in many ways, it *was* exactly what I had dreamed of for so many years. Don't get me wrong; I'm not saying *Glitter* was *Cat on a Hot Tin Roof* or something, but I don't think it deserved what it got. I think it could have been good had it been allowed to be executed as originally conceived, but by the end, it was such a fight just to have it happen at all. But as always, I kept the faith. I told myself, *Everything's going to work out*. I went to that place of hope. *This is hard right now*, I told myself, *it's a struggle, but I'll make it through, no matter what*. And I was stronger than ever on the other side. And though darkness followed, it was in that darkness that I learned to build my own light.

Tommy was furious when I cut the strings he used to manipulate me. There was no way he would allow me to have a huge success after leaving him *and* Sony. He was not going to let me or *Glitter* shine; rather, he was intent on stamping us out. He wouldn't have been satisfied unless I absolutely *failed*. He used to always say, "You do what you do, and then I do my *magic*." He would have me destroyed before I exposed that he was no magician. If the *Glitter* soundtrack had been a monster hit, he would have had to face the fact that he was not omnipotent, he was not indispensable, he did not single-handedly *make* Mariah Carey. To add to his fury, he knew I'd just negotiated the largest cash record deal to date (and my family knew, too, but more on that later). And on top of it, I was making a movie, something he *forbade* when we were together, and that meant my career was expanding, which made him feel like he was shrinking. He had already been publicly humiliated when I left him, but for me to be successful without him too? That was too much for his fragile ego to withstand. What would it mean for his whole empire to be based on intimidation? What would it mean to other artists if I made it without him? I fully believed he was committed to me not having a life he didn't control. That he wouldn't be happy until I was buried in the ground.

I escaped a man and marriage that nearly smothered me to death. I was one of several artists who called Tommy and his flunkies out for working against the best interest of the company because of petty personal vendettas.

Meanwhile over at the new label, all hell was breaking loose because "Loverboy," the first single off the *Glitter* soundtrack, was *only* at number two on the charts, not number one. I didn't understand the panic around a number two single on a soundtrack for a film that wasn't even released yet. But suffice it to say, on the heels of filming *Glitter*, my life and work were once again under tremendous scrutiny and pressure.

And then there was the sabotage. I had written the lyrics to "Loverboy"; the melody was tight, and it had an infectious groove. Super producer Clark Kent and I had chosen "Firecracker," by Yellow Magic Orchestra, as the sample, and the few insiders working on the film's production were really loving it. That did not go unnoticed by Sony executives (and spies). I had chosen the song and paid to have it used in the movie. After hearing my new song, using the *same* sample I used, Sony rushed to make a single for another female entertainer on their label (whom I don't know). They used the "Firecracker" sample and released it before "Loverboy." Ja Rule and I wrote a song together too, and next thing you know, Tommy was calling up his manager Irv Gotti, asking him and Ja to collaborate on a duet for the same female entertainer's record—leaving me to scurry and remake the song. Irv has even discussed it since, in an interview on *Desus & Mero*: "He knows we just did this shit with Mariah . . . and he's trying to fuck with Mariah." This was sabotage, plain and simple.

Look, I was well trained in the art of turning shit situations into fertilizer, but Tommy knew fucking with my artistic choices was particularly low. But I wouldn't let him stop me. I switched gears and turned from the techno influence to a funkier sample from "Candy," by Cameo (you can't go wrong with Cameo), and Clark Kent produced it again. After we were both robbed, he saved the day with a banging track (using some remnants from "Firecracker," which is my favorite part of the song). Da Brat pretty much said it all in her blistering and very *real* rap on the remix to "Loverboy."

> *Hate on me as much as you want to*
> *You can't do what the fuck I do*
> *Bitches be emulating me daily*
> *Hate on me as much as you want to*

You can't be who the fuck I be
Bitches be imitating me baby

—"Loverboy (Remix)"

We even featured Larry Blackmon (in cornrows) in a poppy sexy-kitschy video shot by my good friend, the fabulous David LaChapelle. And we had a good time despite it all.

But the good times were about to turn *real* bad.

RESTING IN PIECES

After leaving Tommy I lived in hotels and on the road before I was finally able to make a home for myself. I came very close to buying Barbra Streisand's exquisite, palatial Central Park West penthouse in an impressive Art Deco building. She famously has a passion for design; her home was decorated with impeccable taste that was totally compatible with what I loved. After all I went through to build Sing Sing it would have been a relief to have a gorgeous turnkey home. But alas, the conservative co-op board was afraid there would be too many rappers, and their entourages, aka big black men, milling about, and didn't approve me. I eventually found a perfect building downtown, in Tribeca, and moved into the kind of home I dreamed of as a child. Having my own glamorous, gigantic New York City penthouse apartment was exciting but also totally disorienting. I was finally in my own space, but I often didn't know where any of my stuff was or where it was supposed to be yet. And I had no time to get my new place in order because I was working nonstop. I had a reputation in the industry for being a beast when it came to productivity. I went hard in the studio, and I went equally hard promoting and marketing. I was an *all-in* artist, and everyone I worked with knew it.

Having a new project on a new label was taking all I had, and I was giving as much as I could. There were all these new people at the label, and my personal management team wasn't properly restructured to accommodate the new demands. And quite honestly, all the change and new, higher stakes overwhelmed them. My schedule was brutal. I would have a shoot or an event until 3:00 a.m., then a 5:00 a.m. press call. It was relentless. Nowhere in my itinerary was there R-E-S-T, and at the time I didn't know how to demand it. When you're working like a machine, there has to be human care built into the process: nutritious food, bodywork, vocal rest, but most importantly, *sleep*. (I knew this, even if the notion of "self-care" was a decade away.)

Of course, the timing of the soundtrack's release couldn't have been worse—something no one could have foreseen. People didn't go see the movie. I still believe *Glitter* was ahead of its time. People may not have been ready to deal with the eighties in the early 2000s, but I knew it was going to be a thing. And then it was! And I still *love* that soundtrack. I am so glad and so grateful that almost two decades later, the Lambs and I got #JusticeForGlitter, making it go to number one in 2018. I'm also glad I get to perform those songs now. The fans gave *Glitter* new shine, new dazzle—the life it *deserved*.

It was late in the summer of 2001. The few critics who were able to preview the *Glitter* movie almost unanimously panned it. The anxiety caused by its bad reception, and the label's reaction to the single only hitting number two, was seeping into my psyche. Honestly, the only other artist I've seen under so much pressure to perform above and beyond their own phenomenal success was Michael Jackson. Like him, I was also used to having unquestionable smashes. It was my idea to make a whole-ass album called *#1's*! But still, number two on a new label, on a soundtrack (*not* a studio album) didn't seem so tragic, if you ask me.

And still the stress was mounting. It didn't seem like the label had a strong promotional strategy, and I didn't have a coordinated management team in place yet. I didn't see anyone around me taking control of what was becoming the "single situation." Worry seemed to outweigh planning and problem solving; internally the project was looking a mess. So my creative survival instincts kicked in. I felt like I had to do *something*—somebody had to do *something*.

High anxiety made what little sleep was allotted for in my schedule nearly impossible. I couldn't get to sleep. I couldn't find my things. I couldn't seem to get anyone to pull it together.

So I made my own move. Admittedly, it was too late and a bit messy, but it was some kind of action. I concocted a last-minute little publicity stunt to garner excitement for "Loverboy": I staged a "crash" of *TRL* on MTV.

In keeping with the vibe of the video and the audience, I thought it would be festive to have a little nostalgic summer moment. Running on pure panic and excitement, I showed up on set with a spunky ponytail, pushing an ice-cream cart full of Popsicles and wearing an oversized airbrushed "Loverboy" T-shirt with a surprise underneath: an eighties *Glitter* look. It was an innocent and silly stunt and highly unrehearsed. I very much freestyled my dialogue, as I tend to do, and I was hoping Carson Daly could play off of me, riff, and involve the audience (as one would expect a host to do). But he didn't play along. (I know he was probably told to act surprised, but he didn't *act* at all.)

I realized I was living in the moment all by myself. So I thought, *Okay, let me pull out a little costume trick to get the energy going.* I awkwardly removed the T-shirt to reveal gold sparkly hot pants and a "Supergirl" tank top. But in response, Carson, acting all aghast, said, "Mariah Carey is stripping on *TRL* right now!" (*Oh,* now *he decides to act.*) I certainly was *not* stripping—I was *revealing.* Granted, my performance was a bit sloppy, and came off as silly. But instead of ad-libbing, Carson was looking at me like I was crazy. My adrenaline was dialed up to 1,000, and Carson asked me, "What are you doing?" *Really?!*

I nervously answered, "Every now and then, somebody needs a little therapy, and today is that moment for me."

The truth is, my fans *are* a part of my therapy. Some people have retail therapy, some have chocolate therapy; I have *fan* therapy. I have *always* gone directly to my fans for energy and inspiration. I established an independent relationship with my fans before social media was even created. I used my website to personally talk to them; I would leave voice messages for them and tell them what I was doing *and* how I was honestly feeling.

It was unfiltered, how I communicated with my fans, and how we communicated with each other. So when I made that infamous call to my fans, while freaked out and feeling alone on a boat in Puerto Rico, leaving a sad message saying I was taking a break—*they* understood. The way it was reported in the press was as if I had a meltdown and made a desperate, random call. Back then, people didn't understand, and wondered why I talked directly to my fans. The media had no concept of the bond I had with my fans. None.

My fans care, and they take note of everything I do and make it their own. The press didn't understand how the fans named themselves "Lambs." The fans paid attention to when Trey Lorenz and I would go into our old-Hollywood affectation and say things like, "Be a *lamb* and fetch me a splash of wine." We would call each other "lamb" as a term of endearment all the time—and that's how the Lambs (the *deeply* devoted fans) were born! Now we are Lambily! My fans saved my life and continue to give me life every day. So honestly, I don't give a fuck if publicists or press thought I was crazy for bringing Popsicles or making phone calls to *my* fans. The Lambs are *everything*, and every song, every show, every video, every post, every festive moment, everything I do as an artist is for *them*.

TRL. Was. A. Stunt. Gone. Awry. And let's be clear and logical, there's no way I, Mariah Carey, or *anyone* could actually *crash* any MTV show, with an ice-cream cart no less. *Maybe* Carson Daly didn't know I was coming, but producers had to schedule my appearance—coordinators, publicists, security, whole-ass *teams* of people knew I was coming. It was a stunt. It seemed like a good idea at the time. *Any* idea was good at that time. I was like a stand-up comic who bombed a set. All performers bomb, but *my* bombing set off a chain reaction that placed a target on my back. The tabloids and the celebrity press at large acted like I'd actually stripped butt naked and given Carson a lap dance on live TV (which is now a mundane routine often performed by reality TV stars and rappers—oh, how the standards have changed)!

The press devoured my silly *TRL* stunt and me right along with it. It was the first time I had experienced the phenomenon of a public fail that woke the monster in the media, that vicious vampire that gains its strength by feeding on the weaknesses of the vulnerable. The bombed stunt mushroomed into a big, nasty, never-ending story. Some mainstream media is a glutton for negative energy and fear. It places a mask over pain and presents it as entertainment news. It was visible, and I was vulnerable. And when the Cinderella of Sony took a fall, no king's horses or men tried to set the record straight, pick me up, or put me back together again. Rather, they fed on the spectacle and just wanted more—more stumbles, more embarrassment, more breaks, more ridicule. The monster in the media is only satisfied when you are destroyed.

This was all happening before the phenomenon of social media. There was no clapping back on Twitter. No "Drag them, Queen!" No organic love mob of the fiercely loyal Lambily to rush to my defense. Thousands of fans and Lambs *did* show me love and support through letters and comments on my website, but the "outside" world didn't take note of that. There was no YouTube and no 'gram. (Although a surprising ally also rose to my defense: Suge Knight (who was *so* powerful then), in an interview on Hot 97, said, "Everybody needs to leave Mariah alone, or they're going to have a problem with me." Trust, back then *nobody* wanted to have a problem with Suge.

Today it's easy to coordinate a promo moment or change the narrative through social media. It was freaking *hard* to penetrate pop culture back then. It was a huge undertaking to get on major TV shows and devise my own "moments"; practically every move you made as an artist was controlled by the "corporate morgue" (as I lovingly call them). Now, when some celebrity mishap goes viral, there's generally a twenty-four-hour media takeover; then it's *over*. Back then, you did one thing, and it dominated the press for what seemed like an eternity. *TRL* was that one thing.

And the press hunted me, ferociously. This was five years after Princess Diana's death by tabloid. I studied how the press hounded her like hyenas. I once had a brief but unforgettable moment with Lady Di when our eyes locked at a *Vogue* party. She was in a stunning sapphire-colored gown, neck dripping in the same blue gems. And she had that *look*—the dull terror of never being left alone burning behind her eyes. We were both like cornered animals in couture. I completely recognized and identified with her. We shared that understanding of how it felt always being surrounded by people, all of whom might not be trying to hurt you, but all of whom are trying to do something. They all want *something*. I didn't know she would be caught and killed shortly after our encounter. I certainly didn't know I would soon be in a dangerously similar position. The hunters were closing in.

With the August heat, my troubled sleep quickly deteriorated into no sleep at all. Sleep had disappeared, as had proper meals. I was barely eating. The panic around "Loverboy" at the label was real, and they were desperate to make another video for the second single right away. We had just spent several exhausting days shooting the "Loverboy" video in the scorching California desert, in harsh conditions, with no water or basic necessities. There had been no covered area to wait in and block me from the sun between takes, which not only fried me, it wasted time, because my makeup kept melting and had to be reapplied. I may have looked super peppy, but "Loverboy" was a technically grueling shoot, and the label wanted me to get on a plane right away, fly back to New York, and start shooting another video for "Never Too Far" the following day!

I was utterly exhausted, baked, fried, and frayed, and certainly wasn't in any condition to make another video. I should have had, at the very least, a three- or four-day buffer between shoots. Besides, there was a whole glamorous performance of the song in the film, which they could've and should've used as a video (ultimately they did). But the label wasn't hearing me.

It didn't matter that I was completely spent—what mattered was that they had spent more than a hundred million dollars on "Mariah Carey." They wanted all their glittery products ready for sale *now*. There was no one around to intervene, to help coach the label on how to pace the projects and my productivity. No one had the strength or power to say no to unreasonable requests on my behalf, and the pressure was steadily rising.

I was exhausted. And the most difficult part was the diabolical delight the tabloid media was milking out of my moment of weakness. It was a nonstop, never-ending circus. I recall watching one entertainment show after the *TRL* debacle where they were talking about me in the past tense. It was so surreal, as if I was watching an "In Memoriam" of Mariah Carey. And all I really wanted *was* to rest in peace.

This, on top of dealing with Tommy and my family, was just too much. I was beyond tired. I was in urgent need of sleep. Sleep, this basic human requirement, this simple comfort, became impossible to obtain. I tried to find refuge in the emptiness of my enormous new penthouse, but the label and "management" were calling me constantly, trying to convince me to do the video. I simply couldn't do it. I had been working for years without a break. It was totally out of the norm for me not to show up, but I really didn't have anything left. I couldn't think. And they couldn't hear me. The phone wouldn't stop ringing. No matter what room I was in—none of which were familiar or comforting to me yet—I could hear the phone, ringing and ringing. Wait. Did Tommy know where I was? Was Tommy trying to torture me too? Were his people following me again? I was getting scared.

I had to find a safe place. I had to find *sleep*. Who could I trust? No one working for me was going to help me find somewhere to go. All I was asking for was a little bit of time. All these people on my payroll, and no one lobbied for me to have one day off. I was trying to tell them I just needed a couple of days blacked out, some time to rest, recuperate, and procure a bit of beauty sleep.

In desperation, I went to a hotel near my penthouse. I thought if I could just get a room, draw the curtains, crawl under the covers, and go to *sleep*, things could be all right.

I had lived in hotels for long stretches of time, and found comfort in knowing people wouldn't bother you. And I had stayed at this particular hotel several times before while my penthouse was being worked on. It never occurred to me to instruct the front desk not to contact my management or tell anyone I was there. Why should I have to? I stumbled into my room and promptly hung the "Do Not Disturb" sign on the doorknob. Even though I'd just been run out of my brand-new, spectacular penthouse to a modest hotel room, I began to feel relief. I drew a bath, slowly sank into the warm, scented water, and put on some soothing gospel ("Yet I Will Trust in Him" by Men of Standard), hoping some of the trauma would dissolve. I began to calm down. The *TRL* incident was still weighing heavily on me. I felt the whole world thought I had lost it. I wrapped myself up in the hotel bathrobe and curled up in the bed. But before I could shut my eyes, I heard a knock at the door. And then there was a *bang*!

I jumped up and stomped to the door, ready to cuss out whoever hadn't read the sign. I opened it to a crowd of people—management people, Morgan, even my mother!

"What the fuck is going on?" I yelled. "I gotta go to SLEEP!" I was panicking. I was hysterical. I was caught. I began to scream—just scream. I couldn't talk. A whole damn delegation had arrived to drag me back to work. All I wanted was a couple of damn days off. So I screamed.

Suddenly Morgan grabbed my arms and pulled me toward him. I became still. He stared at me and quietly said, "This whole thing is just *birthdays at Roy Boy's.*"

I immediately snapped out of it. "Birthdays at Roy Boy's" was an inside joke we had about our father, because he always mixed up our birthdays. Morgan brought me back to our innocent familial language: the jokes and the silly sayings that only we shared, the way we used humor to cope. The words that existed before all of this, all of these outsiders. In that moment I believed Morgan understood how I felt, that he even *cared* about my well-being. "Birthdays at Roy Boy's" took me back to when I felt like he could be an actual family member to me. It was personal and funny, and I was in distress. It was as if he had given me the secret code for "I got you," appearing like a lighthouse in the storm. Emotionally, I had cracked wide open—and Morgan slithered in.

I had been run out of my home *and* a hotel. There was an entire team of people hunting me down to pull me back to work, including my mother. I was beyond desperate and still in need of sleep. My record deal was an over 100-million-pound leash around everybody's neck.

I needed to find someone without any business interests or invest-ments in me—someone who knew me and cared about me, who would help me or hide me. My mind immediately went to Maryann Tatum, aka Tots. She'd been with me as a background vocalist since *Butterfly*, and we became like sisters after her sister died. She was one of my few friends who I thought knew how to contend with really fucked-up situations (and this one certainly qualified!). She was solid and came from solid folk. Tots grew up one of nine children in the projects in Brownsville, Brooklyn. And even though her mother had to deal with raising nine kids on her own, she was always clean, always put together. Tots was sweet and God loving but also knew her way around the streets. I thought she could help me get away from all the people coming after me, and help me get some sleep.

We decided I could go to her apartment in Brooklyn because no one would think to look for me there. By the time I managed to pull it together and sneak out to Brooklyn, I was riddled with anxiety. Not only did I know the label was looking for me, who knew if Tommy was follow-ing me too? It wouldn't have been the first time. (Robert Sam Anson's 1996 exposé "Tommy Boy" in *Vanity Fair* reported on just some of his antics, but it totally helped justify my claims of his maniacal control and surveillance.) And the tabloids were hot on my trail and salivating for my slightest misstep (*still* are).

I took a private car service to Tots's apartment. It was certainly a good place to go incognito, but not to sleep. It was cramped and wasn't exactly comfortable for me, plus my angst and exhaustion were giving me nervous energy. I suggested Tots and her niece Nini, and I all go for a walk to help me wind down.

She said "Girl, wait. You *do* know you're Mariah Carey?"

I guess I couldn't just go traipsing through the streets of Brooklyn. I needed a disguise. Nini braided up my hair, and I put on her Mariah Carey *Butterfly* T-shirt, sweatpants, and a baseball cap with the brim pulled down low. Hiding in plain sight, the three of us strolled down the Brooklyn streets in an attempt to recover some of my last, lost nerves. No one noticed me comfortably flanked between two Black girls in the diverse Brooklyn neighborhood.

Tots assured me I had nothing to worry about, joking, "They probably just think you're some cute Puerto Rican girl who went to a Mariah Carey concert."

We had a little laugh, a little comfort, a little escape—but I still felt like I was being tracked. I couldn't find any relief. I couldn't remember the last time I had slept or had a meal.

Time was collapsing in on me, the days and events all running together. My management and the label somehow discovered I was in Brooklyn with Tots. They called and asked her to convince me to agree to do the video. My emotional instability, as a result of sleep deprivation, was starting to take hold of me. I was cornered and confused. Morgan was again dispatched to come and get me, since the "delegation" at the hotel had surmised that he was the only one I trusted. No one knew that, for me, *trusting* Morgan was a dangerous proposition.

❦

I never knew what to expect with Morgan; he'd been so unpredictable, volatile, and violent for so long. And yet, my mother trusted him the most. He'd become her strong man, her protector, almost a father figure to her—a position that should never be filled by a son. And though he had frightened me so many times as a child, I, too, saw him as a smart, strong man. Morgan was very intelligent and impressive and had developed a treacherous set of survival skills.

He was in the downtown New York scene in the late eighties. He worked in some of the hippest bars and clubs. He was strikingly handsome and occasionally worked as a model. He was well known and well liked. He discreetly supplied the beautiful people with their powdered party favors. He was diabolically charismatic.

At the beginning of my career, Morgan was on a mission to be known as the one who was responsible for "discovering" me. (Seymour Stein, founder of Sire Records and signer of Madonna, actually had an opportunity for that distinction, as he was one of the first to have my demo. Alas, he said, "She's too young"—but that's another tangent.) Morgan had several sketchy contacts in the music industry but also introduced me to some important players in the fashion scene, like the late legendary hair-stylist Oribe. In some circles, I was even known as "Morgan's little sister," though he hadn't seen me as his little sister in a very long time. I was his little ticket to wealth and fame.

I've often publicly recognized Morgan for being the one who loaned me five thousand dollars to pay for my first professional demo, for which I remain grateful and which I paid back five thousand times over. And I would continue to pay and *pay*.

I never thought that modest initial loan made me beholden to him or should allow him to have any say in my career. I was very young, but I knew not to do business with any of the questionable music folks my brother tried to get me to work and sign with. I knew for certain, that for me, business with Morgan would come with *serious* strings. Like a noose.

Less than a month after I signed my first recording contract, my mother and Morgan proposed a family gathering at the shack—maybe to celebrate? Who knew? I really didn't like going back. The shame and fear I had endured while living there was still sticky on my skin. Against my better instincts, I agreed.

The shack was as bleak as ever. The air in the tiny living room was thick with an anxiety and manipulation I could taste. The "wood" paneling had faded and worn down to look more like cardboard from men's shirt packaging. Dingy white polyester lace dime-store drapes hung over the murky windows; the heating vent on the floor coughed up a layer of gray soot that climbed from the hem to midway up those pitiful panels of Irish respectability. My mother and Morgan sat together on the dreary blue corduroy couch. I sat across from them on a run-down beige recliner. Neglect was the overall accent color.

My mother was expressionless, occasionally darting her eyes over to Morgan for approval. He was clearly the "host" of this suspicious home-coming. I could tell he was in straight scheme mode. His eyes had a wild, piercing focus. I could sense his tension, yet he had perfected the art of casting a smooth veneer over his emotions and over his intentions.

Morgan launched straight into a rant about what a conniving low-life my mother's second husband could be, and how they were *concerned* that now that I was on my way to becoming famous, he was likely to pose a "problem." Warning me that he knew all of our family's dirty secrets and threatening that he would spill it all to the press. That he would tell the world about Alison being a drug-addicted prostitute and having HIV. *What?* My mother was silent. I recall Morgan saying that I needed protection—that I needed to be careful, that this guy could end my career before it began—and that he could "take care of it." He could take care of *him*.

In less than ten minutes in the shack, I was back in that familiar storm cloud of fear conjured up by my brother. I certainly didn't need convincing that this man was a horrible person, but I couldn't understand why my mother and brother dragged me back here to talk to me about some alleged threats from *her* terrible husband. I had *just* signed my first record deal! I had *just* pulled myself out of this crazy, scary family drama. What were they even talking about? Why were they doing this? Why was I even there?

The vibe was getting increasingly creepy and claustrophobic. I remember Morgan saying in his quiet sinister way, "I got this plan to shut him up. You don't need to know the details, but believe me I can make him shut the fuck up." He went on to say that all he needed was five thousand dollars. There it was.

I looked over at my mother, hoping to get some clarity. She just kept her eyes fixed on Morgan, who had obviously convinced her to let him run the show. He continued to remind me how mean and vindictive her husband was (and indeed he *was*—he'd been displaying opportunistic behavior since the moment he met me) and that the press would shame me and destroy my career. All I had ever lived for was to be an artist and I had *just signed a record deal*. Maybe it all could be taken away in an instant? And he said it again—for "just five thousand dollars," he could protect me and take care of the threat. "It's just five thousand dollars. No one will ever know." Five thousand dollars for what? To *do* what? A sickening panic began to bubble in my lower belly.

Morgan had a long history of violence, of being mixed up with shady characters and shady situations, and there was no telling what he might do for money. In 1980, he was involved in a scandalous Suffolk County murder case. John William Maddox was murdered by his wife, Virginia Carole Maddox. Their son was an acquaintance of Morgan's. Before the night she shot her husband in the neck with a rifle, she had propositioned Morgan to kill him for her for thirty thousand dollars. He accepted a $1,200 advance but did not carry out the job. According to the court records, her solicitation of Morgan (he was compelled to testify before a grand jury) was key evidence in disproving her claim of self-defense and helped lead to her murder conviction.

I was barely in the third grade when Morgan was involved in a plot to murder a man for money. I remember him and my mother talking about it, and I have a vague recollection of seeing courtroom sketches in the house. Morgan snitched, so he didn't get any time for accepting the payment.

"C'mon, it's only five thousand dollars, no one will ever know" kept ringing in my ears. I sprang to my feet and began pacing the five or fewer steps between the little living room and the even smaller kitchen; both seemed to shrink an inch with each passing second. "You don't have to do anything but give me the money," he said again. I was struggling to process what was *actually* happening here. I don't even think I'd received my first advance check and already, *already* my brother and mother were trying to get money out of me?! And for what? To fuck up my mother's husband?! What the fuck.

Tragically, I wasn't surprised Morgan had begun to try and screw a siphon hose into me right away, but what got me to my feet and blew my mind was that my *mother* was going along with it. She remained savagely quiet the entire time Morgan spewed out conspiracy theories about blackmail, exposing and humiliating both her daughters, and her son arranging to "fuck up" her husband for money. Was she really willing to agree to place all of her children in such grave emotional, spiritual (and possibly legal) peril? Or, equally terrible, was she in on a plot with Morgan to extort money from me? Maybe she was just rendered powerless under his spell.

I was not prepared for the implications all this was having for me and for my position in this family and in this world. Under no circumstances could I ever, *ever* entertain being involved in physically harming *anybody*, even a despicable dickhead like her husband. I categorically refused to even entertain their sick scam. Yet what was really beating me down was that I knew that if I gave Morgan this first five thousand dollars, and if he did something violent or criminal, he would definitely blackmail *me*. This would be the first five thousand drips in a faucet he would use to drain money from me forever.

How delusional of me to even entertain the notion my mother and brother were going to toast me for making my only dream come true. Instead they called me back to gut me. I was in a sad shock. I don't recall exactly what I said, but I remember walking in tight circles, that sick feeling now in my heart and pounding up to my eyes, and I was shaking my head—"No, *No*" . . . and something unseen inside me snapped, and I broke away from that pack.

I stumbled out of the shack, knowing, without a doubt, that I did not belong to any of them. My father was estranged. My sister burned and sold me out. And now there was no more brother and no more mother. Standing alone.

Still bruised, still walk on eggshells
Same frightened child, hide to protect myself
(Can't believe I still need to protect myself from you)
But you can't manipulate me like before
Examine 1 John 4:4
And I wish you well . . .

—"I Wish You Well"

So, by "normal" standards, a record label reaching out to family for help in communicating with an artist was not a risky move. But they did not know the bad, bad moves my family could make.

You, dear children, are from God and have overcome them,
Because the one who is in you is greater
than the one who is in the world

1 John 4:4

To say I was on the edge by the time Morgan got to Tots's would be generous. Exhausted and hungry, I was deprived of all care. Looking into my wild and weary eyes, he tempted me: "Hey, how about a nice trip up to Pat's house?"

Though I hadn't ever had a *nice* trip to my mother's house, in my shattered state, my brother made a convincing argument. Nobody, he contended, would dare to disturb me at my *mother's* house. His voice was sugary sweet, and I was too drained to access my gut instincts. If I were at full capacity, I would've known my mother and her son were the *last* people I should be around when I was so vulnerable.

Even if she cared for me, at that point, my mother knew nothing about me, and nothing about what I was currently going through. She had absolutely no idea of the burden and responsibility of being an artist who generates so much money and energy: To have so many people living off of you, counting on you, and pushing you to constantly work and work. To sing and smile, dress up and twirl, fly and write and work and work! She had no concept of the humiliation I was suffering from the ravenous media monster that was feeding off of me. She couldn't imagine how wounded and hunted I felt. My mother never could acknowledge my fear. In fact, she often triggered it.

But now, I was going to go back with them. Any house my mother was in never felt like a safe haven, especially if Morgan was present, yet I was far too fragile to resist. In my fogginess, it actually made sense to me to go upstate to the house I had bought her, the house I knew so well, where it was quiet and comfortable and there would be plenty of room for everyone. Stripped of my better instincts, I agreed to go. But if I was going, I decided, we all were going. Safety in numbers, I thought. So Morgan, Tots, and I went off on a ride upstate. Over the river and through the woods, to my mother's house we go.

CALAMITY AND
DOG HAIR

My mother wasn't home yet from being in the city with the record-label delegation at the hotel, and I was relieved. It meant I wouldn't run the risk of being provoked by her and Morgan together, and I especially didn't want to use the little energy I had left to try and explain to her why I just needed sleep. Thankfully, I also had my girl Tots as a buffer. As we approached the house, I began to relax a bit. I thought, *This is the house I purchased for my mother and my family to live in, to find comfort in.* Now I was the one who needed it more than anything. I had designed a guest bedroom for anyone in the family who needed a place to stay, that I knew I could surely use now. I could already picture its inviting warmth in my head. All I wanted to do was get a little bit of food in my stomach, get upstairs, close the door, and go to sleep before my mother got home.

As we walked in the house I was struggling to hide how wrecked I was, especially in front of my nephew Mike, who was still living there. He was just a kid and had already been through so much with his addicted mother. I wanted to spare him the traumatic history that was pulsing through me, through all of us. But I was also beginning to panic, realizing I was now isolated from the city and my actual home. I didn't have my driver, I was with Morgan, and my mother would be coming back any minute. They could be poisonous and manipulative together. I felt myself swinging back and forth, out of the house and back to the shack. I was in *their* world now. The past and the present felt the same—unsafe.

The house smelled of calamity and dog hair. I scanned the clutter and disarray. (I never liked the way my mother kept the house; that's why I always had cleaning staff for her.) Like my father, I've always liked things really clean. Mess causes anxiety for me. I began to put things in order, an activity I commonly do to recenter myself. I thought if I could bring some order to the chaos in the house, even in a small way, that I could stay in my body. But I kept slipping.

I'm not helpless, I told myself. This was the beautiful house that *I* had bought, created, and managed as an adult. I was not a little girl in a haphazard shack. *I can bring order to this.* But God, I was so tired. Maybe, I thought, by some loophole of time and space, we really *were* back in the shack. I needed to sleep. Desperately. And I was starved. My mind again began to race.

I went to the kitchen to see if I could scrounge up a little morsel to eat. Typically, when visiting my mother, I would bring all the provisions needed, including disposable plates and cutlery, to ensure everyone would have enough to eat and with an easy cleanup. In the kitchen, I found the sink piled high with dirty dishes. I knew it would help to ground me if I focused on a simple task. Washing the dishes—that would work. *I'm gonna do this. I'm gonna do the dishes*, I thought. *I'm going to eat off a clean plate, then I'm gonna go to sleep.*

Reaching to turn on the faucet, I suddenly remembered. *Six days. I haven't slept more than two hours in six days.* My hands trembled as I tried to begin the task I'd set for myself. All I could hear was my heart slamming inside my chest. *What am I doing? Washing the dishes. Right.* After what seems like an eternity, I finally got one plate done and placed it in the rack. Next I picked up a sudsy bowl, but I felt it slip through my fingers and clatter to the floor. I tried again: I got one done. I dropped one. Now I had to clean up the dish and water on the floor. The sounds of running water, clanging dishes, and people talking swirled together. I was frantically trying to clean up everything and get out of sight before my mother got home. I bent down to get the dish off the floor, and the light went dim and the sounds started trailing off. All the space around me narrowed, and I started to fall away. I blacked out for a split second but was able to recover before I completely collapsed.

I made it. The surges of anxiety were gone, but so was every drop of my energy and every ounce of my will. But hey, if I couldn't go to sleep naturally, passing out would do just fine. With the help of Tots I stumbled up the stairs toward the guest room, picking up clumps of dog hair on the steps along the way (I was barely conscious, but my standards were still awake). I was an exhausted refugee, and I thought that refuge was exactly what I had found. I collapsed onto the cozy bed, surrendering to its softness. Everything quickly turned to a long-awaited dark, and I sank down into it. *Finally, peace.*

"Mariah! What are you doing? They're looking for you!" A booming, dramatic voice violently pulled me out of the pool of quiet in which I had been floating. Lost and sputtering, I was wrenched into consciousness to find my mother hovering over me. My own mother had woken me up from the first sleep I'd had in nearly a week! To make matters worse, she was waking me up to tell me that the record label was looking for me to get me back to work—as if, rather than being my mother and caretaker, she was some kind of agent for the machine that had repeatedly placed my earning potential over my well-being.

That was the last straw. I really did leave my body. Something deep inside me rose quickly up and out of my throat; it was feral with seething rage.

"Well, I did the best I could! 'I did the best I could!' That's all you ever say!" I roared at her, imitating her exaggerated tones. It was a justification I'd heard from her, over and over again, for my entire life. After six days of being hunted down—six days of hiding, anxiety, and near demise; six days of no rest; six days of trauma—I had finally gotten to sleep in the house *I'd* bought, only to be awoken by my own mother. My *mother*, who had found so much rest for herself in that house I worked so hard for!

I wasn't expecting a hug or a kiss on the forehead, homemade chicken soup or baked cookies. I wasn't expecting a warm bath. I wasn't expecting a massage, hot tea, or a bedtime story. I wasn't expecting any comforts a sick child might receive from a healthy mother. I knew my mother didn't have the capacity for that kind of maternal response; after all, I was the one who took care of things. *I* took care of *her*, and everything else. I wasn't expecting her to do anything to help me feel better, but I certainly wasn't expecting her to wake me up! My rage took over. I couldn't see, I couldn't hear, I couldn't feel my body.

As a survival response, I dipped into the depth of my sarcasm and made fun of her, viciously. Cutting to humor when faced with extreme stress or trauma had been a defense mechanism I developed as a child.

"Well, I did the best I could! I did the best I could!" I imitated her mockingly, over and over. I was trying to wake *her* up, with her own words, to the cruel absurdity of the moment. I knew it was wrong, but every filter I might have had to stop me had been ripped away.

I screeched, "I JUST WANT TO GO TO SLEEEEEP!" All my fears, all my resentment, all the years of impressions I'd done of her behind her back—all my anger was thrashing out with each word I hurled at her.

"Well! I! Did! The! Best! I! Could!" I shouted.

No one, and especially not my mother, had ever seen me in such a rage. Throughout my childhood, it was always Morgan and Alison who would throw hysterical fits. *They* would scream and yell and throw condiment bottles at each other. *They* would fight. *They* would shriek and threaten my mother or knock her out cold. My brother and father had fistfights. But now it was *my* turn to let it rip. I wasn't violent or throwing obscenities, but I was still going *off*, for me.

I was in an angry, hysterical frenzy, but I was still also thinking about my nephew Mike. I didn't want to continue the sick cycle we'd all been through. I was standing in front of his door, putting my body between my mother, my tirade, and his innocence. Before we arrived, I had asked Tots to look after Mike; I trusted her because of the countless nieces and nephews she'd taken care of over the years. I never knew what could happen with my family, so she was behind the door comforting him. I was screaming, "This has to stop! We have to break the cycle!"

All the fear and fury I had bottled inside myself was now directed at my mother. She was in the center of the cycle I was desperate to break. My mother was finally experiencing the full bloom of my anger and was ill equipped to understand it or deescalate it. She couldn't even get the *joke*—on the contrary, she felt threatened and embarrassed by it. She shook off her bewilderment; then an iciness consumed her, and she shot me a look that said, *Oh really? You dare mock me? You dare threaten me? You have no idea who you're messing with.*

When my mother feels scared, her complete assurance in the historic evidence that whiteness will *always* be protected activates—and she often calls the cops. At various times, she'd called the cops on my brother, my sister, and even my sister's children. My mother called the cops even when she didn't necessarily feel threatened. One Christmas, I brought my family to Aspen. It was the first year after I left Sing Sing, and I decided I wanted to create my own ultimate Christmas tradition, so I took the whole Carey clan. For me, Christmas means family. I rented a house so I could decorate and have home-cooked meals and we could sing Christmas carols at the top of our lungs if we wanted to, and I put my family up in a fabulous hotel.

At one point we were all hanging out together at the house, and Morgan proceeded to get spectacularly inebriated. When he disappeared for a bit, my mother turned directly to her usual dramatics.

"Where's Morgan?" she bellowed. "I can't find Morgan!" Mind you, Morgan was a thirty-something grown man, but still my mother was in a self-induced panic. "*I can't find Morgan!*" She called his hotel room repeatedly, but there was no answer. So, what did she do? She called the cops. My mother called the cops in Aspen, Colorado, to find my non-white, sometimes drug dealing, been-in-the-system, drunk-ass brother. The cops came to the hotel, and it was a whole big drama. She asked them to break down his hotel door, behind which it turned out Morgan was lying naked, butt up, passed out on the bed. The news spread like wildfire throughout the town, and that, ladies and gentlemen, was the last time Morgan and Cop Caller Mom were invited to spend Christmas with me in Aspen. I really *don't* want a lot for Christmas. Particularly not the cops.

And so, that night in Westchester, she called the cops on me too.

The police arrived quickly, as they tend to do in white, affluent neighborhoods. My mother opened the door. I heard an officer ask, "Is there a problem, ma'am?"

"Yes, we are having a *problem*," she replied, welcoming the two white policemen into the house. I could tell they kind of recognized me, though I was still in quite a state and looked it. I had been passed out, asleep, for the first time in nearly a week. In a tumultuous emotional whirlwind, I had quickly put my hair into a bun. I had on leggings and a T-shirt (as one would, in one's home, when one is trying to rest). I had somewhat pulled it together, because that's what you do when there are police involved. But I didn't have on my superstar mask, which is how almost everyone knows me (except for the Lambs, of course). Without all the wardrobe and glam, I did appear troubled, perhaps a little wild or unwell.

Though the officers were technically in *my* house, their attention was directed toward my mother. She gave them an odd, knowing look, which felt like the equivalent of a secret-society handshake, some sort of white-woman-in-distress cop code. She had been defied, and I had dared to be belligerent. I was being aggressive toward *her*. I was scaring *her*. And they received her signal loud and clear. It was in their training. The code was in her culture. This was her world, her people, and her language. She had control. Even Mariah Carey couldn't compete with a nameless white woman in distress. If I had been given just a day or two to rest, I would've woken up and been ready to make a video. But instead, here I was, standing in my mother's (actually *my*) house with the cops.

The most terrifying part was that I was too worn out to feel my source. The negative energy of my mother, Morgan, and the police—the whole scene—blocked my light. I needed to see Tots. She had a big God in her life too, and if I couldn't access mine, I thought maybe I could feel hers. I believed she could somehow keep me safe in a sisterly, spiritual way. I was trying to hold strong to her, but she was also really scared of the cops. And could you blame her? It's totally understandable. She was the only visibly 100 percent Black person in the house. After successfully keeping out of trouble with police for years in the Brownsville projects, how could she explain to her mother that she'd gotten arrested in an affluent suburb and was in some upstate jail? Lord knows what they would have done to her in there (this was *way* before #BlackLivesMatter and cell-phone activism, although even a movement hasn't stopped most of the brutality). So Tots was trying her best to keep herself and Mike away from the turmoil and out of sight. Against two white cops and one white woman, in upper Westchester, Tots knew she was out-privileged and totally out-powered.

Given his long, turbulent history with law enforcement, Morgan was lying low in the little den we called the "Irish room." No one tried to explain to the police that it was just a family blowout—that everything was okay, and I was just overworked and had lost my temper. I needed care, *not* the cops. But no one defended me. The only thing the cops saw was a scared white woman in a big house full of nonwhite people.

Betrayed, humiliated, and overwhelmed by reliving the neglect and trauma of my childhood, I let go. Not that I had any fight left in me, but I knew better than to fight with the police. I was done. Ironically, I was relieved that the police could take me away from this house of trauma and betrayal. My brother had lured me back into the same depths of dysfunction that he, my sister, and my mother had dwelled in when I was a child. My mother had stolen me from my sleep, then turned me over to the authorities. There was nothing left to do but surrender. I agreed to be removed from my own house by the police, with one simple request—that I be allowed to put on my shoes. My family might have taken my pride, my trust, and the last of my energy, but they weren't going to get my dignity too.

I slipped on some heels (mules, most likely), neatened my ponytail, slapped on some lip gloss, and got in the backseat of the squad car. Being hauled off by cops was certainly no comfort, but I was defeated and needed to get away by any means necessary. The firm seat cushions and the bulletproof protection inside the car provided a twisted sense of security. My body was reminded that it was still in critical need of rest. Morgan slid into the backseat next to me.

I looked at him, empty of everything, unable to accept what my family had just done to me. I couldn't believe it. I had to outsource my pain, to put the blame on a substitute villain. I thought back to how it had all begun—when had things started to unravel?

In a daze, I whispered, "This is all Tommy Mottola's fault."

Morgan's eyes narrowed, and he flashed that sinister smile again. "That's right." He nodded. "That's right."

We drove off into the darkness.

BROKEN DOWN

That night, I did not "have a breakdown." I was *broken* down—by the very people who were supposed to keep me whole. I knew of a place the locals called a "spa" that was very close, and I asked the police if they would take me there. They obliged. I wasn't familiar with the services or reputation of the place, but I figured at the very least I could finally get some sleep, some nutritious food, and perhaps some medical attention. After all I'd been through, I was very concerned about my physical condition. I knew enough to know I needed healing from the compounded trauma I had just experienced. My body was there, but my mind, my emotions, and my spirit were all powered down, in what I now realize was protection mode.

I remember getting out of the squad car and pacing in the parking lot, knowing I didn't belong in that place, but I didn't belong at my family house either. I didn't know where I *belonged*. After a long and groggy battle, Morgan convinced me to go inside. I could feel nothing. I signed myself in, believing I could sign myself out. I had no idea what I had actually signed myself up for. After speaking with some of the staff, Morgan left me there. The size, color, and smell of the place, the names, the faces of the people—I don't have much memory of the details. I was led to a small room at the end of a hall. I perceived it as windowless, though it most likely was not. There was a door to close me in. There was a bed. I curled up tight on top of it.

Terror came quickly.

I could hear the dull thud of a heavy mop hitting and sloshing on the floor in the distance, and the muffled, mingled voices of young girls chatting and giggling. Every once in a while, I clearly heard them say "Mariah Carey." The mop and the voices were getting closer and louder, settling right outside my door. Their laughter was ringing in my head. I coiled tighter into myself, shut my eyes, and tried to disappear. No relief came. I was deeply scared and completely alone. Prayer wouldn't come. Fear was my only companion. The whimpering of frightened people behind doors like mine never ceased as the tortuous night crawled toward morning.

The next day came. I was far from rested or clear-headed, but I was no longer totally numb. I knew I was in need of healing, peace, therapy, food, rest, and restoration. I needed *care*, and the rash decision to come to the closest place possible had clearly not been the right one. I was bombarded with frantic thoughts: *Where is my purse? Where is all my stuff? What the fuck am I doing in this terrible, random place, sharing a bathroom I'm too scared to pee in? How do I get out of here?*

It was clearly not a spa; there was nothing therapeutic or restorative about it at all. It was closer to a prison. Full of confused young people, unruly and unsettling, it was run like an upscale juvenile detention center. The food was disgusting. My mind was racing. Had my mother really called the cops on me? Humiliated me? Escorted me out of the house I *bought*? Was I really here now, in some institution posing as a "spa"?

The most frightening thing was that I had no control over my situation. I didn't have my car, my things, or any money. I didn't have my two-way pager to communicate with my people. There was only one single, shared pay phone. When no one was looking, I tried to call a few people, but to no avail. There was no privacy. I was walking around as a deflated Mariah Carey, stripped of her professional mask and powers, fully exposed to God knows what.

While my memories of my interactions with staff and other patients are mostly vague, I distinctly recall being brought into a bare little office that felt like a police interrogation room, where an older, balding white administrator conducted a haphazard intake interview. I was clearly still upset, and it was difficult to quickly paint a picture of the misunderstanding that had happened at that house the night before, combined with the intensity and severity of all the work obligations I had ahead of me. I went on about having to shoot a video, about the film premiere preparations for *Glitter*, and about all the people dependent on me. I was riddled with anxiety and frustrated that this man wasn't understanding the stakes. Not only was he not caring, he was hostile.

"Looks like you need a dose of humility," was his condescending response to all I had told him. Oh, he thoroughly enjoyed spitting out that line. It was such an obvious and pitiful power grab. I could almost see him puffing up, believing he'd taken the diva down. Not only the tabloids revel in watching stars crash to the ground. I was defenseless—knifed in the back by my ex-husband and stabbed in the heart by my brother and mother. And they all left me to bleed out inside some hellhole.

I went to try to sign myself out, but to my horror, I discovered that I couldn't. I don't know what my brother told the staff, but people were treating me like I was out of control and out of my mind (and most seemed to be enjoying it). It took several days of red tape and paperwork to get out.

I knew Morgan and my mother had been communicating, and I strongly believe they orchestrated the whole thing. I returned to the scene of no crime, my mother's house (correction: *my* house). "Coincidentally," there were paparazzi waiting in the woods to greet me. The cover of the next day's *New York Post* was a photo of me, shot with a long lens through the trees, in pajamas, with little dark sunglasses and a messy bun, sipping juice through a straw. The photo was emblazoned with a giant caption, "World Exclusive! Mariah: The First Photos."

My mother was thrilled. She exclaimed, "Look, it's just like Marilyn!" (It was not.) The *Daily News* cover even gave her a mention: "Mariah's Crack Up! Mother's desperate 9-1-1 call as diva unraveled." When I went back to the house to retrieve my things with my road manager, my mother, in a drab housedress, was sitting on the floor of the porch in the rain, playing jacks, in what appeared to be a trance. It kinda freaked my road manager out. What pathetic irony.

Her glee at the tabloid coverage was no surprise to me. Even though I was the child who didn't break the rules (or laws, or bottles), my mother didn't seem to have the capacity to fully celebrate me as I matured into an accomplished artist. Sometimes I wondered if she couldn't even tolerate my achievements. I often felt like there was an undertow of jealousy pulling on her smile, though I still included her in many of the major events in my life.

One of the greatest honors of my career was receiving the Congressional Award. I'd dreamed of receiving Grammys and Oscars for music or acting, but to be honored by my country for my service to others was a distinction beyond even my dreams—and I dream *big*. I was the recipient of the 1999 Horizon Award, which is given for charitable work focused on promoting personal development in young people, for my work with Camp Mariah, through the Fresh Air Fund. I've never been deeply involved in politics, and at the time I really didn't fully understand the significance of the award and the event. It's one of only two medals legislated by a congressional act (the other being the Medal of Honor). I was being honored along with former secretary of state Colin Powell.

We were hosted like dignitaries, and there was a very elegant, formal sit-down dinner before the ceremony. My mother and I were in high-powered, bipartisan company, including Tom Selleck; former Republican Senate Majority Leader Trent Lott, from Mississippi, and former Democratic House Minority Leader Dick Gephardt (who ran for president a couple of times). This is one of the few events where both political parties put politics aside and proudly participate equally as Americans. On this night, in a room full of politicians, it's understood no one discusses politics (even *I* know that). I was proud that a little girl who grew up feeling like an outcast now had an honored seat at one of the most esteemed tables in the world.

I had my mother all dolled up: hair, nails, professional makeup. I bought her a new, fancy dress—the whole nine. This was an occasion to look our best and be on our best behavior.

Well . . .

She had a few cocktails on the short plane ride from New York to Washington, DC, and continued to booze it on up during the dinner. As the effects of the drinks kicked in, her decorum slipped away. She began to theatrically express her political opinions, which you absolutely *don't* do at a distinguished event like this, even stone-cold sober. Her thoughts descended into insults, which melted down into a small but disturbing tirade. The one thing everyone knew *not* to do was what my mother was now fully engaged in. I was mortified.

My security leaned over and whispered, "We have to get her out of here." I agreed. They whisked her out of the dining area and hid her in my dressing room near the stage for the awards ceremony—apparently just in time, because it was reported to me that when she got into the room she started yelling, "I hate Mariah! I hate my daughter!" When I escaped from the dinner table to go and check on her, she was completely sloshed.

I slid back to my seat and cheerfully performed as if all were well (Lord knows I've had lots of practice). I was escorted to the stage accompanied by two beautiful young Black women from the Fresh Air Fund, who, thankfully, anchored me in the purpose of the evening. I managed to make it through my speech and accept the award. When I got offstage, it was clear we had to get my irate and inebriated mother out of the venue fast, as she was now throwing a full-blown fit. My security worked swiftly to get her into the car, to the airport, and on the plane. On the flight, still decked out in the designer dress I had bought her, she slinked into her first-class seat, continuing to drink and drone, "*Morgan* is the only one I love. *Morgan* is the only one who loves me." Security got my mother safely home and poured her into bed. Alone in the back of a limo, in my black silk gown, hugging an award from my country, I cried.

She may have been in a blackout and unaware of what she did or said. But I had to process the sadness, embarrassment, and pain of the experience. The next morning, I was nervous her booze-induced performance would make it into the press. But it didn't. I had protected her. I don't know who saw her, but mercifully, her congressional calamity did not make it into the tabloids.

She didn't call to apologize. She didn't say anything.

🦋

Being Mariah Carey is a job—*my* job—and I had to get back to it. I knew there would be eyes and lenses everywhere. I needed someone to light the way out of the darkness that place had become. By that time, I trusted only a handful of people. So before I was able to see my way out of the shadowy "Cabin in the Woods," I called on my trusted friend and anchor makeup artist Kristofer Buckle for support. He lifted me up, reapplied my protective public face, and walked with me into the sunlight.

I was wounded, but I got myself back to my penthouse in Manhattan. There was so much recovery and repair to be done. I was still quite fragile, very concerned with the condition of my very new, very big deal at Virgin, and a very short time away from the release of *Glitter*. The coverage of my "crack-up" had everybody understandably shook—not least of all me. I had not regained my emotional or spiritual strength. I was still very much inside the nightmare, and Morgan was still very much in control. But I didn't see him as a puppeteer just yet. I still held a desperate, distorted trust in him. He had snapped me out of my screaming fit at the hotel by saying "birthdays at Roy Boy's." He was not in sight when the cops came in Westchester. He had ridden with me to the "spa." So I didn't associate him with the current collection of catastrophes. He seemed at best an ally, at worst an innocent bystander. I needed *someone*. And I needed to believe that not everyone was against me.

The pedestal I'd erected for my brother when I was a little girl had long since been reduced to rubble, but I kept trying to place him back on top of it. Though I could not see it then, we were clearly in ruins. If I had had my wits about me, or if someone on my payroll had known better, I would have had a team of specialists and professionals lined up to evaluate and treat me at my home. I did have the wherewithal to want to tuck myself away at an actual spa for a few days, where at least I could get some rest, wholesome food, maybe some body treatments—all the things I'd wanted on my way to that first hellish "spa." I also wanted the opportunity to clear my head and protect myself (and the label) from more salacious headlines.

Morgan recommended I go to Los Angeles, where he was currently living, making the case that there were *actual* spas there (true) and no New York newspapers (also true). A spa in LA seemed like a good idea at the time. I allowed Morgan to make the arrangements (not a good idea, at *any* time, but I was desperate).

When we got to LA my anxiety and disorientation was intensified by the tragedy of Aaliyah's sudden and horrific death. Just a few days earlier she had told the press, "I know this business can be difficult, it can be stressful. Much love to Mariah Carey. I hope she gets better soon." The entire music industry was rocked by her death, but the R & B and hip-hop community was devastated. She was indeed our little princess.

So much was happening, and I couldn't fully understand the magnitude of the damage being done to me. Morgan hooked up with some random guy who he said would be helping us. I remember driving around on the highway for what seemed like an eternity. We finally stopped at a place that did not look like a spa at all but, rather, a detox facility. I was still in the hold of extreme exhaustion, so while I wasn't thrilled, I didn't resist. Morgan even went so far as to say, "Come on; it'll be *fun*." It was not fun. It was one of the most harrowing times of my life—and I had seen some *times*.

Once more, I didn't have control of the situation. I could not speak up for myself, and when I could, I was ignored and overpowered.

The facility in LA turned out to be a hard-core detox and rehab center. The first thing that happened to me was they administered drugs—heavy, hard narcotics. They were giant horse pills the color of Pepto-Bismol. At first, I refused to take them, but I didn't have the drive to fully fight. I was so weak. I thought maybe I would just be able to get a little sleep (where was the Ambien when a girl needed it?). Eventually I did sleep, but fitfully. The drugs blocked me from whatever energy and will to fight I had in reserve. They put my big, bright God further in the shadows. They made me sluggish, puffy, and compliant.

I was in a fog much of the time.

Frumpily ensconced in some piece of shit hideous institutional ensemble, I was drained, and my soul was heavy. My face was vulnerable and hadn't had any protection in many days. That's one function of makeup—even while giving a natural look, it can serve as war paint, an invisible force field. It often does for me. It shields me from people literally getting into my pores and under my skin. But I had no such protection in that place.

One morning, I was in my bleak room, feeling drowsy, when an attendant came and brought me into the common area. It was crowded with staff and inmates—I mean, patients—and all were staring up at the large television in silence. On the screen was what looked like the view from the kitchen window in my New York City penthouse in the sky. But the picture was framed in chalky, gray clouds of smoke. Orange and red fireballs were shooting out from the top of the glistening silver Twin Towers like meteors against a vibrant blue sky. Then the proud, monumental buildings crumbled from within. One at a time, they came crashing down in excruciatingly slow motion. The effects of the drugs I'd been kept on were no match for the shock I was experiencing. In that instant, I was stone-cold alert as I watched my majestic skyline disintegrate. My home city was burning and collapsing, and I was thousands of miles away, locked inside a dismal detox—drugged, devastated, and alone.

I was frozen, eyes locked on the horror unfolding before me, when someone from the staff tapped me on my shoulder. They told me it was being reported that terrorists had attacked the World Trade Center, and that they would now be releasing me. I was free to go. Miraculously, it seemed, I was no longer in need of containment or sedatives. I was no longer crazy and out of control.

So I was magically "good to go," because terrorists had attacked America and a "cracked-up diva" wasn't interesting anymore? (*Hello*?!!) But I didn't ask questions. It felt like the world was coming to an end for all of us. And if it was the end, I wanted to get the fuck out of there. Between being there, getting out, and the chaos and terror of the attacks back home, I didn't even realize it was the day the *Glitter* soundtrack was scheduled for release.

The coincidence of my sudden release from "rehab" *and* the release of the *Glitter* soundtrack *and* the 9/11 attacks was haunting. You know how, in a sci-fi horror film, the apocalypse happens and then there's a lone survivor wandering around surveying the devastation? That was me on that warm and cloudy day in LA. On September 11, 2001, I walked out of detox pumped full of toxins. The city of LA was solid, but I was shaky. I felt alone, untethered, and out of my body. I got myself to a hotel and had the first uninterrupted rest I'd had in weeks. With the tiny bit of strength that rest provided, I was able to finally get to an actual spa, because I still had to do "the best I could" to prepare for the *Glitter* movie premiere, which was now only ten days away.

It was a blur, but I pulled myself together. I got some highlights, a cut, and a blowout. I wore a one-shoulder fitted tank top, as I do on the *Glitter* poster, but it had an American flag bedazzled on the front, in honor of the victims and heroes. I paired it with simple low-rise jeans, held my chin high, and hit the red carpet at the Village Theater in Westwood with a smile. I was blessed to have lots of kids and young people at the premiere, as they were the intended audience. *Glitter* was not made for serious cinemagoers and art-gallery hoppers; it was an imperfect, fun, PG flick.

The box-office sales for *Glitter* were dismal, in large part because the country was still reeling from the 9/11 attacks. The tragedy was still fresh, and no one was ready for the lightweight distraction that was *Glitter*. Out of respect for our collective mourning, one would think the media would have turned their obsession away from me as well, but it seemed to only intensify.

After the *Glitter* premiere, I stayed in LA to prepare for the *America: A Tribute to Heroes* telethon, honoring the thousands who died in the attacks. Organized by George Clooney, it would be my first performance since I emerged from that nightmare of family, cops, and institutions. The biggest stars in entertainment—Tom Hanks, Goldie Hawn, Bruce Springsteen, Stevie Wonder, Muhammad Ali, Pearl Jam, Paul Simon, Billy Joel, Robert De Niro, and others—came out, united as Americans. I sang "Hero," as Americans—first responders and so many other brave, unnamed people—showed the world what true heroes really look like. Never had I imagined when I wrote this song that it would mean so much in such a horrific moment in history.

I was anxious to get back to New York. It was inspiring how the city immediately got to work putting itself back together in the wake of the attacks, and I was eager to put my life back together too. I wasn't permitted to resume residence in my penthouse yet, as much of lower Manhattan was still closed off for safety and security reasons. In the meantime, I stayed in a hotel and blocked my family and others from getting to me. I was waking from the nightmare they'd created, and I had to get my own help; I wanted desperately to get back to being okay.

I chose a therapist in upstate New York. He had a profound intellect, but also a deep sensitivity. His insights were not only acute but comforting—he gave me a modern white Buddha vibe. Under his qualified care, I was able to begin to unpack the demoralizing and dehumanizing ordeal I had just been through. Losing my power and being put in scary, inappropriate institutions by my mother and brother while the press ravaged my reputation was almost the end for me.

My therapist named the physical illness I'd been experiencing for so many years—all the nausea from being humiliated by kids and teachers, all the breaking out in hives all over, all the severe upper back and shoulder pain from stress from Tommy, all the dizziness and revulsion from the terror of my brother, all the psychological distress I endured which wreaked havoc on my body had a name—*somatization*. Having a highly respected professional name, it validated that what I was physically experiencing was *real*. It was suddenly all so real.

My career was everything to me, and because of my mother, my brother, and Tommy, it was nearly taken away. Honestly, it felt like they almost killed me. They came close, but they didn't kill me, or my spirit. They didn't permanently damage my mind or my soul. But, *Lawd, they do try.*

There is nothing more powerful than surviving a trip to hell and coming home covered in the light of restoration. It wasn't an easy journey back to myself and to God, but I was back on my feet and walking forward. No one, I decided, was going to stop me or take all my power again. Ever.

In therapy, my emotions were safe to come out of the frigid hold of survival mode, and I was fucking furious. I was supporting *everybody* around me, and they had the audacity to throw me into institutions, give me drugs, and try to take control of my life. When I told my therapist what had happened, he assured me I was absolutely *not* crazy. At most, he said, I'd had a "diva fit." It was a wonder I wasn't permanently emotionally damaged, given what I lived through; however I will probably always struggle with PTSD. He also affirmed that I was completely justified in being enraged. He very candidly suggested I examine the role *money* had played in the experience with my family. I was so wrapped up in the childhood history, the betrayal, the *love* I had once had for everyone involved that I was blind to motive. It was no coincidence that my mother and brother were working on the side of the record company instead of protecting me and advocating for my well-being, and that they just *happened* to claim I was unstable and try to institutionalize me immediately after I had signed the biggest cash record deal for a solo artist in history. I could accept that I was a cash cow for record companies; after all, I was "the Franchise." It's the name of the game—it may be dirty, but I had no illusions that the music business was, first and foremost, a cutthroat *business*. But though I hadn't cut a business deal with my mother or my siblings, they were happy to take me to the slaughter just like the record companies and the media.

I knew for a long time that to my family, I'd been an "ATM machine with a wig on" (a moniker I gave myself). I gave them so much money, especially my mother, and still it wasn't enough. They tried to destroy me in order to take complete control. The therapist made an obvious suggestion: if they could prove I was unstable, they certainly could have believed they would become the executors of my affairs. He asked me to look at them objectively—how they viewed the world, how they never really had consistent, legitimate work but still felt like the world owed them something. We *all* had varying degrees of tough shit to go through in my family, but in this way, we fundamentally differed. I didn't think the world owed me anything. I simply believed I would conquer the world I was born into, in my own way. As I worked myself to extreme exhaustion, they watched and waited for me to fall, like scavengers, so that they might gain control over the fortune I had negotiated, built, and fought for.

🦋

Years later, the pattern still continued, as patterns do. My family didn't change. One of the definitions of insanity, it's often said, is doing the same things over and over and expecting different results. My version of insanity was allowing the same thing to be done *to* me, over and over, by the same people.

"Please change your cast of characters." That was the simple and profound request my therapist eventually made. While I couldn't change the characters of my mother, brother, and sister, I did have the power to change how *I* characterized them in my life. So for my sanity and peace of mind, my therapist encouraged me to literally rename and reframe my family. My mother became "Pat" to me, Morgan, "my ex-brother," and Alison, "my ex-sister." I had to stop expecting them to one day miraculously become the mommy, big brother, and big sister I fantasized about. I had to stop making myself available to be hurt by them. It has been helpful. I have no doubt it is emotionally and physically safer for me not to have any contact with my ex-brother and ex-sister. The situation with Pat, on the other hand, is more complicated. I have reserved some room in my heart and life to hold her—but with boundaries. Creating boundaries with the woman who gave birth to me is not easy; it is a work in progress.

🦋

After I was broken, I received a blessing. The trouble and trauma I endured was not only emotional, it was spiritual as well. As such, I sought healing for my soul. I knew I had to revive and recommit to my relationship with God. I am eternally grateful to have met my pastor, Bishop Clarence Keaton, when I did. I met him through Tots. We used to attend church together at True Worship Church Worldwide Ministries, right across from the Louis Pink Houses projects in East New York. Tots and I were even re-baptized there together. At True Worship, I became a student of the Bible, doing a three-year intensive. We went through it from Old to New Testament. I took notes, and I took the healing words in.

Bishop Keaton used to be a pool shark; he lived a very different life before becoming a pastor. He'd already earned respect in the neighborhood, when at that time it would not be uncommon to duck bullets in broad daylight, so he had protection, and people didn't mess with him. I would have security provided by the church, and the congregation would respect my privacy—the bishop saw to it. I found community in the church and family in my bishop, who treated me like a daughter. He often came to talk to me, even when he was going through health issues toward the end of his life.

It was such an honor to solidify Bishop Keaton's legacy as a great spiritual teacher in my life and in the world by featuring him on two of my songs, "I Wish You Well" and "Fly Like a Bird." He and the True Worship choir joined me on *Good Morning America* to perform "Fly Like a Bird," before he took flight on July 3, 2009.

❦

Having a family in God brought me back to my life in the Light. Pat couldn't understand. She left me a snide phone message on my Blackberry: "What is this with you and your new friends and your *new prayers*?" None of my biological family understood what it meant to care so much about God. But I had to. Returning to God was the only way I made it out of all my trips to hell. I believe my ex-brother and ex-sister have been to a hell of their own; they may still be trapped there. They chose drugs and lies and schemes to survive, but that only seemed to dig them in deeper and to make them resent me more. And I still pray for them.

Maybe when you're cursing me
You don't feel so incomplete
But we've all made mistakes
Felt the guilt and self-hate
I know that you've been there for plenty
Maybe still got love for me

But let him without sin cast the first stone brethren
But who remains standing then
Not you, not I, see Philippians 4:9
So I wish you well

—"I Wish You Well"

So gradually I overcame the dark time that my family had dragged me through. And after all that shit, "Loverboy" ended up being the best-selling single of 2001 in the United States. *I'm* real.

PART IV

EMANCIPATION

MY COUSIN VINNY

After the whole *Glitter* fiasco, Virgin was spooked and wanted to change my deal to make it much less significant. They felt they couldn't justify spending all that money on such an "unstable" person. The woman who had signed me was fired, and they brought in two new people from England to replace her. I remember the first day I sat down with them—basically, they were pretty fucking awful. They were trying to change the deal, and I just knew I had to get out of there.

Getting to Virgin had seemed like a triumph because I was so desperate to get off Sony. Virgin wasn't as big, but it was a boutique label, and I knew how well they had taken care of Lenny Kravitz and Janet Jackson. They offered me such a good deal in part because they weren't as slick and influential as other labels; they didn't know all the tricks that Sony and the other big labels knew. They were eclectic and saw me as a big, shiny star. Initially I chose Virgin over a larger and more cutthroat label for the deal they were offering, but when they wanted to "adjust" it, with all new players, I had no reason to stay. They offered a revised agreement wherein they would pay me much less and have more control. I refused.

Instead, the CEO of Universal Music Group, the genius Doug Morris, and visionary hip-hop music executive Lyor Cohen (we both had come a long way since I met him on the street with Will Smith, singing Rob Base and DJ E-Z Rock's "It Takes Two"), came to my penthouse. The three of us sat in the living room with Marilyn's white baby grand, and over champagne Doug proclaimed, "You know what, Mariah? We're going to do this. I think we're *really* gonna do this." I felt safe and seen. They would have to pay a pretty penny to get me out of the deal I had with Virgin, but they were willing. I was like, *Fuck everybody else; I'm still good, I'm still here.* I mean, I had two of the top music executives in the world on my couch, with no middlemen. We were going to be all right. After all of the trauma I'd experienced, the faith and trust Doug showed in me, and his exciting vision for the future, renewed me. And I *was* going to do it! I had no intention of dying with the nineties, as Tommy had prophesized. I always knew I could be even bigger than he saw. I had so much more music inside of me. Ready to begin again, I signed my new deal.

The first album I made on Universal was *Charmbracelet*. Recording *Charmbracelet* was a chance at restoration and recuperation after the disaster that was *Glitter*. I still believe *Glitter* was ahead of its time. People may not have been ready to deal with the '80s in the early 2000s, but I knew it was going to be a *thing*. And then it was! And I still *love* that soundtrack. I am so glad and so grateful that almost two decades later, the Lambs and I got #JusticeForGlitter, making it go to number one in 2018. I'm also glad I get to perform those songs now. The fans gave *Glitter* new shine, new dazzle—the life it *deserved*.

Waiting at the end of my *Rainbow* bridge to freedom was a kind of paradise, an oasis. Quite literally—I recorded a lot of the album in the Bahamas and on the Isle of Capri (a semi-secret, retro-glamorous getaway like the old Hollywood of Italy). In the Bahamas, we did several live music sessions with Kenneth Crouch (of the legendary Crouch gospel family), Randy Jackson, and a bunch of other talented artists, including 7 Aurelius, who had been making big hits with Ashanti at the time. I was back in my sweet spot laying down light and airy vocals over heavy hip-hop tracks. All of us were there in the gorgeous Bahamas, just writing music.

I loved those sessions. I'm glad I was able to arrange that, because

I needed a palate-cleansing moment. Jermaine and I did "The One" together. I wanted "The One" to be the lead single, but Doug chose "Through the Rain." It was a serious ballad, and Doug thought it would work because it was kind of a sob story, the sort of triumphant Oprah Winfrey moment I needed in the wake of the *Glitter* debacle. It was a good song, but it didn't perform as well as it could have. The label was really invested in the "adult contemporary" genre, which I could do in my sleep. But personally, I had always preferred the so-called "urban contemporary," whatever *that* means.

I went back to Capri, to the gorgeous studio on the top of a hill. It was so great: there are no cars, there is no pollution, the air and the energy are very clean. I didn't have kids at the time, but kids could run around freely there because it was so safe. You can only get there by ferry, and so it made for the perfect hideout for me to hunker down and record. People came out to visit me. Lyor brought Cam'ron out there for a day to record "Boy (I Need You)." Cam snuck in some of that purple (cannabis), and he administered very effective shotguns (I don't inhale directly—the vocal cords, *dahling*). We got fully festive and watched Mel Brooks's *History of the World: Part I* (one of my all-time favorite movies) and laughed our asses off.

One of the songs I love on *Charmbracelet* is "Subtle Invitation." That song is a great example of how I often take the small moments that happen in life and channel their larger significance so that my music can connect to people all around the world who are going through different experiences and coming from different situations and positions. Though the song was about a brief and fleeting fling, it wasn't a resentful song. It was for anyone who could relate to experiences of losing a love but keeping the door open to it.

> *See it's hard to tell somebody*
> *That you're still somewhat attached*
> *to the dream of being in love once again*
> *When it's clear they've moved on*
> *So I sat down and wrote these few words*
> *On the off chance you'd hear*

And if you happen to be somewhere listening
You should know I'm still here . . .
If you really need me, baby just reach out and touch me

—"Subtle Invitation"

Another important song for me was "My Saving Grace":

I've loved a lot, hurt a lot
Been burned a lot in my life and times
Spent precious years wrapped up in fears
With no end in sight
Until my saving grace shined on me
Until my saving grace set me free

Giving me peace
Giving me strength
When I'd almost lost it all
Catching my every fall
I still exist because you keep me safe
I found my saving grace within you

—"My Saving Grace"

Charmbracelet was a real fan favorite. The Lambs have always wanted "Justice for *Charmbracelet*," and it was actually a really good album. It featured Jay-Z and Freeway on "You Got Me," Cam'ron on "Boy," and Westside Connection on "Irresistible." Joe and Kelly Price joined me on the "Through the Rain" remix. The album was a real transition from what I'd left behind into a new chapter. Universal supported me and stuck by my side; it didn't feel like the hostile battle zone that was Sony during Tommy's reign. Commercially, *Charmbracelet* wasn't massively successful, but Doug didn't give up on me—and thank goodness, because liberation was just over the horizon.

It was around 2003, after *Charmbracelet* had been released.

I recall that time as a rare moment when I felt free*ish* and rather unattached. I was kind of seeing a guy, but just seeing, nothing else. I just wanted to have fun. That night it was Cam'ron, Jim Jones, Juelz Santana, and Tots—and me. We'd been hanging out all night—clubbing, cocktails, you know, that whole thing—and we ended up back at my place, up in the Moroccan room. Many things start in the Moroccan room. When I first traveled to Morocco, the country spoke to me. I was inspired by the flavor of everything, the colors, the fabrics, the textures, the smells, the lushness, the exoticness, the glamour it was giving. It was all so mysterious and sensual. The restaurants, the homes, the hotels, they were all fantastically designed, all ultra-comfortable yet dramatic. You must keep it dramatique—*Dramatique!*—for me to love it, *dahling*.

I wanted to re-create that rich, glamorous feeling in my home—to create a beautiful place where I could make an easy escape. Silk pillows everywhere, leather tufts, embellished little tables, hammocks, ornate lanterns. I brought in fabulous North African accouterments to make my own urban oasis, the exotic cherry on top of my beloved penthouse.

It was the height of the ghetto-fabulous fashion era, and we were living it—diamonds and denim galore on all the boys. (Cam'ron was probably wearing a powder-pink leather and flamboyantly furry ensemble. He was in his pink phase.) I'm certain I was in some scandalous micro designer frock. So we're all dressed up and sprawled out amongst a cacophony of cushions. It was almost dawn, and in the IMAX-like view from the wall of windows, the night sky was changing like a mood ring to shades of purple and pink. The whole aura of the room was purple; after all, Dipset (known formally as the rap supergroup the Diplomats) loves everything purple.

All of a sudden, Cam burst out, "Let's go uptown!"

We were still feeling festive, so it sounded like an inspired idea. Cam'ron *is* Harlem, so we trusted he would know of the appropriate shenanigans for late, *late* night into early morning. Me and Cam got in his Lamborghini, which was purple, of course. Everyone else giddily hopped into their own exotic cars. My bodyguard, not so giddy, was trailing us in a big black SUV. There we were, a small convoy of rappers and dolls in unimaginably expensive cars roaring east across a sleepy Canal Street, which soon would be buzzing with Chinese and Senegalese vendors setting up their open-air market of knockoff luxury handbags and watches. But at barely 6:00 a.m., aside from a street sweeper or the occasional trash truck, it was just us, speeding down the wide street, being young and fabulous, cutting through the quiet of the gritty city.

We were headed to the Franklin Delano Roosevelt Drive, which lines the entirety of Manhattan's smooth eastern edge. The FDR doesn't have traffic lights, so I knew Cam and the boys were ready to rip.

Back then—and to this day, for sure—it was life-threatening to be a young Black man in an exotic sports car speeding up the highway, especially on Manhattan's east side. But we were high on a night of frivolity and other purple treats, tearing into the fresh morning. We were feeling young, sexy, and free; the fear of arrest (or death, for that matter) was nowhere in sight. We were chasing fun and freedom, and we captured it, if only for a few miles on a stretch of New York City highway.

As one might imagine, much of my life has been monitored and measured by other people, and in this moment of exhilaration, I got the urge to try and lose my security. Cam eagerly accepted the challenge, shifted gears, and hit that gas. It was like being shot out of a cannon, and the big black vehicle with the big bad bodyguard instantly became a tiny speck in the rearview mirror. Cracking up the whole time, we felt as if we'd just pulled off the hip-hop version of a *Little Rascals*–type caper, with me playing Darla, of course. I've often felt it was a struggle to just have fun, to keep that inner child alive. But I remembered that promise I once made myself, that I would never forget what it felt like to be a kid. I would never let my little girl go.

By the time we peeled off the FDR at 135th Street, the sun had risen. Good morning, Harlem! As we pulled up to the stoplight at the corner of Lenox Avenue, next to Harlem Hospital, I realized we were somewhere close to my great-aunt Nana Reese's church. I only knew of it through stories and a single photograph, but I thought if anyone could help me find this brownstone basement church, it was Cam. And that's exactly what he did.

This wasn't a paper picture in a frame—I was actually there. I could touch the bricks that my family once owned, in the place where they lived, prayed, sang, cried, praised, married, died, and caught the spirit: this is where they had church.

I know much of my parents' families through frozen moments in gilded frames. My family pictures are sacred—they ground me, reminding me who I come from and who has come and gone from me. These photographs are kept in a private little room off my Hollywood-style mirrored and marbled dressing parlor. Behind the endless rows of high heels, the racks of minidresses, floor-length ball gowns, glittering baubles, brooches, and bags, behind all that wardrobe opulence, there's a hidden door leading to my little sanctuary—my personal church of family history. Each picture is a story, evidence that I am connected to all these other people, all different and beautifully complicated. I have them all carefully and strategically placed; I want to piece my family together, to hold them close to me through pictures. I mostly go into this room alone, to look at them and to be with them. In this room, I study my beautiful, fractured, fucked-up family and store their faces in my heart.

The picture that I stepped into that day on 131st Street is of my great-aunt, Pastor Nana Reese. It looks like it was taken in the 1950s. She's tiny and elegant against the weathered brownstone wall: shiny brown skin, deep-set eyes, pressed black hair, no jewelry but a flower corsage near her shoulder. She is wearing a billowing white preacher's robe, white sheer stockings, and square-toed church-lady shoes. She holds a big ol' pocketbook—not a handbag, mind you, a *pocketbook*—with a towel wrapped around the handle, just in case the Holy Ghost busts out and brings the heat during service and she has to mop a sweaty brow. Propped up against the wall by her feet, in rough handwritten capital and small letters that are all the same size, is a sign in white chalk bearing a simple menu: BIBLE SCHOOL, PREACHIN', Y.P.H.A., and NIGHT SERVICE, with corresponding times. Nana Reese was barely five feet tall; her head didn't even come up to the molding on the windowsill. However, she loomed large in the picture and in her neighborhood, robed and ready to preach the Gospel to the congregation.

My cousin Vinny, full name Lavinia, was raised by Nana Reese, so Vinny called her "Mama." It is from Cousin Vinny that most of the stories from that time and that part of my family come down. Both sisters, Nana Reese and Vinny's Aunt Addie, my grandmother, each had one son— Addie's was Roy, my father, the only one who survived. No one ever spoke of Nana Reese's son, but the story, according to Cousin Vinny, is that he died as a child from "consumption." Such a crude-sounding diagnosis, isn't it? Consumption.

"Mama said he was disobedient, wouldn't put on his coat, so he died," Vinny says. Nana Reese was extra-crispy Christian. As a child Vinny lived in one of the apartments above the church. Nana Reese and her husband, the Good Reverend Roscoe Reese, owned the brownstone that housed the church and the one next door, while my grandmother Addie owned two more farther down the block. The church provided typical Pentecostal-style holy-roller storefront-type services on the ground floor, but as Vinny tells it, the real healing was done under the church, in the basement-basement. She recalls, as a child, witnessing a woman who'd come to see the pastor one day: "Her leg was tore up, looked like chopped meat," Vinny claims. "Mama put spiderwebs on that lady's leg and prayed over it, and when the lady came back her leg was perfect. Absolutely perfect." Growing up, I heard of many such miracles happening in that basement. Nana Reese was God-gifted.

My father's mother, Addie, and Nana Reese were close as sisters but far apart in temperament. While Nana was sweet, Addie was strong-willed and set in her ways. She and my mother had issues, to say the least. I remember a time when my mother threw her out of our house. Because of their conflicts, my mother kept me away from this part of my father's family, and my knowledge of them mostly came from spectacular and contradicting stories. I clung tightly to the sketchy scenes and the precious pictures my grandmother saved for her son, Roy. I rescued them when my father died. I love them and I protect them.

So there I stood, that sunny morning, in front of 73 West 131st Street, posing for a picture, just like the pastor, my great-aunt, my blood, had done fifty years before. Only I was hardly in a choir robe; I was most likely wearing a dress the size of Nana Reese's sweat towel—boobs propped up and legs for days, diamonds twinkling. And the man with the camera was one of the flyest and flashiest rappers in the world, leaning against a one-hundred-thousand-dollar whip while he snapped the photo.

This dignified and decaying brownstone I stood before was the site where my mother and father were married. Their wedding was another drama, another story I was told in mismatched pieces. Most of my family can at least agree on this: my mother fainted during the ceremony. Exactly why she fainted is still up for debate. Cousin Vinny was there, and although she was a child at the time, she clearly remembers how beautiful my mother looked on that day. She describes her dress as a "pretty, shiny blue," satin perhaps, and it is in that blue wedding dress that my mother collapsed to the ground, her new groom having to slap her face to revive her. I had once been told my mother lost consciousness after seeing a large rat scurry across the floor during the service, but later I learned that she was pregnant at the time. In either scenario, it's appropriately dramatic for an opera diva's wedding in a Harlem basement church.

As we pulled off the block, I thought about what kind of strong, faithful, and resourceful sisters Reese and Addie had to have been back then. These two Black women—armed with little education—owned four brownstones in Harlem. In addition to the church on 131st Street, Nana Reese also owned a brick church in Wilmington, North Carolina, so big it had its own baptismal pool. Its size and strength (at the time it was the only brick building in Wilmington's Black community) also made it a neighborhood sanctuary: it was the place where all the Black folks would gather and seek refuge from the tornadoes that regularly pummeled the coast.

Nana Reese and the church were a fixture in their town in so many ways. Every morning the choir, called Voices of Deliverance, would sing on the local radio. She was such an influential leader in the community that she was a threat to some, particularly in the days of segregation and violence in the Jim Crow South. One day Nana Reese was visited by some white men in uniform: police and a fire chief. Cousin Vinny remembers their large, imposing bodies towering over her small five-foot frame. Immediately after this "meeting," and without saying a word, she packed up the kids and left her brick church and the congregation it served faithfully for so long, never to return again.

🦋

I thought about those women as I posed for my photo, just before climbing back into the passenger seat of a car that cost more money than they'd ever made in their entire lifetimes. My women elders, who made something from nothing. They had a vision beyond Jim Crow, beyond third grade, beyond fear. I wonder if they ever had a vision of what was in store for their little Roy's baby girl?

So much of the pressure from the recent past had been lifted: I had a new record deal. I had people who were excited and enthusiastic about my comeback. I had thought that *Glitter* would be the death of me, but it gave me new life. I took it as an opportunity to retreat, rest, and renew my purpose. If *Rainbow* was a bridge to safety, *Charmbracelet* was a cocoon, a place of shelter, healing, and growth that made it possible for me to bloom again.

THE LATIN ELVIS

One year, for Christmas, I took a whole chosen family of close friends to Aspen. Unbeknownst to me, the real-estate agent who handled my Aspen rental had gotten together with a coworker to set me up on a blind date. It was a simple scheme: they told the mystery man that I really wanted to meet him, and they told me that he wanted to meet me. He turned out to be international megastar Luis Miguel, the "Latin Elvis."

Our first date was at a restaurant, and it was hardly a date, for me. I was like, *Who is this guy?* He was drinking a lot, and his hair was blown out and all over the place. But a small part of me was intrigued. He had an undeniable passionate flair; I could see the potential for adventure in him. Though he needed to smooth the hair down first. (I did that for him *and* Tommy, by the way—smooth the hair down, figure it out; you know, Hairdressing 101. Five hundred hours!)

After we had both had a few drinks and an awkward dinner, I still couldn't get rid of him. I went to my nephew Shawn's room and told him, "Shawn, you got to come help me figure this out." I had just met this guy, and he was drunk off his ass! I was thinking to myself, *We're not going anywhere with this; it's not going to work.* So Shawn made up an excuse for me and got me out.

The very next day Luis's assistant showed up to my door with a spectacular Bulgari diamond necklace (diamonds aren't my *best* friend, but we're close). I was surprised—and yes, impressed—but in the back of my mind I was also thinking, *What, does he just keep a bunch of diamond necklaces nearby in case he meets a girl?* I know they have jewelry stores in Aspen, but I also knew to be cautious: he'd dated Daisy Fuentes, Salma Hayek—all of these incredibly beautiful and famous Latin women. I soon learned that was his way; he was an authentic, over-the-top Latin lover, for real.

Luis was exciting and extravagant. We were both Aries, and we vibed energetically. He was incredibly romantic and spontaneous. We would go on adventures: ditch security and go for a ride, or pick up and go to Mexico City. He had a phenomenal house on a piece of pristine Acapulco beach, with real pink flamingos! His mansion was majestic, with dramatic carved wooden doors and porches and balconies everywhere. He would often have a full mariachi band serenading us while we had dinner outside on a warm Mexican evening. One of my favorite things to do was jump off the master-bedroom balcony with my beloved dog, Jack, into the sparkling pool below. (Me and Jack were the only ones who didn't speak Spanish, which wasn't always easy.) His staff was so devoted to him; he was like a god to them. Luis was beloved and cherished by all his people.

One time I teased him for not having a hot tub (*I got a pip penthouse with a sick hot tub / We can watch the flat screen while the bubbles filling up*). So what did he do? He surprised me for Christmas with an entire planetarium-style hot tub that you can swim into! We threw a fabulous New Year's Eve party there, going from 1999 to 2000, with the hot tub grotto as a main attraction. Luis didn't hold back in his material displays of adoration. Once, he filled an entire private jet with red roses to surprise me. His dramatic romantic gestures spoke to the eternally twelve girl in me, because they really were like something you saw in the movies.

It was all grand and exciting, but it was far from perfect. For one thing, our relationship was characterized by culture clash. Though we were both young and successful, he was a lot stodgier than me. Our friends were total opposites. His were more conservative, serious and uptight and boring, while I'd have Brat, Tots, Trey, and whoever popping all around. What was more difficult were the cultural gaps between us when it came to race. He would always insist that he didn't see me as Black. We'd have these arguments, and I'd explain, "No, when your dad is Black, it makes *you* Black, so you're going to have to accept that about me." But in his mind, if I didn't *look* Black, I wasn't. For him it was simply skin deep. It was too difficult to explain that for Americans, it's much more complicated. I think for him, easier was better.

Though we made an effervescent couple, it's always hard to live and love in the limelight. He may have been the Elvis of the Spanish-speaking world, but when he came to the United States, no offense, but for the most part I was the "star of the show." He'd been through a lot and lost his mother at a very young age. From what I'd been told, his father was very difficult and controlling. I tried my best to support him emotionally, but I was going through my own shit, and it got to a point where I could no longer deal with it. We were not helping each other heal. At his best Luis was generous, spontaneous, and passionate, but at his worst he was erratic and anxious, and had a dark cloud hanging over his head.

After three years, I knew it was time for us to part ways. We had a good run, and I still have fond memories, but ultimately, he wasn't the one.

As the great Cole Porter wrote, "It was great fun / but it was just one of those things."

> *Okay, so it's five am, and I still can't sleep*
> *Took some medicine, but it's not working*
> *Someone's clinging to me, and it's bittersweet*
> *'Cause he's head over heels, but it ain't that deep*
>
> —"Crybaby"

THE EMANCIPATION
OF ME

After *Charmbracelet*, circumstances forced me into a new place. I said to myself, *I'm going to do what I want to do completely*, and with that I began to work on my next album. I was going to do something from my heart, something empowering. In 2004, L.A. Reid became the CEO of Island Def Jam Music Group. I was so excited because we had always wanted to work together. He heard some of what I had been working on—"Stay the Night," a song I wrote with Kanye. Kanye and I also collaborated with the Neptunes and Snoop on "Say Something." He said, "If this is what you're doing, I'm in!" One night L.A. and I were sitting in the Mermaid Room in my New York penthouse, talking about the essence of the album and how I felt it was going to be all about personal freedom, my emancipation. We discussed the meaning of emancipation—we even looked up the definition in the dictionary. I went on to tell him "Mimi" was a nickname a select few people called me. So, I suggested, "Let's call it *The Emancipation of Mimi*."

L.A. had always loved what I did with Jermaine on "Always Be My Baby." Even though there were already some very good songs for this album, and I had already worked with a bunch of incredible people, including the

Neptunes, Kanye, Snoop, Twista, and Nelly, L.A. was inspired to bring the dream team of me and JD back together to see what our next level would be. I was like, "Let's do it!" I called up Jermaine and said, "Let's get to work." We sat there on the floor at Southside Studios, Jermaine's awesome creative oasis, and within a couple weeks we had written "Shake It Off" and "Get Your Number." In a second session at Southside, we made "We Belong Together," "It's Like That," and then, eventually, "Don't Forget About Us," which was on the platinum rerelease of that album.

For the first time in a long time, I had real vocal rest (something of which Luther Vandross had taught me the critical importance), clarity, and a deep sense of creative control. I initially started writing in the Bahamas and laid down some vocals there; the ocean air and the warm, moist atmosphere were very good for my voice. They were also good for my songwriting. Jimmy Jam and Terry Lewis had previously introduced me to the brilliant musician "Big Jim" Wright, an extremely talented and very special person in my life. At one point, Jim and I were at a house in the Bahamas, doing a writing session. I wanted to have a song that had a seventies live-band vibe; I imagined something Natalie Cole or even Aretha would have done back in the day. Being that Big Jim was a consummate musician, he and I almost effortlessly wrote "Circles." After the session, as he was about to leave—and just as I had written "Hero" on a walk to the bathroom—suddenly a melody washed through my mind as I was walking upstairs.

I came back down very quickly.

"Wait! Wait. Before you leave, I have this idea," I said to Jim. "*Fly like a bird / take to the sky*," I sang. I knew this song was going to be something *meaningful*. I begged him not to leave yet. "Can we write this?" I asked. He loved the idea and stayed put. We laid out the music together, and then I wrote these words:

Somehow I know that
There's a place up above
With no more hurt and struggling
Free of all atrocities and suffering

Because I feel the unconditional love
From one who cares enough for me
To erase all my burdens and let me be free to fly like a bird
Take to the sky
I need you now Lord
Carry me high
Don't let the world break me tonight
I need the strength of you by my side
Sometimes this life can be so cold
I pray you'll come and carry me home

—"Fly Like a Bird"

Big Jim laid down sublime live instrumentation in New York. Later, in the Capri studio, I recorded the vocals. I stayed secluded in the studio for two days working on the backgrounds; I was lost in a song that would eventually be one that would often help me find my way out of the shadows. I worked through the night, so it was dawn when the song was ready for me to listen to all put together. I opened up the big sliding glass doors of the studio, stepped out into the morning air, and looked at the majestic cliffs jutting out of the sapphire sea as the song came pouring out of the booming speakers. The sun was rising as the background vocals were peaking: "*Carry me higher! Higher!*" I closed my eyes, knowing God had laid His hand on the song and on me.

🦋

Later I brought Bishop Keaton in to the studio to anoint "Fly Like a Bird" with a reading of Psalm 30:5: "Weeping may endure for a night, but joy cometh in the morning." Those words were a reflection of all that I had survived. That passage in the Bible really meant something to me. The song is really about how messed up the world is—"Sometimes this life can be so cold / I pray you'll come and carry me home." It's about both difficulty and strength: I can't handle this life alone, but the Lord will help me through it. I'm so grateful to have memorialized Bishop forever with one of my songs that's most important to me.

I give a lot of credit to L.A. Reid, who by then had become a friend, for the success of *Mimi*. He and Universal still believed in me. My album *Butterfly* was an emotional awakening. *Mimi* was a spiritual evolution; there's a lot of my true heart and raw emotion in it. And there are so many good moments. For instance, not everybody knows how much I really love "Your Girl" (it should have been a single). It's innocent, yet still a bit grimy. I first heard Scram Jones's beat while in N.O.R.E.'s studio drinking something out of a Styrofoam cup (I know it's bad for our ecosystem, but that's all they had). There was a little more confidence and a lot more liberation in it: "I'm gonna make you want to / Get with me tonight." And there's a little talking part in the middle of the song "I Wish You Knew," which was inspired by Ms. Diana Ross. There are so many intimate, special, inside, almost intangible details that are specific to me on that album. You can actually feel my authentic emotions; there are no dramatic, overproduced ballads to appease label executives. This was pared down, simple, *real* shit. I think that's why it resonated with so many people.

It was on *Emancipation* where I first started working with a new engineer, Brian Garten (thanks to Pharrell). When we work together, it's seamless. Even though it wasn't televised—because they were in the R & B category—I won three Grammys for that album. (They did the same thing to Usher the year before.) It was still a triumph, because I believe *Emancipation* deserved it. It was a triumph over the fucked-up people who were trying to harm me and use me—my family, Tommy, the record labels, the press, and various others—and it was a triumph over my own trauma and fear.

The Adventures of Mimi tour was so much fun. It had its share of typical mishaps, but largely it felt like a liberation. *Emancipation* had so many hits that at each show the energy was just fire the whole time, thousands of people singing every single word of all the new songs on the album, and some of the hottest artists would come through and do surprise guest appearances. It was a huge commercial success, and it was a real blast.

We took an old-school, almost Motown review approach of packing up a small fleet of busses and driving across America. We did big shows in twenty-five cities (we also did seven in Canada, seven in Asia, and two in Africa). Though there were plenty of people on the road with me—a full band, background singers, dancers, and crew—I was lonely. I was on a huge upswing moment and, as usual, responsible for everyone's liveli-hood. I had to make sure I was in top condition; my voice was rested so I could do my best for my fans first, of course (I never take for granted the money, effort, and time it takes to come to a concert), but also all the folks who depended on me to eat. While I was certainly really friendly with everybody (of course Trey and Tots were there), after each show I would generally retreat to my bus to quietly decompress and rest. This was usually a simple ritual of taking a long, hot, steamy shower and sipping tea with honey. While my big silver bullet of a bus was completely tricked out and outfitted with all the comforts and everything I needed, it didn't provide me with company.

The other performers and crew would have a more typical tour atmo-sphere on their bus—it'd be rocking with raucous laughter, liquor, card games, smoke, jokes, movies, and music. When musicians and dancers ride for hours together down little highways for days, they develop a rowdy family-like culture. And as the "boss" I was often on the outside of the camaraderie they created.

One night I decided I just needed a little levity, and I went to the dancers' bus, which was by far the most popping in our fleet. It was like a basement party happening up in there, just very lively. I easily slipped into the shenanigans. It felt like I was in high school sneaking out with friends and not on my own massive sold-out tour. It was simple and festive.

One dancer stood out. I had seen him before, but something about this night felt different. He was playful and certainly commanding the center of attention with his expressive gestures and buoyant laugh. I'd always thought he was cute, but that night it felt different. There was something really compelling about him—serving a delicious blend of grown-man gorgeousness and boyish charm. I was going to stay on this bus for a while. It was a joy ride, for sure.

It was past the middle of the night, probably close to dawn. We had all been drankin' and singing and carrying on for a few hours when we stopped to go into an all-night diner in some little town in the middle of almost nowhere. We burst into the quiet little local joint about a dozen deep, all loud, laughing, and extremely colorful. What few folks there were in there—maybe a truck driver, a couple of late-shift workers—there were definitely not any of color of any kind. They all stopped chewing and sipping to stare at what probably appeared to be the UniverSoul Circus that had rolled into town and barreled into their spot.

We were all a little too lit to realize we'd lit up that sleepy little diner with our theatrics and flavor. We sprawled out over several tables and booths. That dancer's name was Tanaka. We'd already started shooting flirty glances at each other in the bus about twenty miles back. We sat across from each other in a booth like eighth graders. We softly touched each other's legs under the table, undetected while the rest of the party roared on.

Tanaka and I quickly became friends, and over time a meaningful relationship was built. He is always right there, the effortless life of the party, and when everyone looks to you for something, that can mean *everything*.

✖

Thank God for the transformational "Mimi" era. I needed to have such *massive* success for the public to finally forgive me for the "sin against humanity" that was *Glitter*.

After *Glitter*, many people wrote me off. But as Jimmy Jam said, "Don't *ever* write Mariah Carey off." And I say, "Don't ever write *any-one* off." You don't ever know where strength will come from. I always go to my main source for strength—faith in God, but also love from my fans and all the people who didn't give up on their faith in me. This is not to say I don't struggle with PTSD from the collective events in my childhood, my marriage, and the dark *Glitter* years. I work on my emotional recovery daily. But it is truly fascinating how insignificant the press has become in making or breaking an artist's career, in shaping our narratives. I still feel like parts of the media are patiently waiting for me to have another spectacular meltdown (actually, I've noticed now some people stage breakdowns for publicity), but the difference is, in today's world, *they* don't matter. Now, all artists have an unfiltered voice and enormous public platforms through social media. The tabloids have become the pathetic, rubbish wrapping paper I've always known them to be. They are out of power; they cannot hunt and destroy any more of us. Our fans can come to our defense, bring all the receipts, and create a united front so strong that no bland host or commentator or ravenous paparazzi can even begin to compete with their influence. *We* are the media. I only wish Princess Di had lived long enough to have Instagram or Twitter. I wish she had lived to see the people become the press. Perhaps she and others would have lived to tell their story. I am so grateful to my fans I'm alive to tell mine.

THE FATHER AND
THE SUNSET

Throughout the years, my father kept on living an orderly and disciplined life. He had honorable, steady work as an engineer. He stayed in shape. He hiked and climbed mountains. He ate well and avoided sweets. He drank very little alcohol. He didn't smoke cigarettes (before I was born, he gave up all his vices in one day, and that was it). Alfred Roy was not a man of indulgences. That's why, when I received the news that he had become ill while I was recording *Charmbracelet* in Capri, I was shocked. My strong, invincible father? It was like a blow to the head, quick, sharp, and disorienting. My father called and suggested I come. Not to save him, or finance his care—he didn't need or ask for that; he had always earned and saved his own money. What he needed from me was closeness and closure.

But I'm glad we talked through
All them grown folk things separation brings
You never let me know it
You never let it show because you loved me and obviously
There's so much more left to say
If you were with me today face to face

—"Bye Bye"

I immediately flew to see him at the hospital where he was being treated for abdominal pain related to cancer. I remember that, on that first trip, he still looked like that strong, vibrant, ageless man I knew. But that changed rapidly. Cancer can be a swift bandit, stealing life right out of your body before you even know it has broken in.

After several misdiagnoses, it was concluded that he had bile-duct cancer, a rare form, with no known preventive or curative measures. This cancer grows in the tubes that carry digestive fluid and connect the liver to the gallbladder. It was more than symbolic to me: a healthy man develops a cancer that poisons the part of his body that absorbs and washes away waste. My father held so much inside and had little opportunity to flush out all the bitterness he'd consumed. Now he was in and out of the hospital, and so began my traveling back and forth from recording in Capri to staying at my frail and fading father's bedside in New York.

Strange to feel that proud, strong man
Grip tightly to my hand
Hard to see the life inside
Wane as the days went by
Trying to preserve each word
He murmured in my ear
Watch part of my life disappear

—"Sunflowers for Alfred Roy"

When I visited my father, I would bring massive bouquets of flowers with me to the hospital (any room in any hospital is the epitome of bleak). Yet, as his condition worsened, he developed an intolerance for the fragrance of most flowers. It was hard to fathom that the beauty I thought I was bringing him was making him sicker. On Father's Day the year before, while Shawn and I were driving to his house, on a whim I had stopped at a farmer's market and grabbed a big bunch of bright-yellow sunflowers wrapped in paper to bring him. I was still unable to break the habit of coming to the hospital with flowers, so I brought sunflowers. I figured they couldn't make him sick, because they have no scent, but they have a strong presence. Sunflowers are our symbol.

Quickly, his cancer treatment became ineffective. It was clear there was nothing to be done to stop the toxic disease wreaking havoc in his body. It was almost his time. We knew our time together on this earth was limited, so my father and I got down to the business of talking things through. His sickness made our healing urgent. This was the first time I revealed to him (or any family member) my struggles growing up.

"When I was little," I explained, "it was really hard for me, because white people made me feel ashamed to be what I was. The *hate* I felt from some of them was so real. I didn't have the tools, I didn't have the skill set to know how to handle that. And I don't ever want you to feel like it was because of you."

I tried to explain how alone I felt, trying to handle such a complex situation without guidance. When I was getting ready to start kindergarten, my parents told me I should just say I was "interracial" (that was the word back then, there was no "biracial" or *mixed-ish*). But it wasn't nearly that simple, especially when we were living in white neighborhoods. It would have been much less complicated if we had continued living in Brooklyn Heights, where there was at least some diversity and more progressive ways of thinking. I would not have stood out nearly as much. The kids in the neighborhoods I lived in didn't even know what "interracial" meant. They only knew *they* were white, and that not being white was *other*—and Black was the worst kind of other there was.

I tried to explain to my father that, growing up, I didn't have a sibling or a squad to back me up. Nobody ever gave *me* the compulsory Black instruction, "If anyone calls you a nigger, punch 'em in the face." So when I was cornered and called "nigger" by a group of my "friends," I didn't know what to do. I didn't know what to do when a white boy waited to get me alone on the school bus so he could spit in my face. I didn't know why no parents ever intervened. I didn't know that I couldn't trust parents either, because of how they looked at me. And I couldn't go to the teachers, as some of them were problematic too. Bottom line, I didn't know who to trust, which is a battle I am still waging.

This was hard stuff for a little girl, and I felt so alone—but it wasn't ever his fault. We both needed things we didn't know how to give. I believe deep down my father understood why I had to delve into my music and break away from my family—it was my survival, my identity, my reason to exist. I apologized for not coming to him sooner. "I didn't know where to be," I confessed, "I didn't know who to listen to. I didn't know if you cared."

> *Father, thanks for reaching out and lovingly*
> *Saying that you've always been proud of me*
> *I needed to feel that so desperately*
>
> —"Sunflowers for Alfred Roy"

My father did not want to perish in a hospital. We had to rush to get him to his girlfriend Jean's house, so he could live out his final days in a familiar and comfortable environment. My nephew Shawn was there to support me and help me prepare. We went to his house to gather some personal effects. I was struck by the gray dinginess of my father's place. It wasn't a mess, but it was a distinct departure from the lined-up, spit-shined quality I associated with him. I guess it's hard to keep up such a high standard of orderliness as you get older and weaker.

Seeing how the tight structure of his space had softened made the prospect of his deterioration all the more real to me. As we were going through things around my father's house, I discovered a bundle of newspaper and magazine clippings. I sifted through them and realized that every single one was about me—all stories of my success and accolades. He had written little notes in the margins, underlined and circled different bits he liked. I had no idea he had been keeping up with me from afar. I had no idea he cared about my career. Above all, I had no idea that he was *proud* of me. My eyes welled with tears. That bundle of paper scraps was more validating than all my awards and Quincy Jones's combined.

My aunties, my cousin Vinny, Shawn, and I installed a hospital bed and other amenities in the living room of his girlfriend's house to make his space as comfortable and homey as possible. As the cancer spread and his medication took more control, his desires began to disappear, and I didn't want our memories to vanish with them. I did little things. I cooked his white clam sauce just so he could smell it, so he could smell *us* and remember our Sundays together. To keep us connected to my happiest time, I still make my father's linguine and white clam sauce every Christmas Eve.

His dying wish was that my ex-sister Alison and I would speak again. He didn't know the depths of the hell we'd been through; he didn't know there were ashes where a fragile sisterhood had once stood. Yet, for a limited time, we were able to be in the same room, for him. Perhaps it was made possible by the distraction of the constant traffic of doctors and other family members. Out of respect for my father, people kept their drama tucked in. The only time things came close to tension was when my ex-brother Morgan came to the hospital. Our father refused to see him; the pain they triggered in and caused each other in this life was too dense to unpack, even at the end. Our father had grown weak and visibly smaller by this point, and as their issues were primarily about power, strength, and masculinity, I believe our father didn't want to be seen by Morgan in such a state of vulnerability. Father and son could not find peace on this earth, but perhaps God *the* Father can do it for them, one day.

Now you're shining like a sunflower up in the sky, way up high
—"Sunflowers for Alfred Roy"

Toward the very end my father could no longer speak, but he was still practicing restraint. For his pain meds, he'd hold up one finger, signaling he only wanted to take one milligram. Even on his deathbed he was afraid of addiction, afraid of losing control.

He was more conflicted about religion and faith. Sitting next to him on the edge of the bed, I began reading the Bible to him, which he made clear he did not welcome. His childhood had been steeped in church, but his life was filled with the contradictions of the teachings of the Pentecostal Church and Catholicism.

He made no requests regarding the tradition of the ceremony for his funeral. He had continued to attend the Unitarian Universalist fellowship for so many years that out of respect for his feeling accepted by the unconventional congregation, the funeral was held at the fellowship. But I was determined to bring *church* to the service. He was too often unwelcomed in his life because he was the only Black man in too many places, so I was determined he would not be the only Black person present when we saw him out of this life. He was to have a spiritual send-off. I transformed the church into a glorious garden of sunflowers (which I later re-created in the "Through the Rain" video). My friend the gifted and talented Melonie Daniels, Tots, and I banded together and brought in a full, magnificent gospel choir. I wanted my father's spirit to ride up on the soaring sound that only a gospel choir can deliver. In their majestic robes, the large choir marched and swayed down the aisle and filled the sanctuary. I closed my eyes, and Tots started to sing:

> *If you wanna know*
> *Where I'm going*
> *Where I'm going, soon*

> *If anybody asks you*
> *Where I'm going,*
> *Where I'm going, soon*

> *I'm going up yonder*
> *I'm going up yonder*
> *I'm going up yonder*
> *To be with my Lord.*

The choir swelled that castle with the spirit. It was a whole Pentecostal moment, and the quiet Fellowship congregation didn't know what hit them. It was the power of God's presence in anointed voices. You could feel all the spirits being lifted. I could feel my father's spirit being set free.

Ultimately my father trusted reason to help him exist in an absurd world. Alfred Roy Carey tried hard to love and understand, in a time and place that had little love and understanding for him. And I know he loved me and he was *proud* of me. And that is what I will take with me. I treasure the few possessions he left me: his bronzed baby shoes, family photos, letters, an ashtray, two African sculptures, and the United States flag issued by the US government in honor of his service. For a man who did not worship things, there was one thing he adored, and it is that which I treasure most: his Porsche Speedster. This precious car saw countless hours of his hands fiddling about in its insides, countless hours of our drives and silly songs. Bumper to bumper, his touch, his concentration, his desire for order and elegance are embedded in every inch of that car.

As a tribute to him, I had it restored to its original glory. This required painstaking attention to detail and significant patience and investment. Parts were flown in from Germany, and it was finally returned to its sparkling candy apple red color, with an immaculate finish. It took years, but it is finally in mint condition, as my father always dreamed it would be one day. I mostly keep it in the garage, but every once in a while I'll bring it out. In one of my favorite photos of Rocky, he is sitting in the driver's seat of my father's Porsche. In the two-seater sports car, my son looks like a mini driver, wearing big aviator sunglasses, soft curls, and confidence. He doesn't know the rough roads I, or the grandfather he never met, had to travel to get him into the soft, comfortable leather of that luxurious driver's seat—and he shouldn't. Not yet. He's still a little boy. But I have better tools with which to guide and protect him than were available to me. When I look at that picture today, I can't help but think that though he never knew his grandfather, the look on Rocky's face captures the enduring spirit of Alfred Roy Carey.

PRECIOUS

*P*ush pulled me in immediately. It's one of the few books that, upon finishing it, I turned right back to the first page and read it again. I was on a beach during a girls' trip with my friend Rhonda, who insisted I read it. The voice created by genius author Sapphire completely took me away. She gave such singular and significant expression to a girl and a world that are often invisible. It was challenging and intensely beautiful material.

I first worked with Lee Daniels on *Tennessee*, a film I did in 2008. He was the producer, but he basically ended up directing me, and he totally got *me*. I was thrilled when I learned he had acquired the rights to *Push*, though not at all thinking I would be involved.

A trusted friend, actress and director Karen G, was working as an acting coach with some of the cast, especially the young women, and she let me know that something really incredible was happening on the set. One day, out of nowhere, with one day's notice, Lee asked me to play the social worker character, Ms. Weiss (a role originally intended for the phenomenal Helen Mirren). I was over the moon, but a little freaked out too. I had a little more than one day to prepare. I learned my lines and did some deep, quick-and-dirty improvisation and backstory building with

Karen. I loosely based Ms. Weiss on the upstate New York "Sweetie, it's not *normal*" therapist Tommy and I used to see.

The entire process of filming was renegade and brilliant. Lee believed in me, and I believed in him. I believed in the remarkable cast, and of course I believed in the brilliance that was on the page. Lee's major concern was that I didn't "look like Mariah Carey." He insisted on no makeup and even had a prosthetic nose made for me. We didn't end up using it, but the application aggravated the rosacea around my nose, which, ironically, really worked for the character (now, ain't that some peculiar mixed *ish*, to have both keloids *and* rosacea).

I remember once, on set, Lee caught me applying a little blush and screamed, "NO MAKEUP, Mariah!" Another physical note he gave me was to "walk flat-footed!" (oh, these tippy toes). I was confident in my grasp of the Ms. Weiss character; the most challenging work was not to be emotionally moved by Mo'Nique's amazing and powerful performance. Ms. Weiss had to be detached, but the human being in me struggled with that. There was a moment when Mo'Nique's sublime acting got into my heart, and an involuntary tear welled up in my eye. I discreetly wiped it away, hoping it wasn't caught on camera.

What she and Gabby Sidibe brought to their characters was simply stunning, stellar work. I *loved* working on the film. My management at the time discouraged me from doing it, because it was last minute and low budget, but I knew it was a rare and exquisitely human story. It was also a creative stretch, which was artistically enriching for me. I was so proud to be involved. After *Precious* was screened at Sundance in 2009 and won both an Audience Award and a Grand Jury Prize in the Dramatic category (plus a Special Jury Prize for Mo'Nique), Tyler Perry and Oprah announced they would come on as producers, giving the film the marketing, promotional support, and shine it deserved.

And it got glamorous. Cannes was the epitome of red carpets, with tons of international paparazzi (you better believe Ms. Weiss was left on the screen and Mariah Carey, in full effect, was there). The European press tour was fabulous, full of red carpets, dozens of couture gowns, and a thousand parties, including a secret one on Roberto Cavalli's yacht. *Precious* won awards wherever it went. The biggest night was the 82nd Annual Academy Awards. The film received six nominations, including best picture, best director, and best actress, and won best supporting actress for Mo'Nique and best adapted screenplay for Geoffrey Fletcher—making him the first African American to win in that category.

I also won a few awards for my small but significant role. I won the Breakthrough Performance Award at the Palm Springs International Film Festival, where Lee and I were extra festive, using our pet names onstage (me, "Kitten," and him, "Cotton"), laughing, and whispering to each other. And, okay, maybe we were a little tipsy too, but it *was* one of those bottles-on-all-the-tables award shows! Mostly we were totally *thrilled*.

I was thrilled. Not only did *Precious* give me public validation for my acting after *Glitter*, but because Lee believed in me, I was able to believe in *myself* again as an actress. It was evidence that with the right material and the right people (with the right vision), I could seriously pursue acting. Lee later gave me another unexpected and challenging role as Hattie Pearl, mother of Cecil Gaines (the main character) and field slave in *The Butler*. Lee easily saw in me what so few dared to even look for, and we have a rare and real connection. A trust.

DIVAS

diva (n): *A distinguished and celebrated female singer; a woman of outstanding talent in the world of opera (usually soprano) and by extension in theater, cinema, and popular music.*

My definition of diva is the classic one.

Aretha Franklin is my high bar and North Star, a masterful musician and mind-bogglingly gifted singer who wouldn't let one genre confine or define her. I listened to and learned from *all* of her. When she was in her late teens she moved from singing gospel to jazz—or rather, she added jazz to her repertoire, because she *never* moved from gospel. (One of my favorite albums of hers is still gospel: *One Lord, One Faith, One Baptism.*) And when she sang standards, there was nothing at all standard about her delivery. She brought a soulfulness to everything that was all her own.

Aretha had a bigger vision for herself. Her debut album had "I Never Loved a Man (The Way I Love You)," "Do Right Woman, Do Right Man," *and* "Respect," placing her on top of the R & B *and* pop charts. There was a great Aretha song in every era of my life.

I still believe most people don't understand how amazing she was as a pianist and arranger. I think if you are a woman, with an incredible voice, your musicianship always gets underplayed. I had the distinct honor of working with Big Jim Wright as a producer and musical director. Big Jim had worked with Aretha Franklin, and he told me, when Aretha felt the spirit, she would tap him on the shoulder, and that would be his cue to get up from the piano, where she would sit down and commence to *play*.

The first time I met Ms. Franklin was at the Grammys—my first year, when I was nominated for five awards. What wrecked my nerves was not that I'd only been in the business for about six months, and I was performing at the Grammys for millions of viewers on live TV, and every big music star was in the audience: I was most concerned about the fact that I had to sing in front of *her*. The one who I thought was *the* one, Ms. Aretha Franklin. I had to sing "Vision of Love" with Aretha Franklin sitting in the front row. Many times I had visualized a dream of singing at big awards shows, but I never imagined I would have to do so in front of my idol on my first go-round. I couldn't even sleep the night before. The day of rehearsal, I summoned the courage to go up to her. She was quietly sitting in the front row, on the left-hand side. I knelt down by her seat (because that's what one does in the presence).

"Ms. Franklin, I just wanted to say thank you. My name is Mariah," I said. Humbly, I went on, "I just wanted to say thank you, from all of the singers that you've inspired. Thank you. It's an honor to meet you."

Years later, she said to me, "Mariah, you've always had good manners, and that's the thing that most of these young girls are lacking. It's the manners. They don't have them." I couldn't imagine doing any less for someone who gave the world so much. I got through the performance of "Vision of Love" and won Best New Artist and Best Pop Vocal Performance. Later, I totally scrutinized my performance at the Grammys that night, and I heard every nuance I missed. But I sang before the Queen.

My next great encounter with her was in 1998, when I was asked to perform for VH1's *Divas Live* show, for which they were going to do an Aretha Franklin tribute. Of course I said yes, because it was *Aretha*, and when you are summoned to pay homage to the Queen, you jump, jump, jump to it. When I arrived the day before the show for rehearsal, Aretha was giving the producer something he could feel. Ken Ehrlich is a giant in the industry. He has produced countless honors and awards shows, including more than thirty Grammys (and my *#1 to Infinity* show at The

Colosseum, in Vegas). He and Aretha had history. Good: he produced her operatic debut on the Grammys. Not So Good: they seemed to have had power struggles, like an old married couple. The other "diva" singers selected for the show were Céline Dion, Shania Twain, Gloria Estefan, and Carole King (because of her having written the amazing "[You Make Me Feel Like a] Natural Woman," which Aretha loved and made a classic). Ken told me that on several occasions Aretha said, "Mariah's the only girl that I'll be singing with this evening." Which is why I was the only one to do a duet with her on the show.

Temperatures were rising between Ken and Ms. Franklin because the air-conditioning was on and she doesn't sing with air-conditioning (or outside in the freezing cold).

Luther Vandross was the first artist to warn me of the risks of singing in the cold. He told me that I needed to care for the fragile physical place that holds the muscles, the tendons, and the sensitive strings that vibrate and allow my voice to come through. Listen, if being in the cold can make fingers go numb, imagine what it can do to delicate vocal cords! There's a certain performance of mine in the bitter cold wearing a sheer bedazzled leotard and eight-inch Louboutins at the world's busiest intersection, in intimate proximity to stinking, putrid garbage that everyone seems to want to remember, and that I, quite honestly, often forget. To me, it's as if I was a child playing in the sandbox and I got sand in my eye, wept theatrically, and caused a scene—then arrived twenty years later at my class reunion, after haven gotten a PhD and become a celebrated scholar only to have my classmates ask, "Oh, but how's your eye?"

I was a lot of things in that fleeting moment in the cold, but I knew one thing I certainly was not. I was not broken. Not even close. I had been through so much worse. All debacles are not created equal, *dahhhhling*.

But the Queen of Soul, of course, knew better than to sing in the cold. When I arrived for our rehearsal, I was so excited and nervous. Aretha greeted me with, "Mariah, they're playing games. And I'm not having the games. So we won't be rehearsing this evening," she said, matter-of-factly.

Wait. Who the fuck is playing games? I wanted to scream. *It's enough that I'm going to sing* with *Aretha Franklin, and now I can't* rehearse *with her?!* I could see Ken pacing around, sweating, losing hair, and freaking out. "She's doing what she always does," he sputtered. I don't know what the two of them *always* did, but this was the first time I was going to sing with arguably the greatest singer on the planet, my idol, and I couldn't get a *rehearsal*! Why couldn't they just turn the fucking air off? I was dying.

The night of no rehearsal was a nightmare, except that it was the time she told me she really liked "Dreamlover" and suggested we sing it together. I died again. I was just blown away that she even knew my song, let alone wanted to perform it. Years later, she did sing some of my songs, like "Hero" for Jesse Jackson's birthday and "Touch My Body" on tour, where she ad-libbed all the frisky bits. She said, "Tell Mariah I'm a churchgoing woman, and I can't sing that stuff, now" and the audience sang along with the hook. It was incredible.

But back to *Divas Live*. I humbly asked her if we could please do one of her songs. I didn't think my heart could take *Aretha* singing one of my songs on this occasion. I suggested "Chain of Fools" instead. Mercifully, she agreed. Show day came, and I was brought to her trailer, where she was sitting with a keyboard, so we could go over the song together. We talked for a bit and worked on the song a little bit, but honestly I felt like I was in a bit of a blackout, because it was such an amazing and intimidating experience having that intimacy with her, and the anticipation of performing with her with so little preparation—and for her to trust that I would carry on.

The time for our first number in the show came. She told the audience that she and "my newest girlfriend" didn't get to rehearse, "but she's going to come out and join me." The band began "Chain of Fools," and I walked out on the stage. Her energy was so powerful, I just kept my focus on her and sang when she told me to sing, and we did the song. I ended with a bow and "All hail to the Queen!" How else do you exit a moment like that? And she gestured to me and said, "Miss Carey." That was enough for my soul.

At every tribute there's *always* a big finale with a "We Are the World" moment when all the artists sing some big song together (*we love everybody, but I don't love this part of the show ever, but here we go*). All the other divas were on the stage, set to go out with "(You Make Me Feel Like a) Natural Woman," a natural choice. Everyone knew her part, but we all knew that it was Aretha's song. Well, *almost* all of us knew. Look, if Aretha was going to riff or ad-lib anywhere, that was her prerogative as Queen, but you do not—repeat, *do not*—take it as a challenge. One of the divas didn't understand the culture of the court and tried to come for the Queen a little bit during the song. It was fine. I wouldn't have ever done that. To quote Ms. Franklin, "Something was *askew*."

But at the very end, Aretha decided to take us to church and started to sing gospel. She came and put her arm around me, and I blew out a few big "Jesus!"es because she *invited* me to. It's like jazz: she was the bandleader; you *followed* her. So the dueling diva had gone too far before (in my humble opinion) and appeared to try and outsing Aretha. That. Happened. I couldn't believe anyone would try to upstage Aretha Franklin on *her* tribute, while singing about Jesus, no less. Maybe it was a big culture gap, but it seemed like sheer lunacy to me, and I wanted no part of it. As it was happening, my body began to involuntarily back up out of the Diva lineup and I headed back to join the backup singers, most of whom I knew. It seemed like blasphemy to me, and I wanted to be out of striking distance should the lightning come.

I was mortified, but of course Aretha didn't care. She had more skills, soul, and natural talent than all of us combined and then multiplied. She had so much fun that night and tore it down.

Later I told the story to Patti LaBelle—Godmother, as I call her. (One day she just started calling herself my godmother, after I had the sublime honor of singing "Got to Be Real" with her on her TV special *Live! One Night Only*. She truly is one of the realest singers ever.) She has given me good, seasoned advice and has literally held my hand through some tough situations. So when I called her and told her about the scene, she said, "Mariah, if you would've participated in that hoedown, I would've had to come slap you in the face."

Hopefully the one lesson we all learned on that stage was: R-E-S-P-E-C-T.

Aretha Franklin will always have not only respect from me, but also an ocean of gratitude that will water me forever.

🦋

The year following the "hoedown," *VH1 Divas Live* called me back to do a Diana Ross tribute. The Boss, Donna Summer, and I were supposed to do a Supremes kind of a moment. Of course I lived for the idea, because . . . *Ms. Ross*! However, it would be a bit of a stretch for me, because while I was very familiar with both Ms. Ross and Ms. Summer's iconic disco-diva periods—I grew up with their dance hits—the Supremes era would require research. I loved Ms. Ross's eighties dance anthems like "I'm Coming Out" and big ballads like "Endless Love" (which I *so* loved remaking with Luther); I could capture that feeling. Of course I knew some Supremes classics, like "Stop! In the Name of Love," but I didn't really know their specific performance styles and qualities, or all of the lyrics.

To prepare, I turned to my friend Trey for the Ms. Ross background and backstory. That's when I put it together that Ms. Ross and I were born within the same week in March, a day apart from each other. (Aretha too—when I was with Ms. Franklin in her trailer, trying to learn "Chain of Fools" in a flash, I made some snarky comment (*respectfully*, of course), and she said, "Like the sense of humor. Typical Aries." And Chaka Khan and Billie Holiday have birthdays in that week too!) As much as I loved Diana Ross growing up, Trey is the biggest Diana Ross fan there ever was. He *lives* for her.

Trey and I became friends before my first album came out. I was working in a studio, and he was doing backgrounds next door. I heard this voice going all up in the stratosphere, and I had to find out from whom that glorious sound was coming. It was an instant click with us, not only because of his dynamic vocal abilities that were so complementary to mine but because his spirit was light and full. We also got each other's humor—particularly when it came to impersonating retro film and music stars and parodying great musical moments. And Ms. Ross was an endless reservoir of inspiration; a lot of our sayings—our "-isms"—were derivative of the

Boss. Trey was an expert when it came to her mannerisms, her ad-libs, things he learned watching vintage Motown and Supremes clips, or little gems he picked up from movies and tapes. He just adored everything about her. The way I am with Marilyn, Trey is with Ms. Ross.

Once I was in London, where Ms. Ross and I were both doing the *Top of the Pops* TV show. At the time, and for a very long time, *Top of the Pops* was the most important show to debut a song and make it an international hit record. Your performance of the song on the show could literally make or break it. It wasn't an awards show, it was a televised showcase, and after an appearance, a song could make it to the top of the pop charts. Almost all of the UK and most of Europe would watch. There really is no American equivalent. It was one of the very few places where you could pass superstars like Prince or the Rolling Stones in the hallway.

Ms. Ross was so wonderful to me on set, telling me, "I love you; my kids love you." She was beyond lovely. She even came into my dressing room just to hang out! Instantly I thought, *I'm here* casually *with Diana Ross; I gotta call Trey!* I did, and she left him a really sweet message in that high-pitched but low-volume singsongy voice: "Oh, this is for Trey? This is for Trey. Happy birthday, Trey."

When he heard it, he just about *died*, right on his birthday. He saved that voice message forever. He probably still has it to this day.

To prepare for the *Divas Live* Ms. Ross / Supremes tribute, Trey was schooling me on all these Motown moments, and I was getting into her feeling, but how to integrate with Donna Summer was not as clear. I have such a tender memory connected with Donna Summer. I was quite young and at a publicly funded New York City summer sleepaway camp for kids. Let's just say, it was not the most organized, and the staff were practically kids themselves. It was predominately Black, and I was one of the very few mixed or light-skinned children there, and the only blondish one. But I most certainly was not having more fun. Rather, I was a flash point for animosity. None of the girls liked me. *Why are they mad at me?* I wondered. I didn't understand, then. It wasn't just the light skin and blondish hair—if that weren't enough, *Khalil* liked me. Khalil was the cutest boy in the whole camp.

He had dark, curly brown hair, caramel skin, and greenish eyes. I was also taller than he was, so I think the girls also thought I was too old for him (even though we were the same age).

At any rate, the dreamiest boy at the nightmare camp thought *I* was cute. There was a closing-day dance, and just as the first bird-twinkling-flute sound with soaring strings and the melodic ooohs began, Khalil walked over to me. He took my hand, and "Last dance, last chance for love" slowly started to fill the room. We went out to the dance floor, and our little selves moved in a waltzlike sway until the song broke out into the bright and happy up-tempo part; then we jumped around in our own disco-ball world, letting jealous girls made mean by harsh environments melt away.

I carried that less-than-ideal experience of being at a public camp with me. It inspired me to conceive Camp Mariah, a summer camp focused on career awareness. I intimately understood there were countless children who didn't have access to resources at their hands, space under their feet, and sky above their heads. The first fundraiser was a Christmas concert at the Cathedral of Saint John the Divine in Harlem in 1994, where I performed "All I Want for Christmas Is You" live for the first time. It stood as one of the largest fundraisers ever for the Fresh Air Fund, Camp Mariah's amazing partner. The Fresh Air Fund's Camp Mariah allowed me to create what I didn't have for thousands of deserving children. It has been not only fulfilling but healing.

So for me, Ms. Summer's classic hit was the soundtrack to "Camp Khalil," that innocent childhood moment (and there weren't many). I had never met her. *Divas Live* is a live concert, but it's taped in front of an audience at Radio City Music Hall. There were crew and people bustling all about. Everyone was excited about the arrival of the icon, Ms. Ross, and I was having my own current big pop-culture moment celebrating *Rainbow*, my seventh consecutive album to produce number-one hits on the *Billboard* Hot 100—"Heartbreaker" was my fourteenth. We were doing a walk-through of the staging and preparing for a run-through of the Supremes medley (without Ms. Ross). Donna Summer quietly came up, appearing shy and uncomfortable. No one said much as she went off to the side to have a conversation, I think about the teleprompter, which was scrolling lyrics to "Baby Love." Then someone came and held up three hideous green sequined gowns. They were cheap costume types, nowhere near couture. Putrid.

Who do they think is wearing that? I thought. *'Cause I'm not wearing that.* I was sure Ms. Ross would find them distasteful (to say the least) too. The next thing I knew, someone came over and told me Ms. Summer wouldn't be doing the performance with us. And she left. *Oh, okay.* There was no time to find a Cindy Birdsong (she replaced Florence Ballard in the Supremes). I don't know what made Ms. Summer bow out (if it was the dresses, I certainly don't blame her), but it looked like this year's *Divas Live* was going to be another wild ride.

So now I was adjusting to the notion of doing a duet with Ms. Ross. Of course that was exciting, but the green abominations? No ma'am. I would not be foiled by bad fashion on that particular night—not in front of Ms. Ross, who is a well-documented international fashion icon.

Growing up, I so vividly recall seeing giant black-and-white posters of Diana Ross all over New York City. She was wearing a white T-shirt with rolled-up sleeves and worn-in jeans; her hair was imperfectly perfectly slicked back and tucked behind her ear, and she was in minimal makeup. It was *très chic*—she was so beautiful. My eye couldn't help but focus on her gaze. The poster simply had her first name—"Diana"—written in large lowercase letters off to the side. I pasted that image on my inner inspiration board and subsequently pulled it out for my *#1's* cover. The composition was different, but I was inspired by the poster's simplicity and intensity. From the beginning I sought to make timeless, not trendy, images, and Ms. Ross is a trailblazer in creating modern, classic high-glamour iconography.

I made it known that I would not be wearing the shiny green horror. I don't ever leave the house without my own wardrobe possibilities, because in this business you never really know what might happen—and something very tacky was happening this night. I had a plan. Since Donna Summer had backed out, I offered this to Ms. Ross:

"Well, I have a dress. I actually have *two* dresses that are the same, if you wanted to look at them."

Donatella Versace had made me two fine metallic-mesh-link mini toga-style numbers—one gold and one silver—and I had brought them both with me. (What a perfect night to have options!)

"Yeah, let me see the dress," Diana said.

This was a woman who had been in countless gorgeous dresses, made fashion statements in every language, and I was humbly offering my dress (*fabulous* as it was) to her. Needless to say, I was nervous. I presented the tiny, backless dresses to her, and she took the silver one. *Yes.*

"I promise not to bend over." Those were her first words as she tiptoed out on the stage like a diva nymph with an Afro in the mini metallic silver sheath. She made it her own. I joined her in the gold version, and we stopped! in the name of love for the people. The memory of having her teaching me the hand choreography for the song is sitting in my treasure box of all-time precious moments. I felt a Love Supreme.

Recently, I've been reflecting on something Ms. Ross said to me that time in London. I had sold tens of millions of records, and I was rolling deep, with a big team—makeup artist, hairstylist, wardrobe stylist, publicist, manager, and various assistants. As she was flawlessly putting on her own makeup (she went to beauty school too!), she said, "Mariah, someday, you're not gonna want to have all these people around you."

I believe that "someday" is not far away.

One final "diva" moment. For the 1998 MTV VMAs, Whitney and I were opening the show and presenting the Best Male Video award. It was supposed to be a whole staged "Clash of the Divas" stunt where we would enter from opposite sides of the stage and meet in the middle, only to discover we had on the same dress—a chocolate Vera Wang slip-style gown. We did some cute banter: "Nice dress," and "They *told* me it was a one of a kind." Then I said something like, "It's a good thing I come prepared," and reached behind me to detach the long skirt portion of the dress, revealing an asymmetrical mini as I declared, "Try it on me!"

Then Whitney said, "I can do better" and also ripped away the long piece of her dress, showing a new and different shape. We had a great laugh about it, but the gag is the moment that almost didn't happen. When I showed up at the venue, *my dress had not arrived*. Because the whole opening revolved around the dresses, it wasn't like I or anyone could just whip out a replacement. There was a panic! Apparently the dress was still at the showroom, and so production arranged for a *police escort* for the dress, clearing the streets to get it up to the theater on time.

That day, the police saved my one-of-a-kind-dress moment. If only someone could have saved our once-in-a-lifetime Whitney Houston.

A LITTLE BIT ABOUT
A FEW GOOD MEN

-Karl-

Karl Lagerfeld was always very nice to me, which was not the case with some of the more hauty haute-couture houses. We did a fashion shoot together for *America* magazine—which was a new "luxury urban" publication launched in the early 2000s, when the words "luxury" and "urban" were not common neighbors. The magazine and Karl were willing to go to a newer, fresher visual place with me. Karl produced and photographed the cover shoot. He captured me in both an intimate and a very glamorous light, giving you a little Marilyn-Monroe-by-Eve-Arnold vibe. They are, to this day, some of my most cherished portraits. Karl also photographed my "V Belong Together" *V Magazine* cover during the launch of *The Emancipation of Mimi*. The giant V logo was designed with the pattern from my Dior diamond bracelet—absolute perfection (Love Stephen Gan).

Once, Karl made me a very special couture dress for a big event. It was just beautiful—black satin with a deep V in the back. I wore it with my hair parted down the middle, slicked back (I very rarely wear it this way) and held with an ornament. It was giving a very classic high-fashion look. Because the dress was made of silk satin, though, which can be reflective, it requires proper lighting (in my opinion, *every* situation really does). I looked heavier in most of the photos as I featured the details in the back. The flashes made my ass look huge. Keep in mind, these were the days before ample booties—faux or authentic—were accepted or celebrated in the mainstream. Back then I wasn't allowed to have an ass.

The traditional press was very "Oh. My. God. Becky, *look at her butt*!" It was beyond frustrating. I was in this gorgeous dress, serving a classic couture look, and the press had to criticize my butt and foil the moment. I wasn't that far removed from the time when I couldn't afford actual food and so I had no curves to attack. Mercifully, my then hairdresser Lou Obligini took the picture of me in the dress, sitting with my friend Rachel, and superimposed Marilyn Monroe on the other side of me, altering my original bad feelings about being photographed looking curvy—and illustrating how creativity and vision can change perceptions, people, and points of view. That little black dress had a big impact, as did Mr. Karl Lagerfeld himself, both one of a kind to me.

-Mandela-

When Oprah invites you to go to South Africa, you drop everything and *go*. (When Oprah invites you *anywhere*, you go, but this was super major.) It was something pretty extraordinary even for her—the opening of her Oprah Winfrey Leadership Academy for Girls. It was a once-in-a-lifetime privilege to be among the few people she invited (including Tina Turner, Sidney Poitier, Mary J. Blige, and Spike Lee), and then I was one of the even fewer people she selected to personally meet the phenomenal transformational figure Nelson Mandela.

I was brought into a small, simple, elegant room where Mr. Mandela was sitting in a lone gray wingback chair in one of his signature patterned shirts. He looked like a king. He looked like a father. I was with him for just a moment, but what an incredible, powerful moment. I leaned down to hug him, and in that brief embrace I felt the energy of ancient ancestry and of the future, of struggles and sacrifice, of unshakable faith and vision—of revolutionary love. Mr. Mandela smiled at me, and in an instant I felt my very constitution change.

-Ali-

Muhammad Ali was turning sixty years old, and a CBS television special was being produced in celebration of his triumphant life. It was 2002, right after Will Smith portrayed him in the film *Ali*. I was asked to close the show with the "Happy Birthday" song. I had admired Mr. Ali immensely since childhood. He was one of the few people my entire disjoined family came together on. If he was on TV, we would all gather around; all of us agreed Muhammad Ali was undeniably the *Greatest*. He was a *big* presence to me, like Michael-Jackson-status big.

Inspired by the Marilyn moment when she famously sang to President Kennedy, I did a little rearrangement of the classic and sang soft and breathy at the top: "Happy birthday to you / Happy birthday to you / Happy birthday to the *Greatest*"—after which I moved into a big, vocal gospel-choir-type rendition. Of course I was honored to have the opportunity. However, I did not realize my singing to an icon, inspired by another icon, might have been a bit improper. You see, I was dressed in a simple icy-pink-silk short slip dress, and I did a few kitschy winks and shimmies during my performance. I was thinking, of course, *Everyone is in on the reference*. What I didn't take into consideration was that Mr. Ali was Muslim, as were his wife and daughters. I also didn't know, at the time, that Muslim women dress and act modestly.

Mr. Ali and his wife were seated in special chairs at the foot of the stage. As part of the performance, I was to walk down the stairs and sing right in front of him. I must have appeared to literally be in my underwear to him and his wife. The camera was cutting to him so the audience could see how animated he was, seemingly trying to get out of his chair with excitement—which at that stage in the progression of his Parkinson's syndrome was not an easy task, but which also caused a delighted reaction from the audience (well, *most* of them). Thank God, during the performance I didn't know I was being inappropriate to his family; none of the producers brought this small but significant religious-respect issue to my attention. You know, they could've just said, "Maybe tone down the cute kitten moves and bring the hem down a little—perhaps some sleeves would be nice?" I didn't know. I truly hope the family forgave my youthful ignorance and inexperience.

Legends and heavy hitters like Angela Bassett and Diahann Carroll were there. At the end of my song, Will Smith was to stand on his other side, and he and I would help Mr. Ali walk up to the stage for a finale. All the presenters and performers were gathered, and there was a huge confetti drop, and I was on the arm of one of my absolute heroes. In all the festive mayhem, he leaned over and whispered in my ear, "You're dangerous." Mind you, he wasn't talking very much at that point, but I heard him loud and clear. We both had a private laugh about it.

The man—the people's champion, who knocked out some of the toughest men in the world and knocked down some of the toughest racial barriers—used his precious breath to joke with me that I was *dangerous*. After that experience, proclaiming a moment *legendary* elevated it to a whole new weight class.

-Stevie-

"What color are the lights on the Christmas tree? What do they look like?" I overheard Stevie Wonder ask his brother as he led him through the MGM Grand. We were both there for the *Billboard* Music Awards. He had come to present me with the Artist of the Decade award. Of all the musicians and all the music I've been inspired by, Stevie Wonder would have to be my favorite. As a writer and composer he is a deep diver. He goes all the way to the floor of his soul and brings back treasures so vivid, so full of emotion, they sonically shift your composition. And as a singer, he delivers with complete honesty and heart. He is truly my diamond standard.

I have had the privilege to work with him a few times. Once, he even played me some new material he was working on and asked *my* opinion. One of the greatest songwriters *ever* casually let me listen to his work and was genuinely interested in my feedback—as a musician. A musical moment I will always treasure was an ad-lib he did on my song "Make It Look Good" on *Me. I am Mariah . . . The Elusive Chanteuse*. Right at the very beginning, he says or plays, "I love you, *Mariah*" through his harmonica! And then laughs his sweet, brilliant, healing laugh, and then the song begins. It was like a little blessing before the meal. He played his distinctive harmonica throughout the whole thing, as only Stevie Wonder can.

I often think about that moment when he asked about the Christmas lights on the tree. This man who has brought so much pure joy to people all around the globe, spanning generations, through the power of his incredible musical contribution—a man who has lit up the world with his presence and his songs, a man who has done so much for humanity—was asking to have a twinkle described to him. In that moment, "Mr. Wonderfull" showed me how not to take the simple things for granted and confirmed a Christmas tree can bring happiness, seen and unseen, as long as it is made from love.

When I received the *Billboard*'s Artist of the Decade award, I declared, "Now I can be who I really am," because I had just finished the *Rainbow* album and was on my road to emancipation. Receiving that recognition was a huge accomplishment, yet what I received from Stevie Wonder transcends statues, accolades, and all decades.

-Prince-

Prince gave me a Bible, bound in deep-brown leather, with gold embossed letters. I still have that holy book, sent to me from a brilliant being, a brother angel, who came to my aid in difficult times more than once. Prince defended me as an artist. Around the time of *Butterfly*, a couple of label executives who shall remain nameless (because I don't really know them) were questioning my musical direction in conversation with him. By that time he had reached guru status as a musician (which didn't stop labels from trying to screw him as a recording artist—when it comes to money and power, nothing and no one is sacred, not even music royalty).

They asked him: "Why is she trying to be so urban?" and "What is she doing?"

"I think that's just her shit. That's what she really likes," was his transcendent answer. Exactly right!

It's just her shit. Namaste, suckahs.

When I first met Prince, he told me he loved "Honey." Oh! My! God!

Prince knows my song! I shouted in my head. I was over the moon—the maestro of modern music knew my song! We went on to talk about songwriting and the treachery of "the industry" in subsequent casual meetings at parties or a club (Prince was notorious for randomly, mystically appearing at a nightclub); he was always very giving of his time with me.

One night he, JD, and I stayed up all night talking about the State of the Industry and how, as new leaders, we could gain more independence, agency, and ownership over our work. Then, one day, I got the invitation to Paisley Park. I had frequently fantasized about writing with him, like Wendy and Lisa, or Sheila E.—all incredible, undercelebrated musicians. (I really, *really* wanted to write and record a "Purple Rain"-esque ballad duet. I mean, who didn't, but I know it would've been pretty perfect.) I remember when I arrived at the Paisley Park compound, from the outside it looked like an unremarkable series of big white structures, almost like a big car dealership. But then I went inside and saw the magnificent purple motorcycle from *Purple Rain*. I knew I had entered a whole 'notha world.

I brought Prince sketches of a song I had been playing around with. My process with writing partners is to come in with some concepts—lyrical or melodic sketches—then go back and forth with ideas. We did a lot of talking. I think it was a bit of a test; you see, Prince was a *real* writer and composer—a lot of people claim they are, but we know. I think he wanted to see where my head and my writing chops were. I was already thinking about songs for Silk (the girl band I had in *Glitter*, who I loosely modeled after Vanity 6). I talked to him about how I wanted to use "Nasty Girl," the song he wrote for Vanity 6, as a sample for a film I was working on (similarly to the way ended I up using "I Didn't Mean to Turn You On"). Prince challenged me.

"That's Vanity's song," he said.

He asked me why I couldn't be "inspired" by it, as Puff and Biggie were with "*You nasty, boy / You nasty.*" I let him know rather than just the catchy words, I loved the structure and the beat of the song—the *feeling*. Prince wasn't at all being shady; he was being *protective*. He was being instructive. He told me to finish the song I had begun, and we would work on another new one. I never finished the song, and we never made our song together. I really wish we had (remaking "The Beautiful Ones" would be the closest I would get). Protect your ideas, protect your music, was the message I got from that trip to Paisley Park.

When the *Glitter* debacle was in full swing, Prince reached out to me. He called me often, and what he said to me then I always will cherish inside. He was deeply private, and I will keep the details to myself. But I will say his wise words soothed me. He gave me encouragement, like the big brother I never had. I listened to Prince's music nearly daily (and to this day—Roc and Roe can identify all his G-rated songs!). I don't know if he could ever know what his connecting with me in that storm meant to me. It gave me hope in a desolate time.

Prince had his own singular and wondrous relationship with God. He composed his own concept of spirituality and sexuality, and it was as special and unique as he was. But in the end, when my soul was in need, Prince sent me the sacred scriptures, the beloved books, the Word of God bound together. Prince helped save me on a soul level, when I needed it the most, and through his music he continues to save the day, every day.

DEM BABIES

Boy meets girl and looks in her eyes
Time stands still and two hearts catch fire
Off they go, roller coaster ride

—"Love Story"

Much of the iconic television of the 1990s missed me. I never got to watch *Seinfeld* (now I'm such a stan of *Comedians in Cars Getting Coffee*) and I had no time for—and was isolated from—*actual* friends, let alone sitcom ones. All my time was spent hustling, working, praying, and making "Mariah Carey." I barely watched children's shows when I was a child, so I certainly didn't know of any Nickelodeon shows or their stars. I had no clue *All That* was all that, and I had no idea who Nick Cannon was until 2002, when I saw the film *Drumline* (which I loved). I thought he was very good in it (I also thought he was cute—*very*). That was all.

A couple of years later, Brat was telling me, "He *loves* you. He *always* talks about you," referring to Nick. She was a fan of *Wild 'N Out*, his hip-hop–infused improv sketch-comedy show on MTV, which I also had no knowledge of. *Wild 'N Out* came out the same year as *The Emancipation of Mimi*, which consumed me in a good way—*finally*. It was an incredible moment of long-awaited, phenomenal success. I was hearing one of several of my songs from that album on the radio thirty times a day! It was a massive moment for my fans too. It was what they needed. They need to see me come back like *that*. I really believe, for better or worse, the Lambily, the fans and I, go through things *together*.

"We Belong Together" was a colossal song. It was breaking chart and airplay records all over the United States and internationally. It became my sixteenth number-one record on the *Billboard* Hot 100 (also making me the first woman artist to concurrently hold the number-one and number-two spots, with "Shake It Off"). It ended up staying in a top-ten position for twenty-three weeks and charted for forty-three weeks total. It tied for the third-longest-running number-one song in US chart history (behind "One Sweet Day," *Billboard*'s most popular song of the nineties). *Billboard* named "We Belong Together" song of the decade (song of the *what*?) for the 2000s, and the ninth most popular song of all time.

It won two Grammys, two Soul Train Awards, and Song of the Year at the ASCAP Awards and BMI Awards (among others). It even won a Teen Choice Award—the Choice Love Song award. I didn't know Nick was set to present the award to me (apparently he insisted to the Teen Choice producers). The show was loud, bright, and zany—the award is a surfboard. I recall first seeing Nick and taking in his curious oversized nautical-inspired ensemble, consisting of giant white shorts, a big ocean-blue polo shirt, a lemon-yellow sweater tied around his neck, ankle socks, and sneakers. After he presented me with my board-award, I said, "I heard about all the nice things you've been saying about me." With a genuine beaming smile and a flame in his eyes, he replied, "If you give me a chance, I'll prove all of it is true."

A cute moment—*very*.

More time passed, and Brat wouldn't let up, insistent that Nick and I really connect. We began talking on the phone, almost daily. Then, finally, we did get together, and it was irresistibly fun. And at the time, I was all about having *fun*. I wasn't ready to be grown-up *again*. I had had to be so grown so fast, professionally and especially in my first marriage. (Marrying was something I vowed *never* to do again.)

I missed out on so much as a teen, and Nick, who had a perpetual teen spirit, was charmingly refreshing. He also felt *safe* to me. Look, I was hanging out with Dipset in this era, and while it was a blast, the element of legitimate danger was ever present, okay? Besides, no matter how famous or fine, no matter how well they could rhyme, I held a strict "no rappers" rule. I was very serious about protecting myself from being labeled "that girl." It was critical to me to maintain, most importantly, my self-respect, but also my professional respect from the tight boys' club of artists, producers, and management I collaborated with. I worked with some of the greatest (and some unknown at the time) hip-hop artists of all time. I didn't ever want things to get reality-show messy up in the studio. And the "rap packs" *will* talk amongst themselves (c'mon; they talk for a living!).

It was bad enough there were already a plethora of ridiculous rumors about me sleeping with rappers anyway. If you're not careful, all your business could be all up in somebody's bars ("cause they all up in my business like a Wendy interview"). After Wendy Williams went on a tangent about me on the radio, the *New York Post* picked up the story and I woke up to the headline "Sexcapades," with my photo underneath. They called me, JD, Q-Tip, and some of my creative collaborators the "Hard Partying Rap Posse"—*I can't*. I was not going to give the mill actual fodder. What mattered was that I knew what the truth was, and I was committed to holding to it.

But I regarded Nick as a producer, comedian, and actor—I had no idea he had real rapper aspirations. He laughed a lot, and he made me laugh. We made each other laugh a *lot*. We talked about life and music. I just wanted to be around him. Once, I even left a date with a very handsome and legendary basketball player to ride in the car with Nick so he could be the first to listen to my newest album, $E=MC^2$. I was excited about it, and I wanted to listen to it with *him*.

During this time I was finally pulling my whole self together. I'd already gone through a spiritual cleansing, getting baptized and continuing my therapy. Now I was focusing on my physical self as well. I was working intensely with an amazing trainer, Patricia. The first single for the new album was "Touch My Body," so I had to get "fit in the body" in preparation.

I was feeling stronger, and I hadn't felt good about myself in a while. We were going to cast my new friend Nick in the "Touch My Body" video, since he was a comedian and we were taking a humorous twist with it. (I mean, c'mon, what other direction could I go with a lyric like, "'Cause if you run your mouth / And brag about this secret rendezvous / *I will hunt you down*"? Otherwise, it would've been a stalker movie.) But the role in the video was for a computer geek, and while Nick was really funny, he wasn't a convincing geek. Jack McBrayer, however, was a genius pick, and we had the absolute best time making the video.

Thanks to my fans, who *really* got behind the song, knowing how significant it would be, "Touch My Body" became my eighteenth number-one single. I'm forever grateful to the family of Lambs. I'm also grateful for everybody at the record label who was so devoted to the album and to me. It was my biggest so far; it seemed to do the impossible by pushing me past the record long held by Elvis Presley for the all-time most number-one singles. We did end up casting Nick as the love interest in the next video, "Bye Bye," which we shot in Antigua. Our chemistry was natural, strong, and familiar. The comfort and the intimacy captured on film were real. And after that shoot, we didn't say bye-bye to each other for a long time.

I was enjoying having a fresh, new romantic moment with Nick. We even joked about how we were going to pace ourselves and not rush anything. Once, he sent me a gigantic, gorgeous bouquet of flowers while I was in London, signing the card, "from a *Pace University* dropout," because things were going fast, *fast*. We'd quickly established a solid friendship, then even more quickly hopped on our own underground love roller coaster. We could share our layers with each other. We connected on some very core things. He was a good guy. He was faith based. He was ambitious. He had been in the entertainment industry for a long time, so he understood the madness. He paid attention to me. The power dynamics between us felt even.

I was clear with Nick that I was not at all interested in becoming physically vulnerable again. I was *not* going there unless there was complete commitment, which at the time meant marriage. (So, obviously I would

have had to break the vow I made to myself about never marrying again.)
Nick respected my position.

I sincerely thought I would never have kids. Our relationship changed
that. We talked very seriously about having children, and that changed
everything. Having children together became our reason. Our desire to
have children became a force of nature and why we got married so quickly.

> *Way back then it was the simple things*
> *Anklets, nameplates that you gave to me*
> *Sweet Tarts, Ring Pops*
> *Had that candy bling*
> *And you were my world*
>
> —"Candy Bling"

The whole world is pink yet lavender when you're in a good swirl, and
we were in a sweet swirl (a swirl is the opposite of a spiral). Nick's proposal
to me was wrapped in childlike romance. He was always eating candy,
which the "eternally twelve" in me found totally acceptable for a grown
man. On the evening the Empire State Building was scheduled to be lit
up in my signature "pink yet lavender" colors, in celebration of a native
New Yorker making history with "Touch My Body" setting a new record,
Nick and I were chilling in the Moroccan room, talking, laughing, and
listening to music. With that enormous, luminous smile of his, Nick gave
me one of those big candy Ring Pops; it was among other confections
inside a little metal Hello Kitty lunch box. I thought, *Okay, this is cutely
festive—I'll eat some celebratory candy with him.* Disguised as a candy pop
ring was a large, clear emerald-cut diamond, flanked by two moon-cut
diamonds, surrounded by smaller pink diamonds—a very real ring! It was
dazzling and matched the situation. I wore a lavender dress with a pink
cardigan, and we took a helicopter ride over the city and marveled at the
lights and reveled in our moment. That night, Nick and I sparkled and
shined brighter than the Empire State Building itself.

Our wedding was just about the absolute opposite of my first. It was a total spiritual celebration, not mostly an industry production. It was intimate—maybe a dozen people in all. I had my pastor, Bishop Clarence Keaton, come in from Brooklyn to officiate. We held it at my beautiful house in Eleuthera, Bahamas. The white silk matte jersey gown I wore was custom-made for me by Nile Cmylo, an independent women's designer I'd worked with for years, not by a high-profile fashion house. It had a simple, form-fitting silhouette, and my shoulder-length veil required no handlers, only a few bobby pins. My ex-sister's first son, Shawn—whom I lovingly refer to as my nephew-slash-brother-slash-uncle-slash-cousin-slash-grandfather, because he really has been the blood family member who has been with me and for me in so many capacities, and I cherish him—walked me down the sandy, salmon-colored aisle. And after the ceremony, I kicked off my Manolos and twirled barefoot in the fine pink grains, allowing the hem of my cloud-colored gown to swish and sway in the aqua-blue waters. We basked in the glow of the Bahamian sunset and genuine love. It was *ours* to have and to hold. We didn't overstage anything. We didn't even really care about photos (though, ironically, they ended up as a cover story for *People*). This time, I was sipping fine champagne with fine friends—no more lonely, salty tears in sad, sugary daiquiris.

It was near Christmastime, and I was ten weeks pregnant. It was our Christmas miracle! Nick and I were beyond excited. We kept our little secret just between us, but of course I planned to make the revelation an event over our Christmas vacation. I was even designing tree ornaments as the announcements for friends and family. But on a routine checkup at our obstetrician's office, the sonogram was silent. The sacred, rhythmic swoosh of our baby's heartbeat was gone—and in that silence I could hear my own heart crack. I survived my miscarriage, but I will never forget it.

After the devastation I made it my mission to prepare my body to healthily hold and sustain new life. I totally detached from the industry machine and went underground to heal and build. It was the first time in my entire career when I turned down work to concentrate on my well-being (I passed on some big acting opportunities, and after *Precious*, that's really where I wanted to go). I employed mostly non-Western medicinal practices, like Chinese herbs and acupuncture. I had meditation moments (and it's hard), whatever it took. Nothing mattered except putting myself in the best possible position to become and stay pregnant.

All my efforts paid off double—the next time, we were blessed with the miracle pregnancy of the twins! Growing two humans was rough on my body. I gained over a hundred pounds and got very ill. I developed poisonous edema—I was dangerously swollen full of toxic fluid. I also developed gestational diabetes. But the most damaging of all my afflictions was the loneliness. All my fun party friends were nowhere around, because I couldn't twirl around the city, I couldn't partake in splashes of wine and late-night gallivanting. On the contrary, I was in constant discomfort. Again, I didn't have a team that knew how to surround me with the proper care. I was often by myself. But fortunately, this time I *did* have a mother-in-law who was there for me more than anything else. Nick's mom, Beth, would come and rub my back (the backaches were debilitating) and feet, which were under excruciating strain from all the weight. She helped me slather on my very special cream that I developed with my dermatologist on my giant, tight drum of a stomach (over a hundred pounds gained, and no stretch marks 'pon de tummy!). She would just sit with me and her grandbabies growing inside my big belly. A kindness.

Nick, on the other hand, didn't quite comprehend the enormity of what I was going through. Once, we were at an appointment with our specialist for high-risk pregnancies. While I was hooked up to a machine, with the weight of two human beings and a small lake of fluid filling my entire body, the memory of comfort of any kind far in the distance, my kind, older doctor, in his thick Middle Eastern accent, looked over at my sulking second husband and said, "Poor Nick; *he's* so exhausted."

The recording of *Merry Christmas II You* is what held me together during my treacherous pregnancy. I loved creating the first Christmas album so much; I thought doing another would keep me from slipping into sadness. I totally immersed myself in the writing and recording. I wanted this album to be more diverse and the production lusher. I was collaborating with a broader range of producers, like James Poyser from the Roots (we made "When Christmas Comes" as a classic R & B song, and it's one of my all-time favorites) and Broadway musical producer Marc Shaiman (the 1950s-esque standard "Christmas Time Is in the Air Again"), in addition to my own go-to favorite partners like Randy Jackson, Big Jim Wright, and JD. The doctors wanted me to be on bed rest, but how, tell me, how do I *rest*? As I was being pulled down from the loneliness and the fluid I was retaining, working on this album was lifting me.

I recorded most of it in our house in Bel Air, which once belonged to the late, legendary Farrah Fawcett. In my many imaginative roles as a child, one of my all-time favorites was private investigator Jill Munroe of *Charlie's Angels*. No surprise, I was fascinated by her hair: the perfection of the color and cut, just *laid*. (I've paid it several homages in my career.) I recall my mother telling me her hair was "frosted," which my six- or seven-year-old mind heard as "frosting." And I just knew someday I would slather my hair with a chocolate-and-vanilla swirl and come out looking just like Jill.

One of the highlights of the album was arranging the "O Come All Ye Faithful / Hallelujah Chorus" duet with Patricia Carey, where I was able to blend opera and gospel. We performed it on my ABC Christmas special, with a full orchestra and choir (and with me *very* pregnant—three generations onstage together!). During this time I also recorded "When Do the Bells Ring for Me" with the incomparable Tony Bennett for his *Duets II* album; the timeless icon himself came to my home studio to record. I squeezed my big pregnant self into my little pink vocal booth, and we set up microphones outside in the studio for Mr. Bennett, so that our voices would be separate and smooth, but we could be in the same room, which was very important to Mr. Bennett. I recall looking out my little window at a living legend singing with me in my house—a moment. "I never sang with a trio before" was his witty remark (as there were technically four hearts beating in the session), a memory that will always remain with me.

I promoted and performed *Merry Christmas II You* while enormously and dangerously pregnant. One invitation I simply could not turn down was performing a song I wrote called "One Child" for the twenty-ninth annual *Christmas in Washington* special. It was filmed in the majestic National Building Museum, and I was singing with a full choir of beautiful and hope-filled young people backing me up. President Obama, the First Lady, Sasha, and Malia were in the front row, directly in my line of sight, beaming with dignity. It was such an honor to perform for the Obamas, and by extension the country, again. For the finale all the performers were gathered on stage and the First Family joined us. Earlier Nick had suggested I tell FLOTUS our then secret. She and President Obama were going down the line, thanking all of us, and when she came to me, I seized the moment and whispered in her ear that I was having *twins*. After I sang "One Child," Michelle Obama, our forever historic First Lady, became the first to know we were having two children. What a blessing.

Monroe and Moroccan got their names because I wanted them to have the initials MC, like me. My precious daughter was obviously named after my childhood hero (the sonogram revealed her posed like a Hollywood starlet, reclining on a chaise in the womb!). We arrived at Moroccan because both Nick and I loved the name Rakim (because he is one of the greatest rappers to ever do it). "Moroccan" was a bit of a hybrid name: it rhymed with Rakim, it's a gorgeous, mystical country where I had a special experience, and it's the name of the room where so many creative and magical moments happened, including Nick presenting me with my candy bling.

It was wonderful and fun when "dem babies" were little. Together, Nick and I lavished them with as much joy, attention, and safety as we could. But along with double the joy came double the responsibility. It was a lot of work, and a lot of having to be home and be available. Making the necessary adult adjustments to being working parents in entertainment took its toll on our relationship, and the end of our marriage came fast, as it began. Even though we had prenuptials in place, the divorce took two years to become final and cost hundreds of thousands of dollars in legal fees.

I call your name baby subconsciously
Always somewhere, but you're not there for me

—"Faded"

Honestly, I think Nick and I could have worked it out between the two of us, but egos and emotions got inflamed (which can translate into many billable lawyer hours, and ultimately it did). It was tough. We both wanted to make sure everything was cool for our family. We will *always* be family, and we make it work. We still have fun, reminisce, and joke. And we both are certain that Roc and Roe are indeed are our light. Every day they give us new life.

I've often wondered if there's ever been a perfect family

—"Petals"

I don't wonder anymore. Now, I know for certain that there's never been and probably never will be a "perfect" family. But I have finally found stability in the family I created. There are times I cannot believe I was a little girl who lived in shacks, who always felt unsafe, under-cared for, lonely, and perpetually scared. I have wanted to go back in time to protect and rescue that little girl from the precarious world she was trapped in. And now, I marvel at my own wonderful children, Monroe and Moroccan, and the safe and abundant environment that has been created for them. Rather than being uprooted thirteen times, they live in multiple gorgeous, pristine, and palatial homes. Instead of exposed nails in the stairs and filthy carpeting, they run freely down long, shiny marble hallways, slide in their socks, and squeal with delight. In lieu of a three-legged rocking couch, they watch films on a cinema-style screen from a steady, luxurious custom-made one of goose-down cushions that's bigger than my first apartment.

My children are surrounded by my uninterrupted love. I have never been away from them for more than twenty-four hours, and when I am working, they are watched over by a loving family of friends and professionals. They have never, *ever, ever* been left alone. They have never wondered where I am or if their father knows what their lives are really like. They have multitudes of memories and images of being with two loving parents *together*. Their lives have never been threatened. Cops have never stormed our house. They probably have three hundred shirts to rotate and donate, and their sweet, soft curls are deeply understood. They do not live in fear. They have never needed to escape. They don't try to destroy each other. My children are happy, and they play with each other, learn with each other, joke, laugh, and live with each other. And no matter what, they will always have each other. They are Roc and Roe for life.

Of all the many gifts God has blessed me with—my songs, my voice, my creativity, my strength—my children are a vision more beautiful than I could have ever conceived. It is by divine design that the children of a wayward child (who as a child professed she would *never* have children) are so extraordinarily fortunate. And though I've worked so hard for so long, it is still miraculous to me that in one lifetime such a leap has been made for my mixed-up lineage. We have broken a cycle of brokenness.

Guided by grace, I am emancipating myself from the bondage of all the dysfunction of my past—rerouting my legacy and rooting it in pure love. And the blessings keep flowing. Twenty-five years after writing a love song for Christmas that came out of a deep desire for joy and peace in my own family, I have all I ever wanted—topped with *big*, happy, festive family holiday celebrations.

SNOW GLOBE OF JOY

I was standing decked out in a bedazzling red sequined gown inspired by the dress Marilyn wore in the "Two Little Girls from Little Rock" number in *Gentlemen Prefer Blondes*, on a spectacular, cheerfully decorated stage, at my sold-out 2019 Christmas show in Madison Square Garden. My face was aglow from the joy of the occasion, but mostly as a result of the gifted hands of my gorgeous longtime makeup artist, kiki—confidant and dear friend Kristofer Buckle. Roc and Roe, in their own little merry ensembles (they performed a special rendition of "Rudolph the Red-Nosed Reindeer" that night!) were on one side, and Tanaka was on the other. Behind me were my "singing siblings"—my brother, Trey, and sisters Tots and Tekka, who have been with me through all my seasons, tumultuous and tranquil. And in front of me, yaaaass, in front of me, were tens of thousands of my amazing, diverse, enormous family of loving fans.

I looked out and saw fabulous flocks of Lambs in sequined onesies and other such glitzy garb (the arena was overflowing with sequins, studs, and crystals!), holding signs and holding hands. There were little girls in crushed-velvet dresses on their fathers' big shoulders; there were old men with no hair next to young women in head wraps; there were Black people, white, indigenous, Asian, Middle Eastern, and countless mixes and variations; gay, straight, fluid, trans, nonbinary, people who were liberal, conservative, devout, agnostic, abled and disabled; people of every shape, hue, persuasion, and belief you could imagine.

And as I gazed upon the marvelous multitudes, as if a lone, bright star was shining right down on her face, I saw Liron, a woman who was once a twelve-year-old girl who had the lyrics to "Looking In" written on the door of her bedroom in Tel Aviv, now a woman who is an invaluable member of my inner team and a treasured, loyal friend. I saw the knowing eyes of girlfriends and colleagues—people I have worked with, laughed and cried with during every era of my life. My universal family of fans, who have given me unparalleled, unstoppable, unconditional support since Day One, were spread out before me like a crystal-clear ocean of love.

For so long I wished I could get five people to be in harmony at Christmastime, and here I was in a family of thousands of Lambs, fans, and friends, and *everybody* was singing "All I Want for Christmas Is You" together! They were singing with me; they were singing *to* me. Our voices were ringing so loudly and jubilantly all of New York City could've heard us and joined in. In that moment we were all united in our own universe of the Christmas spirit. Tons of white confetti flakes came floating down on top of us from the ceiling. It was like the whole world was with me in one big snow globe of joy!

The next day I was utterly exhausted and entirely exhilarated as I woke up to the *Billboard* headline: "Wish Come True: Mariah Carey's 'All I Want for Christmas Is You' Hits No. 1 on Hot 100 After 25-Year Wait."

Wait. What?!

Right at the end of 2019, I got my nineteenth number one! The Lambs made it happen again! My fans made it the most streamed song globally in a single day *ever*! I had worked hard and focused with my small team to give the song big energy on its shining silver anniversary, but making it to number one—that's huge! That's only something genuine fans, not just marketing plans, can do.

After the wonderful whirlwind of "All I Want for Christmas Is You" ended I made my traditional sojourn to my own winter wonderland, Aspen. With blood and chosen family—Roc and Roe, Tanaka, Shawn and his wife, two of my dogs, Cha Cha and Muttley, in tow, I was ready to nestle in and let our new traditional festivities begin! The days were sparkling and crisp. The grassy fields outside our homey-yet-sprawling chalet were blanketed with thick crystal-white snow, as if glittery clouds had settled down to sleep in our backyard. Content to stay in our cozy onesies all day, the kids and I put on our puffy coats and ski boots right on top of our PJs and dashed out into the fluffy blanket of flakes to make snow angels. Eyes pointed up at the bright-blue sky, we let the fresh smell of pine waft over our faces and tickle our noses.

Inside, the beautiful bustle of family warmed the whole house. From Handel's *Messiah* to the Jackson 5, Christmas music was the infinite soundtrack (with laughing, dogs barking, and kids scurrying as the backgrounds). The halls, the walls, everywhere was decked and decorated, and fires roared in the fireplaces. In the living room the massive tree was filled with white lights, gold balls, cherubs, and gilded butterflies and topped with a beautiful angel star with gold-tipped wings and cream gossamer fabric flowing down from them. (In the family room is always another old-school-style tree with big, multicolored lights, giving a fuller, much happier Charlie Brown vibe. We decorate it with homemade ornaments and happy Polaroid pictures of each other; I also add cherished ornaments Lambs from all over the world have sent me over the years.) Garlands and lights cascaded down mantels and doorways, and white candles and poinsettias were all about. Cups were filled with rich hot cocoa and yummy butterscotch Schnapps.

At Christmas I have time to cook my favorite dishes—my father's linguine with white clam sauce (for Christmas Eve, of course) and stuffed shells. Santa comes by the house to spread some cheer, and we ride and sing on a two-horse open sleigh, hey! We sing carols and actually frolic in the snow. It is real. It is loud. It is fun. It is Joy. It is my world.

I was already feeling full of gratitude (and hot chocolate and Schnapps) during our Aspen getaway holiday when another *Billboard* headline broke: "Mariah Carey Becomes First Artist at No. 1 on *Billboard* Hot 100 in Four Decades, Thanks to 'All I Want for Christmas.'" Yes, *thank you* to the fans who have loved my little Christmas love song so deeply—so much so that it held the number-one spot on the charts for three weeks, making it the last number-one song of 2019 and the first number-one song of 2020, the first year of a new decade . . . Really, what *is* a decade again?

After all the swirling, toasting, singing, and celebrating. folks peeled off to cozy up into their places for the night. The kids were snuggled up in the family room, watching a movie, and everyone else was content in their bedrooms. I tiptoed quietly into the living room and sat by the fireplace. All was dark except for the stars twinkling outside of the big windows against the black-blue sky and the warm amber glow from the fire. I reveled in a sweet, quiet, private moment with myself. I took it all in.

I am peaceful.

I am complete.

EPILOGUE

Lord knows
Dreams are hard to follow
But don't let anyone
Tear them away
—"Hero"

In the middle of a violent storm, very young, I was given a glimpse of God's vision for me. As a child, awakened to my dream, I believed with my entire being in what I was meant to do and who I was meant to be, long before anyone else did. And holding on to that belief required everything I had. Along the way I was given signs of hope, but mostly I faced chaos and calamity, heartbreaks and brutal betrayals to derail me. Some almost killed me, or worse, almost killed my spirit. The toughest truth was that the people I loved the most hurt me the worst. The ones closest to me were the ones who came closest to stripping me of my dreams. If I have learned anything in this life worth sharing, it is, protect your dreams. Even in the face of disadvantages and dysfunction, you can't let *anybody* define, control, or take away your vision of *your* life— not your mother, brother, sister, father, spouse, boyfriend, girlfriend, fake friend, boss, bully, bigot, manager, partner, assistant, critic, cousin, uncle, auntie, classmate, mogul, predator, influencer, president, false preacher, fake teacher, coworker, frenemy with a phone, coward with a camera, or chicken with a keyboard.

For I assure you: If you have faith the size of a mustard seed, you will tell this mountain, "Move from here to there," and it will move. Nothing will be impossible to you.

—Matthew 17:20

In the end, and in the beginning, it's all about faith for me. I can't define it, but it has defined me.

ACKNOWLEDGMENTS

This book would not be possible without the loving guidance of God.

In loving memory of Lavinia Cole aka "Cousin Vinny." Thank you for holding our family history and sharing it with me. Your participation in this book and in my life were invaluable.

Thank you to my tribe of angels: Alfred Roy, Addie Mae Cole, Nana Reese, Mother Emma Cutright, and The Bishop. I feel you with me every day . . . carrying me higher.

And for the people, the precious people, and there are many, who lift me up and hold me down, daily: I thank you for all you have done and undone to help me bring my life to life.

I am eternally grateful. (And please forgive me if I have left out your name. You are in my heart.)

My nephews/brothers/cousins/uncles/grandfathers Shawn and Mike, I treasure you endlessly.

The gorgeous and gifted Kristopher Buckle. The loving and caring Ms. Ellen Greene. G.G. "I said Good Night." The solid and steady Al Mack and the "hate to be boring" Michael Richardson and the incredible Brian Garten and his ever tolerant family. Your collective support and protection have been vital to me, and I am eternally grateful.

Without the deep understanding and friendship of Karen G, Rhonda Cowan, Stephen Hill, and Lee Daniels (aka Cot), I would not have made it.

My cousins Cee Cee and Chris—our fun was like cooked food to me. Still love you like rice and beans.

To my four-legged family throughout the years who gave me unconditional love: Princess, Duke (got dem balls, ha!), the ever-present Jackson P. Mutley Gore III (I love you always), the Good Reverend Pow, Jill. E. Beans, Squeak. E. Beans, J.J. aka Jack Jr.Dat Boy, Mutley !!!!!! Jackie E. Lambchops, Pipity, Dolemite, QUEEN CHA CHA the good girl, the *baby* and the O.G. Clarence of Centerport SWYWT (Shit Where You Want To) my friend (heart).

And the wonderfully unique Tanaka, thank you for providing a beautiful and steady shoulder to lean on (IFLY).

Jay-Z, thank you for believing, thank you for leading, and Sir Jay Brown, Mr. Hank, and the entire Roc Nation team. Rob Light and the folks at CAA, Allen Grubman, Joe Brenner, the Stewarts, and my entire legal team, Burt Dexler, Lester Knispel, and Rosemary Mahtawossian at Boulevard Management. I so appreciate all of your work on my behalf.

My very special publisher and festive friend Andy Cohen, love you much! My editor, James Melia (*dahling!*), and all at Henry Holt. Thank you for your patience, diligence, and good nature through it all.

And to my writing partner Michaela angela Davis, sisterhood is a strong, precious, spiritual, and powerful place. It is where we have lived together to tell this story.

To Liron, thank you for being so brilliant, inspiring, and most of all a *true* friend and wonderful human being. Thank you for encouraging me to listen to my songs and more than anything for reigniting me with my music—that's everything.

And finally, but firstly and always, to my family of fans, there really are no words, but I will try. Many don't understand how real our relationship is, but for me, it is the *realest* I have ever known. You have literally given me life and saved my life time and time again. You can never know how I cherish every letter, poem, and book you've ever given me, every video, poster, and piece of merch you've made for me, and every single tattoo you've put on your body. Thank you for crying with me, thank you for crying for me. Thank you for cheering me on and cheering me up. This book is for YOU, my truth is for you, and I hope it inspires you to live in yours.

SONG CREDITS

"Sunflowers for Alfred Roy" written by Mariah Carey and Lionel Cole © 2002 Universal Tunes (ASCAP) on behalf of itself and Beyondidolization & Songs Of Universal, Inc. (ASCAP) on behalf of Rye Songs

"Bye Bye" written by Mariah Carey, Tor Hermansen, Mikkel Eriksen, and Johnta Austin © 2008 Universal Tunes (ASCAP) on behalf of itself and Beyondidolization & Sony/ATV Music Publishing (UK) Limited and EMI Music Publishing LTD, administered by Sony/ATV Music Publishing LLC (ASCAP)

"White Rabbit" written by Grace Slick © 1994 Irving Music, Inc. (BMI) on behalf of Copperpenny Music

"Far from the Home I Love" written by Jerry Bock and Sheldon Harnick © 1964 Trio Music Company (BMI), administered by BMG Rights Management (US) LLC, Mayerling Productions (BMI), a Division of Rodgers and Hammerstein, a Concord Company, Alley Music Corp. (BMI) & Bock IP LLC (BMI)

"The Art of Letting Go" written by Mariah Carey and Rodney Jerkins © 2013 Universal Tunes (ASCAP), on behalf of itself and Beyondidolization & Rodney Jerkins Productions Inc. (BMI), administered by BMG Rights Management (US) LLC

"Petals" written by Mariah Carey, James Harris, Terry Lewis, and James Wright © 2000 Universal Tunes (ASCAP), on behalf of itself and Beyondidolization & Kobalt Songs Music Publishing (ASCAP), administered by Kobalt Songs Music Publishing

"Looking In" written by Mariah Carey and Walter Afanasieff © 1995 Universal Tunes (ASCAP), on behalf of itself and Beyondidolization, Sony/ATV Music Publishing LLC (ASCAP) and Tamal Vista Music (ASCAP), administered by Sony/ATV Music Publishing LLC & Kobalt Songs Music Publishing (ASCAP), administered by Kobalt Songs Music Publishing

"Can't Take That Away (Mariah's Theme)" written by Mariah Carey and Diane Warren © 1999 Universal Tunes (ASCAP), on behalf of itself and Beyondidolization & Realsongs (ASCAP)

"Close My Eyes" written by Mariah Carey and Walter Afanasieff © 1997 Universal Tunes (ASCAP), on behalf of itself and Beyondidolization, Sony/ATV Music Publishing LLC (ASCAP), administered by Sony/ATV Music Publishing LLC & Kobalt Songs Music Publishing (ASCAP), administered by Kobalt Songs Music Publishing

"Make It Happen" written by Mariah Carey, Robert Clivilles, and David Cole © 1994 Universal Tunes (ASCAP), on behalf of itself and Beyondidolization & WC Music Corp. (ASCAP)

and David Cole Pub Designee (ASCAP), all rights on behalf of David Cole Pub Designee administered by WC Music Corp.

"I Am Free" written by Mariah Carey and Walter Afanasieff © 1995 Universal Tunes (ASCAP), on behalf of itself and Beyondidolization, Sony/ATV Music Publishing LLC (ASCAP), and Tamal Vista Music (ASCAP), administered by Sony/ATV Music Publishing LLC & Kobalt Songs Music Publishing (ASCAP), administered by Kobalt Songs Music Publishing

"Hero" written by Mariah Carey and Walter Afanasieff © 1993 Universal Tunes (ASCAP), on behalf of itself and Beyondidolization & WC Music Corp. (ASCAP) and Wallyworld Music (ASCAP), all rights on behalf of Wallyworld Music administered by WC Music Corp.

"Always Be My Baby (Mr. Dupri Mix)" written by Mariah Carey, Manuel Seal, James Harris, Terry Lewis, and Jermaine Dupri ©1996 Universal Tunes (ASCAP), on behalf of itself and Beyondidolization, Universal Music Corp., Kobalt Songs Music Publishing (ASCAP), all rights administered by Kobalt Songs Music Publishing and Songs of Kobalt Music Publishing, & EMI April Music Inc. (ASCAP), EMI Full Keel Music (ASCAP), and Air Control Music (ASCAP), all rights administered by Sony/ATV Music Publishing LLC

"Side Effects" written by Mariah Carey, Scott Storch, Crystal Johnson, and Jay Jenkins © 2008 Universal Tunes (ASCAP), on behalf of itself and Beyondidolization, Reservoir Media Music (ASCAP), Published By Reservoir Media Management, Inc. & EMI April Music Inc. (ASCAP), EMI Blackwood Music Inc. (BMI), CStyle Ink Music Publishing (ASCAP), Slide That Music (ASCAP), Young Jeezy Music Inc.(BMI), All rights on behalf of EMI April Music Inc., EMI Blackwood Music Inc., CStyle Ink Music Publishing, Slide That Music, and Young Jeezy Music Inc., administered by Sony/ATV Music Publishing LLC

"Butterfly" written by Mariah Carey and Walter Afanasieff © 1997 Universal Tunes (ASCAP), on behalf of itself and Beyondidolization, Sony/ATV Music Publishing LLC (ASCAP), administered by Sony/ATV Music Publishing LLC & Kobalt Songs Music Publishing (ASCAP), administered by Kobalt Songs Music Publishing

"Everything Fades Away" written by Mariah Carey and Walter Afanasieff © 1993 Universal Tunes (ASCAP), on behalf of itself and Beyondidolization Wallyworld Music (ASCAP) and WC Music Corp. (ASCAP), all rights on behalf of Wallyworld Music administered by WC Music Corp.

"The Roof" written by Mariah Carey, Mark Rooney, Kejuan Muchita, Albert Johnson, Samuel Barnes, and Jean Olivier © 1997 Universal Tunes (ASCAP), on behalf of itself and Beyondidolization, Songs Of Universal, Inc. (BMI), on behalf of itself and Second Generation Rooney Tunes, Inc., Universal Music - MGB Songs (ASCAP), on behalf of itself and Juvenile Hell, Universal Music—Careers (BMI), on behalf of itself and P. Noid Publishing,

Jelly's James LLC (ASCAP) and Jumping Bean Songs (BMI), administered by Sony/ATV Music
Publishing LLC & Cloud 9 Holland Music Publishing, Next Era, Slam U Well (ASCAP), and
Twelve and Under Music (BMI)

"My All" written by Mariah Carey and Walter Afanasieff ©1997 Universal Tunes (ASCAP), on
behalf of itself and Beyondidolization Sony/ATV Music Publishing LLC (ASCAP), administered by Sony/ATV Music Publishing LLC & Kobalt Songs Music Publishing (ASCAP),
administered by Kobalt Songs Music Publishing

"Honey" written by Mariah Carey, Kamaal Fareed, Mohandas Dewese, Bobby Robinson, Stephen
Hague, Malcolm McLaren, Larry Price, Ronald Larkins, Sean Combs, and Steven Jordan ©
1997 Universal Tunes (ASCAP), on behalf of itself and Beyondidolization, Universal Music
- Z Tunes LLC (ASCAP) on behalf of itself and Jazz Merchant Music, EMI April Music Inc.
(ASCAP), EMI Songs LTD (ASCAP), Justin Combs Publishing Company Inc. (ASCAP),
and Charisma Music Publishing Co LTD (ASCAP), all rights administered by Sony/ATV
Music Publishing LLC, Steven A. Jordan Music, Inc. (ASCAP), all rights on behalf of Steven A. Jordan Music, Inc. administered by WC Music Corp., Peermusic (UK) Ltd. (ASCAP),
administered by Songs of Peer Ltd., Songs of Reach Music (BMI) & Bobby Robinson Sweet
Soul Music (BMI)

"Justin Playin (Dreams)" by Christopher Wallace and Rashad Smith. © 2004 EMI April Music
Inc. (ASCAP), EMI Blackwood Music Inc. (BMI), Big Poppa Music (ASCAP), Justin Combs
Publishing Company Inc. (ASCAP), Janice Combs Publishing Inc. (BMI), & Sadiyah's Music
(BMI), all rights administered by Sony/ATV Music Publishing LLC

"Fly Away (Butterfly Reprise)" written by Mariah Carey, Elton John, Bernard Taupin, and David
Morales ©1997 Universal Tunes (ASCAP) on behalf of itself and Beyondidolization, Universal Songs Of PolyGram Int., Inc. (BMI), on behalf of HST Publishing Ltd., Universal
PolyGram Int. Publishing, Inc. (ASCAP), on behalf of Rouge Booze, Inc. & EMI Music Publishing LTD (ASCAP), administered by Sony/ATV Music Publishing LLC

"Crybaby" written by Mariah Carey, Teddy Riley, Aaron Hall, Gene Griffin, Timothy Gatling,
Calvin Broadus, and Trey Lorenz ©1999 Universal Tunes (ASCAP), on behalf of itself and
Beyondidolization, Universal Music - Z Tunes LLC (ASCAP), Sony/ATV Music Publish-
ing LLC (BMI), My Own Chit Music (BMI), administered by Sony/ATV Music Publish-
ing LLC, Donril Music (ASCAP), administered by BMG Rights Management (US) LLC &
Smitty's Son Productions (SESAC)

"Loverboy (Remix)" written by Mariah Carey, Larry Blackmon, Thomas Jenkins, Christopher
Bridges, Shawntae Harris, Pierre Jones, and Rashawnna Guy © 2001 Universal Tunes
(ASCAP), on behalf of itself and Beyondidolization, Fox Film Music Corporation (BMI),
Universal PolyGram Int. Publishing, Inc. (ASCAP), on behalf of Universal Music Publish-
ing Int., Universal Songs Of PolyGram Int., Inc. on behalf of Universal Music Publishing

Int. B.V., EMI April Music Inc.(ASCAP), Air Control Music (ASCAP), Ludacris Music Publishing Inc. (ASCAP), and Thowin' Tantrums Music (ASCAP), all rights administered by Sony/ATV Music Publishing LLC & Rashawnna Guy Music (ASCAP)

"I Wish You Well" written by Mariah Carey, Mary Ann Tatum, and James Poyser © 2008 Universal Tunes (ASCAP), on behalf of itself and Beyondidolization, Songs Of Universal, Inc. (BMI) on behalf of itself and Rye Songs, Jajapo Music, Inc. (ASCAP), administered by Songs of Peer, Ltd.

"My Saving Grace" written by Mariah Carey, Kenneth Crouch, Trevor Lawrence, and Randy Jackson © 2002 Universal Tunes (ASCAP), on behalf of itself and Beyondidolization, EMI April Music Inc. (ASCAP) and Eekobolishasha Soundz (ASCAP), administered by Sony/ATV Music Publishing LLC & Dream Merchant 21 (ASCAP), administered by BMG Rights Management (US) LLC

"Fly Like A Bird" written by Mariah Carey and James Quenton Wright © 2005 Universal Tunes (ASCAP), on behalf of itself and Beyondidolization & James Wright Publisher Designee (ASCAP)

"Goin' Up Yonder" written by Walter Hawkins © 1976 Bud John Music (BMI), administered by Capitol Christian Music Group, Inc.

"Love Story" written by Mariah Carey, Manuel Seal, Jermaine Dupri, and Johnta Austin © 2008 Universal Tunes (ASCAP), on behalf of itself and Beyondidolization, Universal Music - MGB Songs (ASCAP), on behalf of itself and S.L.A.C.K.A.D. Music & EMI April Music Inc. (ASCAP), administered by Sony/ATV Music Publishing LLC

"Candy Bling" Words and Music by Mariah Carey, Ahmad A. Lewis, Terius Youngdell Nash, Carlos Alexander McKinney, John Theodore Klemmer, and Stefan Kendal Gordy © 2009 Universal Tunes (ASCAP), on behalf of itself and Beyondidolization, Universal Music Corp. (BMI) on behalf of itself and Ahmad Music, Deep Technology Music (ASCAP) and Remohj Music Co. (BMI), all rights administered by BMG Rights Management (US) LLC and Intellectual Don (NS), all rights on behalf of Intellectual Don administered by WC Music Corp., Remohj Music (BMI), Bonefish Music (BMI) & Sony/ATV Music Publishing LLC (BMI), EMI Full Keel Music (ASCAP), and Kendal's Soul Music (ASCAP), all rights administered by Sony/ATV Music Publishing LLC

"Through the Rain" written by Mariah Carey and Lionel Adam Cole © 2002 Universal Tunes (ASCAP), on behalf of itself and Beyondidolization & Songs Of Universal, Inc. (BMI) on behalf of Rye Songs

"Subtle Invitation" written by Mariah Carey, Marcus Aurelius, Irving Lorenzo, Randy Jackson, Kenneth Crouch, Robert Bacon, and Trey Lorenz © 2002 Universal Tunes (ASCAP), on behalf of itself and Beyondidolization, Sony/ATV Music Publishing LLC (BMI), EMI April Music Inc. (ASCAP), D J Irv Publishing (BMI), and Eekobolishasha Soundz (ASCAP), all rights administered by Sony/ATV Music Publishing LLC, Dream Merchant 21 (ASCAP), administered by BMG Rights Management (US) LLC, Reservoir Media Music (ASCAP), published by Reservoir Media Management, Inc., ChandLora Music (ASCAP) & Smitty's Son Productions (SESAC)

"Faded" written by Mariah Carey, Michael Williams, Marquel Middlebrooks, and Denisia Andrews, © 2014 Universal Tunes (ASCAP), on behalf of itself and Beyondidolization, Sounds From Eardrummers LLC (ASCAP), administered by WC Music Corp., Marquel Middlebrooks BMI Pub Designee (BMI), Warner-Tamerlane Publishing Corp. (BMI), WC Music Corp. (ASCAP), and Eardrummers Entertainment LLC, administered by Warner-Tamerlane Publishing Corp., & BU Music Publishing LLC (SESAC), administered by Kobalt

"Fantasy" written by Mariah Carey, Tina Weymouth, Christopher Frantz, Steven Stanley, Adrian Belew, and Dave Hall © 1995 Universal Tunes (ASCAP), on behalf of itself and Beyondidolization, Universal PolyGram Int. Publishing, Inc. (ASCAP), on behalf of Metered Music, Inc., Stone Jam Music (ASCAP) and WC Music Corp. (ASCAP), on behalf of itself and Stone Jam Music, administered by WC Music Corp.

PHOTOGRAPH CREDITS

All photographs courtesy of the author with the exception of the following:

"Looking in": courtesy Denis Reggie

"Behind the scenes at a genuine diva moment with the incomparable Ms. Whitney Houston": courtesy Daniel Pearl

"The Two Dresses and Ms. Ross": New York Daily News Archive/ Getty

"Theater producer Kermit Bloomgarden with Arthur Miller and Marilyn Monroe with the piano": photographer/artist: Robert W. Kelley/ Getty

"With the Queen": photographer/artist: Kevin Mazur/INACTIVE/ Getty

"Backstage 'moment' at the World Music Awards in Monaco": courtesy of Kristofer Buckle

"Backstage in Taipei on the *Butterfly* tour": courtesy of Kristofer Buckle

"Me and Kris surviving *Glitter*": courtesy of Kristofer Buckle

"Living for my Lagerfeld dress with Rae Rae and Kris": courtesy of Kristofer Buckle

"Serving a dip with my dear friend Treymond": courtesy of Kristofer Buckle

"At the Lanesborough hotel in London with Bailey the puppy": courtesy of Kristofer Buckle

"Alternative 'Riah'": courtesy of Kristofer Buckle

"With Luis Miguel, the Latin Elvis": photographer/artist: Dave Allocca/ Getty

"Bianca after Dark": courtesy of Kristofer Buckle

"Ms. Carey with President and Mrs. Obama": Beatrice Moritz Photography

"President Obama making Roe laugh": photographer/artist: Saul Loeb/ Getty

"Prince helped me on a soul level when I needed it the most": photographer/artist: Patrick McMullan/ Getty

"With my all-time favorite, Stevie Wonder": photographer/artist: Paul Morigi/ Getty

"Liron and I having a laugh": Bill Boatman

"My son, Rocky, in his grandfather Alfred Roy's car": courtesy of Bryan Tanaka

ABOUT THE AUTHOR

Mariah Carey is an American artist of Black and Irish ancestry. She is an award-winning singer, songwriter, producer, actress, entrepreneur, and philanthropist. She has recorded fifteen studio albums and holds numerous industry records, including the most number-one singles of any solo artist in history.

She has received many accolades, honors, and distinctions throughout her career, including the Congressional Award for her charitable work with youth through the Fresh Air Fund's Camp Mariah. She is an inductee into the Songwriters Hall of Fame. Carey remains forever thankful and fiercely loyal to her global family of fans.

Ms. Carey is the mother of two children, Moroccan and Monroe.

About Michaela angela Davis

Michaela angela Davis is an award-winning writer, image activist, producer, and cultural commentator. She is a veteran fashion, beauty, and culture editor with a particular focus on elevating stories about Black women's identity and culture.
@MichaelaangelaD